SO-ARB-008

TIME FOR KIDS

ALMANAC

2012

TIME FOR KIDS

ALMANAC 2012

Produced by

DOWNTOWN BOOKWORKS INC.

PRESIDENT: Julie Merberg
EDITORIAL DIRECTOR: Sarah Parvis
MANAGING EDITOR: LeeAnn Pemberton
SENIOR CONTRIBUTORS: Kerry Acker, Marge Kennedy, Jeanette Leardi, Mickey Steiner
SPECIAL THANKS: Beth Adelman, Patty Brown, Stephen Callahan, Mike DeCapite, Amanda Culp, Morris Katz, Nathanael Katz

Designed by
Brian Michael Thomas/Our Hero Productions

TIME FOR KIDS
PUBLISHER: Bob Der
MANAGING EDITOR, TIME FOR KIDS MAGAZINE:
Nellie Gonzalez Cutler
EDITOR, TIME LEARNING VENTURES:
Jonathan Rosenbloom

HOME ENTERTAINMENT

PUBLISHER: Richard Fraiman
GENERAL MANAGER: Steven Sandonato
EXECUTIVE DIRECTOR, MARKETING SERVICES:
Carol Pittard
EXECUTIVE DIRECTOR, RETAIL & SPECIAL SALES:
Tom Mifsud
EXECUTIVE DIRECTOR, NEW PRODUCT DEVELOPMENT:
Peter Harper
DIRECTOR, BOOKAZINE DEVELOPMENT & MARKETING:
Laura Adam
PUBLISHING DIRECTOR: Joy Butts
ASSISTANT GENERAL COUNSEL: Helen Wan
BOOK PRODUCTION MANAGER: Susan Chodakiewicz
DESIGN & PREPRESS MANAGER:
Anne-Michelle Gallero
ASSOCIATE MARKETING MANAGER: Jonathan White
ASSOCIATE PREPRESS MANAGER: Alex Voznesenskiy

Special Thanks
Christine Austin, Jeremy Biloon, Glenn Buonocore, Jim Childs, Suzanne Janzo, Rose Cirrincione, Carrie Frazier, Christine Font, Lauren Hall, Jacqueline Fitzgerald, Raphael Joa, Malena Jones, Mona Li, Robert Marasco, Kimberly Marshall, Amy Migliaccio, Nina Mistry, Dave Rozzelle, Ilene Schreider, Adriana Tierno, Vanessa Wu, Time Imaging

For information on TIME FOR KIDS magazine for the classroom or home, go to TIMEFORKIDS.COM or call 1-800-777-8600.

For subscriptions to SI KIDS, go to SIKIDS.COM or call 1-800-889-6007.

Published by TIME FOR KIDS Books, an imprint of Time Home Entertainment Inc.
135 West 50th Street
New York, New York 10020

ISBN 13: 978-1-60320-883-3
ISBN 10: 1-60320-883-6
ISSN: 1534-5718

TIME FOR KIDS is a trademark of Time Inc.

THIS EDITION PRINTED IN 2011 EXCLUSIVELY FOR WS PACIFIC PUBLICATIONS, INC.
Manila, Philippines

We welcome your comments and suggestions about TIME FOR KIDS Books. Please write to us at:

TIME FOR KIDS BOOKS
ATTENTION: BOOK EDITORS
P.O. BOX 11016
DES MOINES, IA 50336-1016

If you would like to order any of our TIME FOR KIDS or SI KIDS hardcover Collector's Edition books, please call us at 1-800-327-6388.
(Monday through Friday, 7:00 a.m.–8:00 p.m. or Saturday, 7:00 a.m.–6:00 p.m. Central Time).

CONTENTS

8–15 WHAT'S IN THE NEWS?
- **8** Around the World
- **10** Around the Country
- **12** Health, Science, and Technology
- **14** Sports and Entertainment

16–25 ANIMALS

- **16** TIME For Kids Story Gators, Go Home!
- **17** Pets!
- **18** Vertebrates
- **18** Animals with Jobs
- **19** Invertebrates
- **20** Warm-Blooded or Cold-Blooded?
- **21** Camouflaged Critters
- **22** Endangered Animals
- **23** TIME For Kids Story A Safe Place for Salamanders
- **24** Animal Communication
- **24** Tool Users
- **25** Daring Defense
- **25** TIME For Kids Game Tiger Match

26–29 BODY AND HEALTH
- **26** TIME For Kids Story Get Some Sleep!
- **27** Why Exercise?
- **28** What Are You Made Of?

30–33 BOOKS AND LITERATURE
- **30** Types of Literature
- **32** Award-Winning Books

34–37 CALENDARS AND HOLIDAYS
- **34** 2012 Calendar
- **36** Major Holidays in 2012
- **37** Year of the Dragon
- **37** TIME For Kids Game Pass the Pie

38–45 COMPUTERS AND COMMUNICATION

- **38** TIME For Kids Story A Wired World
- **38** Web Address Endings
- **40** Shape Up Your Photos with Special Software
- **40** Hard vs. Soft
- **41** Electronic Trends
- **42** TIME For Kids Story Txtng Can B Gr8!
- **42** IM Dictionary
- **43** Webby Awards
- **44** Internet Resource Sites for Kids

Contents

3

46-81 COUNTRIES
46 TIME For Kids Story A Big Discovery in Egypt
47 The World's Nations from A to Z
80 Cool Landmarks Around the World

82-91 ENERGY AND THE ENVIRONMENT
82 TIME For Kids Story Coral Crisis
83 Environmental Threats
84 Nonrenewable Energy Sources
85 The Dangers of Fossil Fuels
86 Renewable Energy Sources
86 Wind Power on the Rise
87 Energy Use in the United States
88 The Three Rs
89 Energy Use at Home
90 Habitats and Wildlife

92-95 FOOD AND NUTRITION
92 TIME For Kids Story What's Eating Michael Pollan?
93 Superfoods to the Rescue
94 Nutrition Basics

96-113 GEOGRAPHY
96 The Seven Continents
97 Our Changing Planet
98 The Five Oceans
99 TIME For Kids Story One Salty Place
100 What's That?
101 Time Zones of the World
102 Maps of the World

114-121 GOVERNMENT
114 Symbols of the United States
116 Separation of Powers
116 Checks and Balances
117 The Legislative Branch
118 The Executive Branch
120 The Judicial Branch
120 TIME For Kids Story America's Newest Top Judge
121 Famous Supreme Court Cases

122-133 HISTORY
122 TIME For Kids Story Time Line of Women's History in the United States
124 Ancient History
125 World History
130 U.S. History

134-137 INVENTIONS
134 TIME For Kids Story Budding Inventors
135 The Coolest Inventions of 2010

138-143 LANGUAGE
138 TIME For Kids Story Learning Chinese
139 Speaking Without Sound
140 2010 Scripps National Spelling Bee
141 Update Your Dictionary
141 Easily Confused Words
142 Poems
143 Word Words
143 TIME For Kids Game Using Language to Win Wars

144-149 MATH AND MONEY
144 Geometric Terms
144 Geometric Puzzles
145 Common Formulas
145 Easy As Pi?
146 What Is an Integer?
146 Making Sense of Fractions
147 Everyday Math
147 TIME For Kids Game Apple Picking Time!
148 Handling Money
148 The Value of Money
149 Paper Trail
149 Incomes Around the World

150-153 MOVIES AND TV
150 TIME For Kids Story Looking Back on Harry Potter
151 Teen Choice Awards
152 Academy Awards
152 Nickelodeon Kids' Choice Awards
153 People's Choice Awards

你好

Contents

5

154–159 MUSIC

154 TIME For Kids Story Bieber Fever
155 The American Music Awards
155 2010 Nickelodeon Kids' Choice Awards
156 Teen Choice Awards
157 MTV Video Music Awards
157 TIME For Kids Story Broadway Royalty
158 Grammy Awards
159 Top 5 Musical Instruments

160–169 PRESIDENTS

160 TIME For Kids Story JFK's Life of Service
161 Presidential Shake-Ups
162 U.S. Presidents in Order

170–175 SCIENCE

170 Branches of Science
172 What Is Ecology?
172 Rocks and Minerals
173 Botany and Trees
174 How Science Helped Solve the Mystery of King Tut
175 TIME For Kids Game Pioneers in Science

176–179 SPACE

176 TIME For Kids Story Found: An Earthlike Planet, at Last
177 The Solar System
178 Space Waste
178 Milestones at Zero Gravity
179 Space Time
179 TIME For Kids Game Astro-nuts

180–195 SPORTS

180 TIME For Kids Story Star on Ice
181 Winter Sports
182 Football
184 Baseball
186 Basketball
188 Hockey
188 Soccer
189 Auto Racing
190 Tennis
190 Golf
191 Gymnastics
191 Surfing
192 Cycling
192 Swimming
193 Horse Racing
193 Dogsledding
194 X Games
195 TIME For Kids Game Gift Mix-Up

196–199 TRANSPORTATION
196 Will You Drive an Electric Car One Day?
197 Alternative Fuels
197 Tilt and Travel
198 Milestones in Transportation History
199 TIME For Kids Game Get Moving!

200–229 UNITED STATES
200 The 50 States
225 Washington, D.C.
226 U.S. Territories
226 Spotlight on Puerto Rico
227 TIME For Kids Game U.S. Monument Matchup
227 Top 10 U.S. Baby Names
228 U.S. Map

230–233 VOLUNTEERING
230 TIME For Kids Story Kids Lead the Way
230 Top 5 U.S. States for Volunteering
232 Lend a Hand!
233 Raising Money for Donations
234 A Little Sure Can Help A Lot

234–237 WEATHER
234 TIME For Kids Story Tracking Tornadoes
234 Inside a Tornado
236 Wild Wind
237 Droughts and Floods
237 Five Fun Facts About Winter Weather
237 TIME For Kids Game Find the Flakes

238–241 WHAT'S NEXT?
238 Science and Technology Outlook
240 Health News on the Horizon
241 Future Fun!

242–243 ANSWERS

244–246 PHOTO CREDITS

247–256 INDEX

Contents

What's in the News?

AROUND THE WORLD

FLIGHT TROUBLES

Eyjafjallajökull (ay-uh-fyat-la-yuh-kuht), a volcano in southern Iceland, erupted on April 14, 2010, causing massive disruptions to European air travel. Flights to and from many European cities were grounded as an ash cloud rose between 20,000 and 36,000 feet (6,096 and 10,973 m) high into the sky. European air officials declared a six-day flight ban in many areas, which left tens of thousands of travelers stranded. The ash cloud posed several dangers to airborne planes, including engine failure and limited visibility.

guess what? Experts estimate that there are between 500 and 1,550 active volcanoes in the world. Counting the exact number is impossible. Many of Earth's volcanoes are underwater, and they may erupt without anyone knowing.

CRISIS IN JAPAN

On March 11, 2011, a powerful earthquake rocked Japan. Buildings buckled, highways fell, and fires broke out. The quake hit in the Pacific Ocean, off Japan's east coast, and caused a tsunami (soo-nah-mee). Waves as tall as three-story buildings swept away entire cities. Experts believe more than 10,000 people died in the tragedy. An estimated 500,000 people were made homeless.

In addition to shortages of food, water, and fuel across the country, Japan also faced a serious nuclear threat. The quake and tsunami caused major damage at the Fukushima Daiichi nuclear power plant. Explosions at the plant caused some radiation to escape. High levels of radiation are dangerous.

A CHILEAN RESCUE

On August 5, 2010, a mine collapsed in northern Chile, trapping 33 miners underground. The miners spent more than two months 2,300 feet (701 m) beneath the surface of the Atacama Desert. (That's more than twice as deep as the Eiffel Tower is tall!) Scientists found a way to get some light into the rescue shelter so the men could feel the difference between night and day. The miners exercised to stay healthy, and were able to pass notes up to their loved ones on the surface.

Engineers from around the world worked together to come up with a successful rescue plan. After 69 days, the first miner was rescued using a narrow steel capsule called Fenix. One by one, the miners were brought out of the collapsed mine over a period of 22 hours and 36 minutes.

8

REVOLUTION IN TUNISIA

Tunisia is a small country in North Africa, bordered by Algeria and Libya. For 23 years, the country was run by President Zine el Abidine Ben Ali. Many Tunisians were fed up with the high rates of unemployment, rising food prices, political corruption, and poor living conditions in the country. Demonstrators took to the streets in mid-December 2010, demanding change. In mid-January 2011, President Ben Ali resigned from office and fled to Saudi Arabia.

guess what? Some people refer to the events in Tunisia as the Jasmine Revolution, after the country's national flower.

A NEW GOVERNMENT IN EGYPT

Beginning on January 25, 2011, huge numbers of Egyptians began calling for Hosni Mubarak, who had been President for 30 years, to step down. Protesters were angry about the widespread poverty in the country and the lack of jobs. They spoke out against police brutality and food shortages. Many of the protesters were young and tech savvy. They used social networking sites like Facebook and Twitter to help spread their message. In response to the uprising, the government blocked access to the sites, prohibited the use of text messages, and even shut down the Internet throughout the country. Demonstrations grew larger and more widespread, and finally, on February 11, 2011, Mubarak stepped down.

A poster of Hosni Mubarak is taken down in Egypt.

CIVIL WAR IN LIBYA

Following the dramatic events in Tunisia and Egypt in early 2011, huge demonstrations were also held in Bahrain, Yemen, Syria, Iran, Jordan, and other countries in North Africa and the Middle East. Events in some countries remained largely peaceful, but violence in Libya led to international intervention. The conflict started brewing on February 15, 2011, when protests broke out in Libya's second-largest city, Benghazi. Many Libyans demanded that longtime dictator, Muammar Gaddafi, step down. Gaddafi refused to resign and ordered attacks on the protesters.

On March 17, the United Nations Security Council authorized the use of "all necessary means" to protect civilians. The U.N. also imposed a no-fly zone, prohibiting Libyan fighters from flying. A coalition of countries that includes the United States, Britain, France, and Qatar, began enforcing the resolution. On March 19, the coalition began launching air strikes on the North African nation in order to prevent attacks on civilians. President Barack Obama promised to "continue to support the efforts to protect the Libyan people."

What's in the News?

9

What's in the News?

GULF OF MEXICO OIL SPILL

The United States faced the worst accidental oil spill in its history when the Deepwater Horizon oil rig, owned by BP (British Petroleum), exploded and sank 5,000 feet (1,524 m) into the Gulf of Mexico, on April 20, 2010. Experts estimate that more than 4.9 million barrels of oil from the rig leaked into the water, threatening more than 400 species of turtles, sea birds, and other marine life. Eventually, the oil reached the coasts of Louisiana and the other states bordering the Gulf. In addition to its devastating environmental impact, the spill took a toll on fishermen, as well as hotel and restaurant workers, and other people who live and work in the affected areas. After nearly three months of unsuccessful attempts to control the leak, BP finally managed to temporarily halt the flow of oil by capping the well. The well was officially declared dead in September.

A GIANT FIND AT GROUND ZERO

An 18th-century ship was found buried under the World Trade Center site in New York City. While working to build a parking garage, bulldozers uncovered a 32-foot (9 m) piece of the ship 20 feet (6 m) below street level. Based on the remains of marine organisms found in tiny holes in the ship's wood, one historian said the ship may have sailed the Caribbean. Experts believe the ship was probably weighted down and intentionally sunk to be part of a landfill that would help support city piers. This isn't the first time a ship was found under New York City. In 1982, archaeologists found an 18th-century cargo ship buried under Water Street, on the east side of lower Manhattan.

A NEW JUSTICE

Elena Kagan was sworn in to the Supreme Court in August 2010. She is the fourth woman in U.S. history to sit on the high court.

DON'T LET THE BEDBUGS BITE

Bedbugs are tiny, flat insects that feed on the blood of humans and animals. In the 1940s, a chemical called DDT was used on crops, as well as on items like wallpaper and mattresses, to kill insects, wiping out much of the bedbug population in the United States. But because of health risks posed to humans and animals, the use of DDT was banned in the 1970s. Now, bedbug populations are on the rise. The situation got so bad that some hotels, movie theaters, and even shoe stores in New York City shut down so experts could get rid of the pests.

Bedbugs come out at night and nibble on sleeping people and animals. Their bites can trigger allergic reactions in some people, but most often people just notice small, mildly itchy bite marks. Bedbugs do not transmit diseases, but they are incredibly hard to get rid of. They have developed a resistance to some of the chemicals used to kill them.

EVERYONE COUNTS!

The U.S. government distributed a Census form to all U.S. residents in 2010. The forms ask questions about each person living in a residence, including each person's age, date of birth, race, and gender. The information collected during the Census is used to help the government know where people live so it can distribute funds for education, law enforcement, and the building of new roads, among other things. It is conducted every 10 years.

Most Bedbug-Infested U.S. Cities

1. New York, New York
2. Philadelphia, Pennsylvania
3. Detroit, Michigan
4. Cincinnati, Ohio
5. Chicago, Illinois
6. Denver, Colorado
7. Columbus, Ohio
8. Dayton, Ohio
9. Washington, D.C.
10. Los Angeles, California

Source: Terminix

IMMIGRATION BATTLES

In order to live in the United States legally, a person must be born in the U.S., have a visa (which is a paper allowing him or her to stay in the country for a particular amount of time), be given a green card (which usually allows a person to stay in the country for 10-year periods and can be renewed), or be granted citizenship. Becoming a citizen can be a long and expensive process.

Experts estimate that there are between 7 million and 20 million people living in the United States illegally. Many of them cross into the southwestern United States from Mexico. To combat illegal immigration, the governor of Arizona signed a strict immigration bill into law in April 2010. The law requires people to carry papers at all times to prove their citizenship status. It also gives police the power to stop anyone they think might be in the country illegally. A federal court insisted that immigration is a federal issue, not one to be dealt with by the states, so many of the stricter measures of the law will not be enforced. Supporters of the original bill have vowed to appeal the federal ruling and to find other ways to combat illegal immigration in their state.

What's in the News?

What's in the News?

HEALTH, SCIENCE, AND TECHNOLOGY

STUDYING THE SUN

In February 2010, NASA (National Aeronautics and Space Administration) launched the Solar Dynamics Observatory (SDO), a satellite that will collect information about the sun. During its five-year mission, the craft will send detailed images to scientists to help them better understand how the sun works and how it affects Earth's climate.

The surface of the sun is a turbulent place. Solar flares are explosions of gases in the sun's atmosphere that release huge amounts of energy. They can disrupt radio waves and damage communications satellites. The amount of energy given off in a solar flare is 10 million times greater than the energy released when a volcano erupts. The images and information coming from SDO will help scientists to predict and prepare for the wild weather in space.

An image of the sun taken by SDO

guess what? Scientists who study the sun are called heliophysicists.

STREAMLINING CPR

You've probably seen someone perform CPR (cardiopulmonary resuscitation) in a movie. It is an emergency procedure used to help a person who is unresponsive or not breathing. Until recently, health experts recommended that CPR be a combination of pressing down on a person's chest quickly 30 times and mouth-to-mouth breathing. The American Heart Association (AHA) has issued new guidelines for CPR. They say focusing on pushing on the chest is usually just as effective as conventional CPR. However, the combination of pressing on the chest and mouth-to-mouth breathing is still recommended for children.

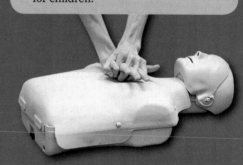

PORTABLE COMPUTERS

Apple's iPad is a tablet computer. With a touch screen that is about 10 inches (25 cm) tall (or wide, depending on how you hold the device), the iPad is like a cross between a smartphone and a laptop computer. It is less than ½ inch (1 cm) thick, weighs less than 2 pounds (1 kg), and allows users to access the Internet. Users can read e-books, store and view photos, download and watch movies, listen to music, and play games on the iPad. Many people are opting to buy tablet computers like the iPad instead of smartphones or laptops.

12

UPGRADES IN AIRPORT SECURITY

In an effort to upgrade airport security, the Transportation Security Administration (TSA) introduced Advanced Imaging Technology (AIT) machines in airports around the country. Known as a full-body scanner, the AIT machine creates a computerized outline of the person standing inside. Some air travelers worried that the machines created images of them that showed them without their clothes. They felt that the TSA was violating their right to privacy. Some passengers even organized a boycott during a busy travel weekend. Passengers who refused to pass through the AIT machines had to be patted down by a security officer instead. The TSA plans to install about 1,000 machines by the end of 2011.

guess what?

Doctors performed the first complete face transplant in 2010.

A NEW DISCOVERY

Two partial skeletons were discovered in an area of South Africa called the Cradle of Humankind. Scientists examined them and determined that the bones belonged to an adult female and a male child, and that the remains are about 1.95 million years old! Not only are the bones incredibly old, but they belong to an entirely new species of human ancestor. Members of the new species, called *Australopithecus sediba*, stood upright, and had human-like hips and pelvises. But they also had ape-like arms, which indicates that they spent time climbing or living in trees.

Researchers assembled the bones they believe belonged to a young boy about 4 feet 2 inches (127 cm) tall. This partial skeleton includes an extremely well-preserved skull.

What's in the News?

13

What's in the News?

SPORTS AND ENTERTAINMENT

WHAT'S THE BUZZ ABOUT?

South Africa hosted the FIFA World Cup in the summer of 2010. In the final match, Spain beat the Netherlands, one goal to none. But the biggest buzz came from the vuvuzelas, South African horns. Vuvuzelas are made from brightly colored plastic, and are roughly 3 feet (1 m) long. With thousands of fans blowing these horns at the same time, each match sounded like it was surrounded by a giant swarm of bees. The constant buzzing angered some fans, who argued that the noise made it impossible to hear commentators' voices, national anthems, and referees. There was even talk about banning them from the World Cup. But FIFA's president, Sepp Blatter, wanted to keep them. "I have always said that Africa has a different rhythm, a different sound," he said. "I don't see banning the music traditions of fans in their own country. Would you want to see a ban on the fan traditions in your country?"

DECISION 2010

When LeBron James's contract with the NBA Cleveland Cavaliers ended in 2010, he became a free agent. Teams from around the country wanted to hire him. In the end, it was up to James to pick the team he wanted to join. On July 8, 2010, he made his announcement in a live 75-minute television special, *The Decision*. Ten million viewers tuned in as James finally announced, "I'm taking my talents to South Beach." While Miami Heat supporters cheered the decision, Cleveland fans were angry that James chose to leave the Cavaliers. And many more basketball fans were disappointed that he wouldn't be joining the New York Knicks, the Chicago Bulls, or any of the other teams he had been considering.

FIRST FOR THE GIANTS

The San Francisco Giants took home their first World Series championship since 1954. They defeated the Texas Rangers, four games to one.

LONGEST TENNIS MATCH EVER

In June 2010, U.S. tennis player John Isner and Nicolas Mahut of France faced off during a match at Wimbledon, in England. Neither athlete was particularly well known before the match, but now they will go down in history for playing the longest tennis match ever recorded. The match lasted 11 hours and five minutes, and had to be spread out over three days. Isner won.

Isner

14

BIEBER FEVER REACHES NEW HEIGHTS!

Justin Bieber began his career as the star of homemade YouTube videos. Within a few years, he has become one of the hottest teen recording stars of all time. He was named Artist of the Year and Favorite Male Artist (Pop or Rock) at the American Music Awards, Choice Male Artist at the Teen Choice Awards, and Best New Artist at the MTV Video Music Awards. He published an autobiography titled *Justin Bieber: First Step 2 Forever: My Story* and saw his life on the big screen with the 3-D film *Justin Bieber: Never Say Never*. The movie was part concert footage and part documentary about Justin's superfast rise to pop stardom.

THE END OF HARRY POTTER?

The final two installments of the Harry Potter films, *Harry Potter and the Deathly Hallows, Part 1* and *Part 2*, were released in 2010 and 2011. The first film in the popular series hit screens in 2001. That's 10 years of big-screen Pottermania! Many fans have followed the story of Harry, Hermione, and Ron since 1997, when the first book in the series was published in the United Kingdom.

3-D MOVIES ARE A HIT!

From *Toy Story 3* and *How to Train Your Dragon* to *Alice in Wonderland* and *Green Lantern*, films showing in 3-D are hot tickets in theaters. There will be many more in 2011 and 2012.

GOING GAGA FOR GAGA

Catchy songs and outrageous outfits have kept Lady Gaga at the top of the pop charts and on the covers of magazines. In one of her craziest moments yet, she attended the MTV Video Music Awards in a dress made out of meat!

E-BOOKS ON THE RISE

Sales of e-books, which can be read on devices like the Kindle, Nook, iPhone, and iPad, jumped dramatically. In fact, readers spent $39.9 million on e-books in 2010. That's a 158% increase over the year before.

What's in the News?

15

Gators, Go Home!

By Suzanne Zimbler

Imagine an alligator crawling through the snow. Seem strange? There's a reason. The reptiles don't normally live in cold climates. Their natural home is in the southeastern part of the United States.

But lately, gators have been popping up far from where they belong. In August 2010, one was seen swimming in the Chicago River, in Illinois, and another was spotted strolling down a street in Brockton, Massachusetts. In the same week, a baby alligator was found hiding under a car in New York City.

EX-PETS

Experts say the creatures are most likely pets that have been abandoned by their owners. "People buy them as pets, and then they get too big," says Kent Vliet, an alligator expert from the University of Florida. "At some point, they decide they just can't deal with it."

According to Franklin Percival, a wildlife biologist for the U.S. Geological Survey, alligators are often abandoned when they become 3 feet (1 m) long. "People wonder why they made the early decision [to buy them]," he says.

Keeping alligators as pets is allowed in some states, including Massachusetts, as long as the owner has a permit. Illinois used to issue alligator permits, but stopped three years ago because of problems with illegal ownership and people releasing unwanted pets. New York also does not issue alligator permits.

REPTILES AT RISK

Chicago's reptile intruder drew crowds. The creature peered up at the people gathered by the river, then swam away

Baby alligators (known as hatchlings) are only about 6 to 8 inches (15 to 20 cm) long at birth.

when a duck got too close. "It's not scary," said 8-year-old Caleb Berry afterwards. "It was a baby, and it wasn't eating anything."

According to Vliet, baby alligators do not pose much of a threat to people. They eat snails, frogs, and small snakes. However, they would probably bite if handled, he said.

The lost reptiles are the ones that are really in danger, experts say. Alligators are cold-blooded creatures. They cannot control their own body temperature. To warm themselves, alligators bask in the sun. The creatures cannot survive for long in northern climates.

Some of these creatures are captured by authorities and handed over to reptile specialists. But other pet gators abandoned by their owners may not be so lucky. That is why many experts advise against owning alligators. "Ecologically, it's not responsible," said Percival. "And maybe ethically it's not a good idea either."

Alligators sun themselves in Everglades National Park in Florida.

1. Labrador retriever

2. German shepherd

3. Yorkshire terrier

4. Beagle

5. Golden retriever

TOP 10 MOST POPULAR DOG BREEDS

6. Bulldog

7. Boxer

8. Dachshund

9. Poodle

10. Shih tzu

Source: American Kennel Club

TOP 10 DOG NAMES

1. Bella
2. Bailey
3. Max
4. Lucy
5. Molly
6. Buddy
7. Maggie
8. Daisy
9. Charlie
10. Sophie

1. Persian

2. Maine coon

3. Exotic

4. Abyssinian

5. Siamese

TOP 10 MOST POPULAR CAT BREEDS

6. Ragdoll

7. Sphynx

8. Birman

9. American shorthair

10. Oriental

TOP 10 CAT NAMES

1. Max
2. Bella
3. Chloe
4. Oliver
5. Lucy
6. Smokey
7. Shadow
8. Tiger
9. Tigger
10. Charlie

Source: Cat Fanciers' Association

Animals

17

VERTEBRATES

There are two basic kinds of animals: vertebrates, which have backbones, and invertebrates, which don't.

FISH are cold-blooded, live in water, and breathe using gills. Their skin is scaly and, with the exception of sharks (which give birth to live young), they lay eggs. Carp, swordfish, **betta,** flounder, tuna, and eels are some examples of fish.

AMPHIBIANS are cold-blooded and begin life in the water, breathing through gills. When they are fully grown, they breathe through lungs and can walk on land. They lay eggs. Some examples of amphibians are frogs, **toads,** newts, and salamanders.

REPTILES are cold-blooded and have lungs. Their skin is scaly. Most reptiles lay eggs. Reptiles include lizards, **turtles,** snakes, alligators, and crocodiles.

BIRDS are warm-blooded, and have wings and feathers. All birds lay eggs, and most can fly (though **ostriches,** kiwis, and penguins cannot). Some other examples of birds are eagles, ducks, swans, pelicans, doves, finches, hummingbirds, cardinals, and flamingos.

MAMMALS are warm-blooded and, with the exception of the platypus and the echidna, give birth to live young. Mammal mothers breast-feed their young. Most mammals have hair or fur and live on land (except for porpoises, dolphins, and whales, which live in the water). Bats, lions, giraffes, squirrels, dogs, horses, anteaters, **koalas,** grizzly bears, otters, and humans are all mammals.

ANIMALS WITH JOBS

Humans have been training animals for centuries. These furry and feathery friends have been taught to entertain audiences, transport people and goods, carry messages, and save lives. Carrier pigeons are known for their incredible ability to find their way home. During World War I and World War II, they carried messages back and forth between soldiers. They've also been used to get medication to hard-to-reach sick people. From 1860 to 1861, the Pony Express mail service employed 400 horses carrying saddlebags of letters 2,000 miles (3,219 km) across the United States.

Today, dromedary camels, elephants, and donkeys perform many tasks. They carry heavy loads, assist in farming, and are ridden by humans. Several dog breeds have been very helpful to humans. Bloodhounds help track lost or missing persons. Saint Bernard dogs are famous for their mountain rescue skills, and Labrador retrievers are often used as guides for blind people.

German shepherds make great police or rescue dogs.

INVERTEBRATES

SPONGES live in water and are immobile. They get their food by filtering tiny organisms that swim by.

COELENTERATES (sih-*len*-teh-rates) have stinging tentacles around their mouths. They use their mouths not only to eat with but also to eliminate waste. Examples of coelenterates are corals, hydras, jellyfish, and **sea anemones.**

ECHINODERMS (ih-*keye*-nuh-derms) live in the sea and have exoskeletons, which means that their skeletons or supporting structures are located on the outside of their bodies. Echinoderms include sea urchins, starfish, **brittle stars,** and sand dollars.

WORMS live in a variety of places, including underwater, in the ground, and even inside other living creatures. Examples of worms include tapeworms, flukes, pinworms, **leeches,** night crawlers, and earthworms.

MOLLUSKS (*mol*-usks) have soft bodies. To protect themselves, some have hard shells. **Clams,** oysters, octopuses, scallops, squids, slugs, and snails are all mollusks.

ARTHROPODS have bodies that are divided into different parts, or segments. They also have exoskeletons. Arthropods include crustaceans (such as lobsters, crabs, shrimps, and barnacles), arachnids (spiders, scorpions, and ticks), centipedes, millipedes, and all insects (such as butterflies, ants, bees, **dragonflies,** and beetles).

INSECT PARTS

HEAD

THORAX

ABDOMEN

There are more insects on Earth than all other kinds of animals combined. Scientists have identified more than 1 million species of insects, but generally agree that there are many more out there. From ants to beetles, fireflies to houseflies, stick bugs to stink bugs, insects vary greatly in shape, size, color, diet, habitat, and behavior. But insects are all alike in three major ways.

- They have six legs.
- Their bodies are divided into three sections (head, thorax, and abdomen).
- They have hard outer skeletons, known as exoskeletons.

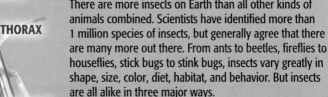

Animals

19

WARM-BLOODED OR COLD-BLOODED?

The temperature of an animal's body depends on whether the animal is warm-blooded or cold-blooded.

WARM-BLOODED ANIMALS (birds, mammals) are able to keep their body temperature constant. In cold weather, they turn the food they eat into energy that creates heat. In hot weather, they sweat, pant, or do other things to help cool their outsides and insides. Most of the food they take in is devoted to maintaining their body temperature.

TOP 5 Birds Sighted

From February 18 to 21, 2011, tens of thousands of people across the United States and Canada filled out checklists as part of the Great Backyard Bird Count. The results are in. Here are the most-reported birds.

1. Northern cardinal: 45,538 checklists
2. Mourning dove: 40,139 checklists
3. Dark-eyed junco: 39,419 checklists
4. Downy woodpecker: 34,618 checklists
5. American goldfinch: 31,923 checklists

SOURCES: THE CORNELL LAB OF ORNITHOLOGY AND THE NATIONAL AUDUBON SOCIETY

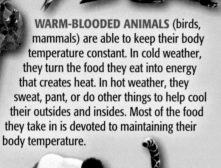

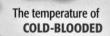

The temperature of COLD-BLOODED ANIMALS (reptiles, fish, amphibians, invertebrates) is the same as that of their surroundings. Because of this, they are able to be very active in hot weather but are sluggish in low temperatures. When it is hot, chemicals in their bodies react quickly to help their muscles move, but these reactions slow down as the outside temperature drops. Most of the food cold-blooded animals take in is devoted to building their body mass.

TOP 5 Longest Snakes

A reticulated (reh-*tik*-yoo-lay-tid) python grows to be an average of 35 feet (10.7 m). That's as long as a school bus. Here are some other extra-long snakes.

1. Reticulated python		35 feet (10.7 m)
2. Green anaconda		28 feet (8.5 m)
3. Indian python		25 feet (7.6 m)
4. Diamond python		21 feet (6.4 m)
5. King cobra		19 feet (5.8 m)

20

CAMOUFLAGED CRITTERS

In order to stay safe from predators, many animals have developed ways of blending into their environments. If a larger or more dangerous animal doesn't see them, they have a better chance of surviving. Some animals, such as the chameleon, can change color to look like the leaves and trees around them. Others have shapes or textures that make them hard to see. Here are a few amazing camouflaged animals.

Many types of moths look similar to tree bark.

The arctic fox's white fur helps it blend into its environment.

This geometrid caterpillar mimics a tree branch.

It is hard to tell where the plant ends and this stick insect begins.

Katydids are expert camouflagers. They look just like leaves, so insect-eaters may not notice them. For added protection, they resemble unhealthy or dying leaves. Since most animals prefer to eat healthy leaves, the insects are often skipped over by the leaf-eaters, too.

Like chameleons, octopuses can change color. They can also alter their normally smooth skin to look bumpy like the rocks and sand around them.

Decorator crabs are not able to change the color of their shells. Instead, they cover themselves with shells, rocks, pieces of seaweed, and other things they find on the seafloor.

Animals

21

ENDANGERED ANIMALS

In 1973, the Endangered Species Act was passed by the U.S. Congress to protect various plants and animals from vanishing from the United States and its territories. The U.S. Fish and Wildlife Service keeps track of the populations of all known species in the country, adding or removing their names as their survival numbers change. Here are some endangered species on the list.

Fishing has almost wiped out the white abalone, a marine snail, along the coast of California. It is the first marine invertebrate to get endangered species protection.

White abalone
Gray wolf
Alabama cavefish
California condor
Piping plover
American crocodile
Bald eagle
Ocelot
Desert pupfish
Tooth cave spider
Hawaiian hoary bat
Lesser long-nosed bat
Grizzly bear
Mount Hermon June beetle
Yellow-shouldered blackbird
Jaguar
Bay checkerspot butterfly
El Segundo blue butterfly
Woodland caribou
Mona boa
Amber darter
Ivory-billed woodpecker
Green sea turtle
Steller sea lion
Chinook salmon
Hawaiian duck
California tiger salamander
Carolina northern flying squirrel
Arroyo toad
Wood stork
Polar bear

Bald eagles build their nests, called aeries (*air*-ees), at the top of tall trees. Many return to their nest each year, adding more sticks, twigs, and grass. Bald eagle nests can weigh more than 4,000 pounds (1,814 kg) and be as large as 9 feet (3 m) wide!

Unlike most cats, jaguars love the water and are often excellent swimmers. They even go fishing by waving their tails over water to attract hungry fish. Fur hunters are the biggest threat to jaguars' survival.

Ivory-billed woodpeckers were believed to have been extinct, but some were spotted in 2005 in an Arkansas swamp forest. Their enormous white bill is made of bone, not ivory.

In February 2011, some land in California was set aside as protected in an attempt to save the arroyo toad, which has been on the endangered species list since 1994.

Polar bear fur does such a good job of keeping the animals warm that they can actually overheat in their icy, cold environment. They will jump into the chilly Arctic water to cool off.

A Safe Place for Salamanders

By Suzanne Zimbler

The axolotl (*ak*-suh-lot-ul) is often called the Mexican walking fish. But make no mistake. This strange-looking creature with featherlike gills and a slight smile is not a fish at all. It is a salamander.

To see one in its natural habitat, you would have to travel to Mexico City, Mexico. There used to be millions of axolotls in the lakes there. During the time of the Aztecs, the creature was a common sight. It was an important part of the Aztec diet and a key character in their tales.

But today, axolotls are hard to spot. Human actions are to blame. One lake where the salamanders once lived dried up from overuse. Another is badly polluted. To make matters worse, fish from China and Africa were introduced to the area. Officials hoped people would eat the fish. Instead, the foreign fish ate the axolotls' eggs.

Scientist Luis Zambrano is trying to save the creature from extinction. "As a Mexican, protecting this animal is very important to me," he told TFK. As a

Scientist Luis Zambrano warns that without help, the axolotl could be extinct in nine years.

scientist, Zambrano knows the axolotl is valuable for another reason—it has the amazing ability to regrow body parts that are lost or damaged.

Zambrano and his team set up five axolotl refuges in canals. A barrier of plants and sand surrounds each refuge, keeping out fish and pollution. If these havens are successful, Zambrano plans to build more. At the moment, less than 5% of the area is a suitable habitat for axolotls. He hopes that people who learn about the salamander will support efforts to save it. "Polar bears are more famous," he says, "but the axolotl needs our help, too."

What's That?

Many scientists work with animals. Each different field has its own name. Here are a few. Try saying ichthyologist five times fast!

A **coleopterist** studies beetles.
An **entomologist** studies insects.
An **ethologist** studies animal behavior.
A **herpetologist** studies reptiles and amphibians.
An **ichthyologist** studies fish.
A **malacologist** studies mollusks.
A **mammalogist** studies mammals.
An **ornithologist** studies birds.

An entomologist examines the antenna of a tiny sawfly.

Animals

23

ANIMAL COMMUNICATION

Animals do not talk to one another like humans do, but that does not mean they do not communicate in other ways. Birds call to one another and sing particular songs to attract mates. Prairie dogs use many different calls to let other members of their colony know when danger is approaching. They use different noises for coyotes, hawks, humans, and other potential threats. Dolphins, among the smartest animals on the planet, work together to surround schools of fish to eat them. To coordinate, they communicate using a variety of clicks and whistles.

Gorillas bark, growl, and pound on their chests to get their point across. Honeybees do an elaborate in-air dance to tell one another where to find nectar. Scientists have even trained some gorillas, chimpanzees, and bonobos (a type of ape similar to the chimpanzee) to communicate using sign language.

Prairie dog

Whales communicate by making high-pitched squeals and almost cowlike moos. Each species of whale has a different type of song. Some sing alone and others in groups. You can listen to whale songs online at *whalesong.net*.

TOOL USERS

Humans aren't the only animals to pick up objects and use them as tools. Chimpanzees insert long, thin sticks into beehives or termite nests to get at the honey or termite snacks inside. Sometimes they even strip the sticks of leaves and twigs that may get in the way.

Rocks are the tools of choice for sea otters. These playful animals use rocks to break open clam, crab, and other shells to get at the meat inside.

Otters aren't the only ones using rocks to get to food. Some birds will find hard-to-crack eggs and soar high in the air before dropping them. These birds have learned to aim for rocks rather than soft ground so that the eggs will be sure to break open. And some birds have learned to break open eggs in a less messy way. Egyptian vultures like to eat ostrich eggs. They are large and full of protein, but they are also tough to open. This type of vulture will hold a rock in its beak and bang the rock against the ostrich egg until it breaks open. And then, dinner is served!

Egyptian vulture

Chimpanzee

Using their trunks, elephants snap off tree branches and use them to shoo away flies.

24

DARING DEFENSE

Many animals have ways to discourage predators from eating them. **Porcupines** are covered in quills. Normally, these spines lie flat along a porcupine's body, but when the porcupine is threatened, the quills rise up. With raised quills, not only does the animal look much larger, but it now has a body covered with sharp, pointy weapons that it can use to poke its enemy. Sea urchins are also covered with sharp spines. Animals from starfish to seabirds to humans like to eat the soft body of the sea urchin, but they must first get past a lot of sharp spikes to get to the fleshy body underneath.

Other animals employ smells or poison rather than spikes. A skunk will spray nasty-smelling liquid at a creature that looks threatening. **Monarch caterpillars** nibble on the poisonous milkweed plant, which makes them toxic to eat. The caterpillars later become beautiful monarch butterflies, and they *still* taste terrible to predators. The hooded pitohui and the blue-capped ifrita are two types of birds, both found in New Guinea, that have poisonous skin and feathers. Who would want to eat them?

Some of the most toxic animals on Earth are poison dart frogs. The 2-inch-long (5 cm) **golden poison dart frog** contains enough poison in its tiny body to kill 10 adults. Scientists believe that these frogs get their unique poison from the toxic plants and insects they eat. When a golden poison dart frog is raised in captivity, it does not become poisonous.

TOP 5 Biggest Cats

Tigers are the biggest cats in the world. How much does a tiger weigh? Multiply your weight seven times! Here are the heavyweight champs of the cat kingdom, by the top weight of the males.

1. Tiger: 673 pounds (305 kg)

2. Lion: 550 pounds (249 kg)

3. Jaguar: 264 pounds (120 kg)

4. Puma: 227 pounds (103 kg)

5. Leopard: 198 pounds (90 kg)

SOURCES: WALKER'S MAMMALS OF THE WORLD

TIME FOR KIDS GAME

TIGER MATCH

Here are eight pairs of tigers. Some are walking, some are roaring, and some are resting. Can you find the matching cats? Draw a line from each tiger to its identical twin.

Answers on page 242.

Animals

Body and Health

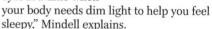

Get Some Sleep!

By Vickie An

Are you tired during the day? Do you have trouble focusing? Do you feel like a grouch? If so, you might not be getting enough sleep.

On weekday mornings, Jeilun Liao, 8, wakes up around 7:40 a.m. He brushes his teeth and gets dressed. Then he heads to class at P.S. 124 Yung Wing School, in New York City.

Jeilun gets between eight and 10 hours of sleep a night. On most nights, he has a hard time falling asleep. Waking up in the morning isn't easy for this fourth grader. "I don't want to get out of bed," Jeilun says. "I'm so tired."

Jeilun is not alone. Kids across the United States aren't getting enough sleep. Experts say children ages 5 to 12 should get 10 to 11 hours of sleep each night. But according to the National Sleep Foundation, kids are only sleeping an average of nine and a half hours a night. An extra 30 minutes of slumber may not seem like a lot. But it can make a big difference for kids.

SLEEP WELL, DO WELL

The amount of sleep you get can affect how well you learn. Students who are well rested tend to score higher on math and writing tests. Kids who don't get enough sleep have a harder time paying attention in class. This can affect future test performance.

Lack of sleep can also affect your mood and how you act, says Jodi Mindell. She is a sleep expert. "You're more likely to be cranky if you don't get a good night's rest," she says. "Sleep affects everything." Yolanda Oredel, 10, is a fifth grader at Clara Barton Elementary School in Anaheim, California. Yolanda and some of her classmates kept a sleep journal for a week. She says she was in a better mood on the days she slept more. "I paid more attention in class, too," she told TFK. Yolanda's teacher, JoAnne Winnick, says she can tell when her students are tired. "I've even had kids who lay their heads on their desks and doze off," she says.

WIRED AWAKE

What is keeping kids up at night? One big sleep stealer is the use of electronics, says Mindell. More kids are using computers, playing video games, texting friends, and watching TV at bedtime. "It's a lot of bright light to your eyes at a time when your body needs dim light to help you feel sleepy," Mindell explains.

It's never too late to change your sleep habits, says Mindell. Put sleep on your to-do list. Go to bed at the same time every night. Pull the plug on electronics in the bedroom. Try this challenge: Go to sleep early for a week. "Then see how you feel," Mindell says. "You will be stunned at the difference."

guess what? According to the National Sleep Research Project, teenagers and young children need the most sleep: 10 to 11 hours. The average adult age 25 to 55 should aim for eight hours. People over 65 need the least amount of shut-eye: about six hours.

WHY EXERCISE?

Exercising is one of the most important ways to keep your body healthy. When you exercise, you strengthen your bones, muscles, and heart. You also burn off extra fat, improve your balance, improve your mood, and regulate your body's metabolism, which is the process that turns the nutrients in food into energy and heat.

Today, many kids don't get enough exercise. Does that sound like you? If it does, it's time to get up and get moving! Whether you choose to play soccer, go for a swim, ride your bike, or challenge your neighbor to a game of tag, you can always find a workout that is fun for you. In addition to organized sports like football or baseball, you can work out alone by doing yoga, stretching, or skipping rope.

Even doing your chores can help keep you fit! You burn calories by putting away the dishes, raking leaves, vacuuming, or folding laundry.

BURNING CALORIES

People gain weight because they take in more calories through eating and drinking than they burn off through exercise. Calories are units of energy that you take in when you consume food (see "Food and Nutrition," page 95). Here are some examples of activities and the number of calories they burn in 30 minutes. These numbers are based on a person who weighs approximately 70 pounds (32 kg).

ACTIVITY	CALORIES BURNED	ACTIVITY	CALORIES BURNED	ACTIVITY	CALORIES BURNED
Aerobics, general	103	Gardening	63	Playing catch	40
Bagging leaves and grass	63	Gymnastics	63	Running	127
Ballet	76	Hacky Sack	63	Shooting baskets	71
Baseball	79	Hiking	95	Skateboarding	79
Basketball	127	Horseback riding	63	Sledding	111
Bicycling	127	Ice skating	111	Soccer	111
Bowling	48	Jogging	111	Softball	79
Canoeing	56	Jumping rope	159	Swimming	95
Chores	48	Karate	159	Table tennis	27
Doing homework	29	Kickball	111	Taking out the trash	40
Frisbee	48	Making the bed	32	Tennis	111
				Touch football	127
				Walking	100
				Washing the dog	56
				Yard work	79

Going green

Scientists have found a way for humans to generate their own energy while they work out. A 30-minute workout on a treadmill could create enough electricity to run a laptop for an hour. If this technology goes mainstream, health clubs could keep the environment healthy while the people inside get in shape!

Body and Health

Bone Up on Bones

Bones have two major purposes: to give shape and structure to your body, and to protect internal organs.

WHERE ARE YOUR BONES FOUND?
- 27 are in each hand.
- 26 are in each foot.
- 14 are in your face.

 Your funny bone isn't a bone at all. It's a mass of nerves that runs along the long bone in your arm—a bone called the humerus.

Growing, Growing, Grown!

At birth, you have more than 300 bones, but by the time you are an adult, you'll have just 206. Where do those additional bones go? Some bones fuse together, making one bone where there had been two.

Some bones grow a lot during a person's lifetime. Just think how short a baby's arms and legs are compared to the limbs of an adult. The longest bone in your body is the thighbone, or femur. It's about one-fourth of your total height. It keeps growing as long as you do. Your spinal cord, however, stops growing when you are about 5 years old.

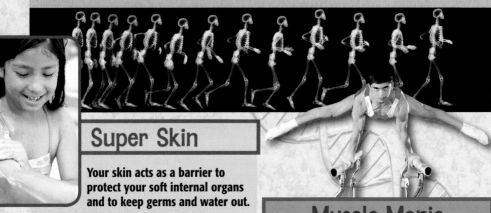

Super Skin

Your skin acts as a barrier to protect your soft internal organs and to keep germs and water out.

- An average-size adult has about 20 square feet (1.9 sq m) of skin.
- Skin gets its color from a pigment called melanin.
- Skin is the body's largest organ.
- Three main layers make up your skin: the **epidermis** (the outer layer that constantly flakes off), the **dermis** (located beneath the epidermis and containing blood vessels, sweat glands, and hair follicles), and the **hypodermis,** or subcutaneous tissue (the deepest layer of skin, which stores fat and helps keep you warm).

 The average person will shed about 40 pounds (18 kg) of skin in a lifetime.

Muscle Mania

Muscles enable you to move by pulling and pushing your skeleton along. Some muscles, such as your heart, are involuntary. That means they work without your doing anything about it. Other muscle movements are voluntary, like when you move your hand to pick up and clench a ball.

- You have 30 muscles in your face.
- Your largest muscle is called the *gluteus maximus* (another name for buttocks).
- Your heart muscle beats about 70 times a minute.
- Your eye muscles move more than 100,000 times a day.

BRAAAAINS!!

Your brain is the boss of your body. It sends signals down the spinal cord and through the nerves to all of the organs in the body. Different parts of the brain specialize in processing thoughts, memories, feelings, dreams, speech, physical coordination, balance, hunger, or sleep.

The cerebrum (suh-*ree*-brum) is the largest part of the brain. It controls your memory, reasoning, and voluntary muscles. When you play a video game, solve a math problem, kick a soccer ball, or high five your friend, you are using your cerebrum. The cerebrum is made up of the frontal lobe, parietal lobe, occipital lobe, and temporal lobe.

The **frontal lobe** deals with intellect, behavior, problem solving, and creativity, among other things.

The **temporal** (*tem*-per-uhl) **lobe** helps regulate hearing, memories, and fear, as well as other things.

The **brain stem** connects the brain to the spinal cord and handles involuntary body functions like breathing, circulating blood, and breaking down food.

The **parietal** (puh-*reye*-ih-tul) **lobe** controls the sense of touch and helps you understand senses and language.

The **occipital** (ok-*sip*-ih-tul) **lobe** handles vision and reading.

The **cerebellum** (sair-uh-*bell*-um) controls balance, coordination, and movement. When you stand on one foot, walk on the balance beam, or aim the perfect free throw, your cerebellum is in charge.

Have a Heart

The heart is a muscle with a very important job: to pump blood through your arteries to all the parts of the body. Oxygen, digested food, hormones, and nutrients are carried by the blood to the cells that need them. The blood also carries waste materials and carbon dioxide away from the cells.

Blood is carried to and from the heart in three kinds of tubes, or blood vessels: arteries, veins, and capillaries.

- Arteries carry blood away from the heart.
- Veins carry blood to the heart.
- Capillaries connect arteries and veins.

The aorta is the body's largest artery. It carries oxygen-rich blood from the heart to the abdomen, where it branches off to supply blood to many organs (but not the lungs).

The pulmonary artery carries oxygen-poor blood from the heart to the lungs. The lungs remove the carbon dioxide from the blood as you exhale. As you inhale, your lungs replenish the oxygen in the blood.

The heart has four chambers. The upper chambers (right atrium and left atrium) receive the blood that enters the heart. The lower chambers (right ventricle and left ventricle) pump blood out of the heart.

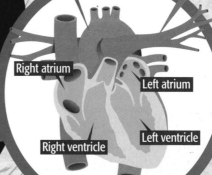

Right atrium

Left atrium

Right ventricle

Left ventricle

Body and Health

29

Books and Literature

Types of Literature

The two biggest categories of literature are fiction, which features made-up characters and stories, and nonfiction, which includes facts and is about real people, places, and events. Here are some of the most common types of writing that you may come across, along with a few recommendations from some TFK kid reviewers.

TFK Kid Reporter Tara Lynne Moon read and recommended *The Star Maker*, by Laurence Yep. The book tells the story of a kid named Artie who is constantly picked on by his cousin Petey. Tara Lynne wrote, "Laurence Yep does a very good job of telling the story using details and emotions, and his strong words and wisdom stand out."

TFK Kid Reporter Frannie Salisbury enjoyed the biography *Alexander Hamilton: The Outsider*, by Jean Fritz. She explained, "Hamilton was sometimes considered an outsider because of his birthplace, which was in the West Indies." The book is packed with facts, dates, quotes, and letters from Hamilton's lifetime. Franny reports, "It would be a great resource for a school project. . . . The author captures the interesting side of Hamilton and makes it fun to read about him."

NOVEL
A piece of fiction, written in prose (which means it is written in language that resembles everyday language instead of being written in rhyming verse, for example). Novels are full-length narratives as opposed to short stories.

SHORT STORY
A prose narrative about the length of one chapter in a novel

AUTOBIOGRAPHY
The factual account of a person's life told by that person

BIOGRAPHY
The factual account of a person's life told by another person

ESSAY
A discussion of a particular topic from a personal perspective

MYSTERY PERSON

I was born on August 1, 1779. I was a lawyer, but I wrote poetry as a hobby. On September 14, 1814, I wrote an important poem about the U.S. flag. The words of my poem became the lyrics of "The Star-Spangled Banner." In 1931, Congress officially named the song the U.S. national anthem.

WHO AM I? _____

Answer on page 242.

SCIENCE FICTION
A novel that takes place in the future or in a setting in which science and technology play important roles

HISTORY
The factual recording of past events

FANTASY
An imaginative story with bizarre characters that takes place in an unnatural setting

ROMANCE
A novel in which love is the central theme

MYSTERY
A novel in which a crime, often a murder, is solved

HISTORICAL FICTION
Fictional stories or novels that take place during specific historical periods, often featuring actual historical people, events, and settings

POEM
A reflection or narrative written in lines of verse that may or may not rhyme

PLAY
Written in dialogue. The actions in a play are meant to be acted out onstage.

TFK Kid Reporter Claire Julian gave high marks to *The Gecko and Sticky: Sinister Substitute*, by Wendelin Van Draanen. According to Claire, "Thirteen-year-old Dave Sanchez and his talking gecko, Sticky, make a great superhero team. When a mysterious substitute teacher fills in for the evil Ms. Veronica Krockle, who has never missed a day in her nine years of teaching, Dave and Sticky know something is up. Soon, they figure out that the substitute teacher is not a teacher at all, and their quest to save Ms. Krockle begins."

For historical fiction, TFK Kid Reporter Andrew Ravaschiere recommended *Woods Runner*, by Gary Paulsen. The book begins on the western frontier of Pennsylvania during the American Revolution. "Thirteen-year-old Samuel Lehi Smith returns from hunting for food for his family and finds that his colonial settlement has been attacked by the British," Andrew writes. "The British, aided by the Iroquois, take Samuel's parents away as prisoners. This thrilling book takes you on Samuel's journey as he strives to rescue his parents."

Reference Books
—and What They Tell You

Thesaurus: Synonyms and antonyms of words

Dictionary: Words' spellings, pronunciations, origins, meanings, and examples of usage

Encyclopedia: In-depth explanations of various topics

Almanac: Quick-and-easy access to facts, figures, charts, and other data for a specific year

Atlas: Political, topographical, and historical maps

Books and Literature

31

Award-Winning Books

2011 Newbery Medal
Moon over Manifest
by Clare Vanderpool

2011 Caldecott Medal
A Sick Day for Amos McGee
by Philip C. Stead, illustrated by Erin E. Stead

2011 Coretta Scott King Author Award
One Crazy Summer
by Rita Williams-Garcia

2011 Michael L. Printz Award
Ship Breaker
by Paolo Bacigalupi

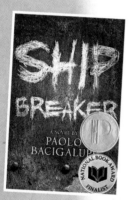

2011 Robert F. Sibert Informational Book Medal
Kakapo Rescue: Saving the World's Strangest Parrot
by Sy Montgomery, photographs by Nic Bishop

2011 Pura Belpré Award
The Dreamer
by Pam Muñoz Ryan, illustrated by Peter Sis

2011 Margaret A. Edwards Award
The Amazing Maurice and His Educated Rodents
by Terry Pratchett

2011 Scott O'Dell Award for Historical Fiction
One Crazy Summer
by Rita Williams-Garcia

2011 Odyssey Award for Excellence in Audiobook Production
The True Meaning of Smekday
by Adam Rex, produced by Listening Library

guess what?
One in 10 Americans owns an electronic reading device such as a Kindle, Nook, or iPad.

32

The 2011 Yalsa Award for Excellence in Nonfiction
Janis Joplin: Rise Up Singing
by Ann Angel

2010 National Book Award for Young People's Literature
Mockingbird
by Kathryn Erskine

2010 Indies Choice Award for Young Adult Book of the Year
Catching Fire
by Suzanne Collins

2010 Edgar Allan Poe Award for Best Young Adult Book
Reality Check
by Peter Abrahams

2010 Boston Globe–Horn Book Award for Fiction and Poetry
When You Reach Me
by Rebecca Stead

2010 Boston Globe–Horn Book Award for Nonfiction
Marching for Freedom: Walk Together, Children, and Don't You Grow Weary
by Elizabeth Partridge

Books and Literature

MYSTERY PERSON

I was born on April 3, 1783. As an author, I sometimes used the pen name Dietrich Knickerbocker. *The Legend of Sleepy Hollow*, a tale about a headless horseman, is one of my most famous stories.

WHO AM I? _____

Answer on page 242.

33

Calendars and Holidays

2012

JANUARY

S	M	T	W	T	F	S
1	2	3	4	5	6	7
8	9	10	11	12	13	14
15	16	17	18	19	20	21
22	23	24	25	26	27	28
29	30	31				

FEBRUARY

S	M	T	W	T	F	S
			1	2	3	4
5	6	7	8	9	10	11
12	13	14	15	16	17	18
19	20	21	22	23	24	25
26	27	28	29			

MARCH

S	M	T	W	T	F	S
				1	2	3
4	5	6	7	8	9	10
11	12	13	14	15	16	17
18	19	20	21	22	23	24
25	26	27	28	29	30	31

APRIL

S	M	T	W	T	F	S
1	2	3	4	5	6	7
8	9	10	11	12	13	14
15	16	17	18	19	20	21
22	23	24	25	26	27	28
29	30					

MAY

S	M	T	W	T	F	S
		1	2	3	4	5
6	7	8	9	10	11	12
13	14	15	16	17	18	19
20	21	22	23	24	25	26
27	28	29	30	31		

JUNE

S	M	T	W	T	F	S
					1	2
3	4	5	6	7	8	9
10	11	12	13	14	15	16
17	18	19	20	21	22	23
24	25	26	27	28	29	30

JULY

S	M	T	W	T	F	S
1	2	3	4	5	6	7
8	9	10	11	12	13	14
15	16	17	18	19	20	21
22	23	24	25	26	27	28
29	30	31				

AUGUST

S	M	T	W	T	F	S
		1	2	3	4	
5	6	7	8	9	10	11
12	13	14	15	16	17	18
19	20	21	22	23	24	25
26	27	28	29	30	31	

SEPTEMBER

S	M	T	W	T	F	S
						1
2	3	4	5	6	7	8
9	10	11	12	13	14	15
16	17	18	19	20	21	22
23	24	25	26	27	28	29
30						

OCTOBER

S	M	T	W	T	F	S
	1	2	3	4	5	6
7	8	9	10	11	12	13
14	15	16	17	18	19	20
21	22	23	24	25	26	27
28	29	30	31			

NOVEMBER

S	M	T	W	T	F	S
			1	2	3	
4	5	6	7	8	9	10
11	12	13	14	15	16	17
18	19	20	21	22	23	24
25	26	27	28	29	30	

DECEMBER

S	M	T	W	T	F	S
						1
2	3	4	5	6	7	8
9	10	11	12	13	14	15
16	17	18	19	20	21	22
23	24	25	26	27	28	29
30	31					

guess what? A popular Southern twist to the traditional Thanksgiving turkey is turducken, a turkey stuffed with a duck stuffed with a chicken.

Calendars and Holidays

35

MAJOR HOLIDAYS
IN 2012

JANUARY 1: New Year's Day

JANUARY 16: Martin Luther King Jr. Day

JANUARY 23: Chinese New Year

FEBRUARY 2: Groundhog Day

FEBRUARY 14: Valentine's Day

FEBRUARY 20: Presidents' Day

FEBRUARY 21: Mardi Gras

FEBRUARY 29: Leap Day

MARCH 11: Daylight Saving Time Begins

MARCH 17: St. Patrick's Day

APRIL 1: April Fools' Day

APRIL 7–14*: Passover

APRIL 8: Easter

APRIL 22: Earth Day

MAY 5: Cinco de Mayo

MAY 13: Mother's Day

MAY 28: Memorial Day

JUNE 17: Father's Day

JULY 4: Independence Day

SEPTEMBER 3: Labor Day

SEPTEMBER 17–18*: Rosh Hashanah

SEPTEMBER 26*: Yom Kippur

OCTOBER 8: Columbus Day Celebrated

OCTOBER 31: Halloween

NOVEMBER 4: Daylight Saving Time Ends

NOVEMBER 11: Veterans Day

NOVEMBER 22: Thanksgiving

DECEMBER 9–16*: Hanukkah

DECEMBER 25: Christmas

DECEMBER 26–JANUARY 1: Kwanzaa

*All Jewish holidays begin at sundown the evening before.

36

YEAR OF THE DRAGON

The Chinese calendar is based on the lunar calendar, and the Chinese New Year starts on the first day of the lunar calendar. In 2012, the Chinese New Year begins January 23. People celebrate by wearing red, setting off fireworks, and sharing meals with their families.

Each year on the Chinese calendar corresponds to one of 12 animals in the Chinese zodiac. 2012 is the Year of the Dragon. Other Years of the Dragon include 1916, 1928, 1940, 1952, 1964, 1976, 1988, and 2000. People who are born under this sign are thought to be energetic, healthy, honest, sensitive, stubborn, and brave. In what year were you born? How about your brothers, sisters, and friends? See the chart on the right to find out where your birth year falls on the Chinese zodiac.

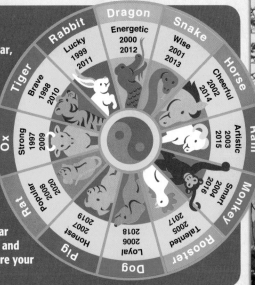

TIME FOR KIDS GAME

PASS THE PIE

Someone at this Thanksgiving dinner table took an extra piece of pie. There were eight slices, but only seven people. Use the clues to find out who gobbled up an extra piece.

1. The person has brown hair.
2. The person is not wearing glasses.
3. The person is holding a fork.
4. This person's eyes are closed.

Answer on page 242.

MYSTERY PERSON

I sailed with the Pilgrims on the *Mayflower* from England to the New World in 1620. Our group started a colony called New Plimouth. I was its military leader. In 1621, we shared a feast with the Wampanoag Indians. It was the first Thanksgiving.

WHO AM I?

_____

Answer on page 242.

Calendars and Holidays

37

Computers and Communication

A Wired World

By Suzanne Zimbler

Many kids spend hours each day on cell phones, computers, and other electronic devices. Fitting in other activities can be a challenge.

At 10:30 p.m. on a weeknight, 11-year-old Brandon Blanco is sound asleep in his Naples, Florida, home. Suddenly, a loud noise wakes him up. Instinctively, Brandon reaches for his cell phone. He blinks twice, and the message on the dimly lit screen becomes clear: "R U awake?"

But the late-night text does not annoy Brandon. He gets frequent messages and calls, even after bedtime. And he can't imagine life without them. "If I didn't have a cell phone, I wouldn't be able to talk to my friends or family as often," he told TFK.

Brandon's use of technology does not stop there. He also has an iPod, a computer, a TV, and three video-game consoles in his room. With so many choices, it is no surprise that when he is not at school, he spends nearly every waking minute using one or more of these devices.

Brandon is hardly alone. According to a recent study by the Kaiser Family Foundation, young people ages 8 to 18 are spending more time than ever using electronic devices. How much time? More than seven and a half hours a day on average, the study found. That is about an hour more than just five years ago.

GAGA FOR GADGETS

The jump is the result of a huge explosion in mobile devices, says Victoria Rideout, the lead author of the study. Today, nearly seven out of 10 kids have cell phones. Just five years ago, it was four out of 10. And the number of young people with MP3 players has more than quadrupled in that time.

"These devices have opened up many more opportunities for young people to

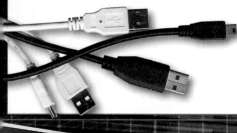

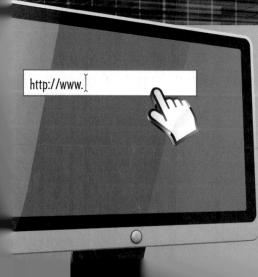

Web Address Endings

There are five main endings for Web addresses in the United States: *.com*, *.gov*, *.edu*, *.org*, and *.net*. These endings tell you something about a website before you even visit the home page. For example, addresses ending in *.edu* are for the websites of educational institutions. Those ending in *.gov* are sites for government agencies, and those ending in *.org* are created by and for nonprofit organizations.

use media, whether it's on the bus, on the way to school, or waiting in line at the pizza parlor," says Rideout. Often, kids multitask, or use more than one device at a time. Media expert Cheryl Olson is not surprised. "If you've got a chance to do something on your computer and take a phone call and have the TV on in the background, why not?" she says.

PLUGGED IN AND TUNED OUT?

Most experts agree that technology has much to offer kids. But some worry that plugged-in kids could be missing out on other activities, such as playing outside or hanging out with friends. "It's a matter of balance," says Olson. "You've got to work on it."

Multitasking while doing homework is another concern. Some kids listen to music, watch TV, or use the phone while completing assignments. "It is important to make sure that you can stop and concentrate on one thing deeply," says Rideout.

Logan Jones, 11, of Maumelle, Arkansas, is a self-proclaimed "game freak." Still, he is glad not to have unlimited time with his

PlayStation 2. "I'll tell my mom I'm going to play a game, and she'll say, 'Okay, but only for 30 minutes,'" Logan told TFK. With new and exciting devices hitting stores every year, keeping technology use in check is more important than ever. "Kids should try," says Logan. "But parents might have to step in sometimes."

TOP 5 High-Tech Activities

What are plugged-in kids doing with all their electronic gadgets? Here are the ways they spend the most time each day.

1. Watching TV — 4 hours, 29 minutes
2. Listening to music — 2 hours, 31 minutes
3. Using a computer — 1 hour, 29 minutes
4. Playing video games — 1 hour, 13 minutes
5. Talking on a cell phone — 33 minutes*

*This does not include time spent text messaging.

SOURCE: KAISER FAMILY FOUNDATION

Computers and Communication

39

Shape Up Your Photos with Special Software

Computer programs like Adobe Photoshop are used to change digital photos, either to fix problems or to make the photos look different. Here are some of the basic things that can be done with a photo-editing program.

- Cropping, or cutting, a picture down to a different size or shape
- Making an image lighter or darker
- Reducing or eliminating the red-eye effect that sometimes happens when a flash is used

You can also do creative, silly, or wacky things. For example, if your aunt cannot make it to the family reunion, you can use photo-editing software to pluck her likeness from one picture and add her to a group portrait. You could even dress up George Washington and add a new face to Mt. Rushmore!

Hard vs. Soft

Your computer, monitor, mouse, and keyboard are some of the items referred to as hardware. They are the devices you can touch. Usually made of plastic, metal, and wiring, hardware allows you to run software, or the programs that enable computer users to write stories, play games, watch videos, edit movies, and do many other things.

Hard copy is a term for a printed copy of the information created and stored on a computer. Soft copies, on the other hand, are the digital versions of documents or files.

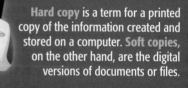

40

Electronic Trends

People have been sending more e-mails than handwritten letters for a long time now, but what are some other e-trends?

Online Journals

Many magazines and newspapers are still printed on paper and distributed as hard copies, though most have online versions as well. Newspaper editors can update news much more quickly on websites than in print. Creating an online-only news source is also less expensive than producing a print edition of a newspaper. These are two of the reasons that some newspaper companies have opted to release online-only editions.

Editors and computer programmers are also hard at work developing new ways for newspapers and magazines to be read. For example, in 2010, TIME released a special new version of the magazine for the iPad.

TV on the Computer Screen

First there were cable stations to play movies. Then there were VHS videotapes. DVDs came next, and while some people still buy DVDs or their higher-definition cousins, Blu-ray discs, or rent them from services like Netflix or Red Box, a growing number of computer users are simply downloading movies and TV shows directly onto their computers and watching them there.

Interactive Maps

Rather than pulling paper maps from the glove box, more and more drivers are relying on the Global Positioning System (GPS) to help them travel from one place to another. A GPS device (such as TomTom or Garmin) relies on satellites that orbit about 12,500 miles (20,200 km) above Earth. There are currently 28 of these satellites in orbit. A GPS device on the ground receives signals from four or five of these satellites to pinpoint its exact location. Then it matches up its current location with a map to give the user precise directions. GPS units usually have built-in speakers so driving instructions are broadcast out loud. That way, a driver can keep his or her eyes on the road instead of on the map. Smartphones and iPhones often include GPS applications as well.

guess what? Police in South Africa are using GPS to keep endangered animals safe from poachers. By implanting GPS chips into the horns of South African rhinos, authorities can track the rhinos' movements. The tracking system can also send an alert if an animal has left a protected area or if it is acting strangely.

Computers and Communication

41

Txtng Can B Gr8!

Naomi S. Baron, a professor at American University in Washington, D.C., is the author of *Always On: Language in an Online and Mobile World.* Baron believes that text messaging can be an effective way to communicate. But you need to know when to use special texting language and when not to.

Does text messaging lead to the acceptance of bad grammar and poor spelling? Many young people write messages with abbreviations (like "U" for "you"), no capitalization ("i saw leslie"), and phonetic spellings ("sez" for "says"). Some people think that text messaging is wonderful. However, others worry that texting language is harming written English.

2 TXT OR NOT 2 TXT?

Part of learning any language is figuring out which style to use when. We write more informally when we leave a note for our parents than when we compose an essay for school. But some kids are using texting language like "lol," "2," or "sez" in their school writing, rather than saving it for texting friends. That's a mistake!

It is important to know when *not* to use texting language: not in formal schoolwork and not when writing Grandma a thank-you note. It's easy to figure out what kind of language to use. You do it all the time when you speak. Think about your audience before you write, and then decide whether it is okay to use texting language. If it is, then have fun!

FROM

TIME **FOR KIDS** MAGAZINE

IM Dictionary

Sending messages back and forth over computers or cell phones can take a lot more time than having a quick conversation out loud. To save time, many people use acronyms (words formed from the first letter of each word in a phrase or name) and Internet shorthand.

?4U	question for you
2nite	tonight
AFC	away from computer
B4	before
BBS	be back soon
BFN	bye for now
BRB	be right back
DUST	did you see that
EOD	end of discussion
F2F	face to face
FOAF	friend of a friend
FYEO	for your eyes only
G2G	got to go
GBH	great big hug
GFETE	grinning from ear to ear
GFU	good for you
HAGD	have a good day
HB	hurry back
IMO	in my opinion
J/C	just checking
L8R	later
N2M	not too much
NP	no problem
OIC	oh I see
OTP	on the phone
SYS	see you soon
VBS	very big smile
W8	wait

guess what? Many students assume that the language often used in texting originated with cell phones. Actually, most of these shortcuts have been around for decades. Some abbreviations, like "b/c" for "because" or "btw" for "by the way," were used long before there were computers.

Webby Awards

Every year since 1996 (when the Internet was still quite new), the International Academy of Digital Arts and Sciences has given out awards to recognize excellence on the Internet. Here are some of the winners of the 14th Annual Webby Awards.

- **Lifetime Achievement:** Vinton Cerf
- **Person of the Year:** Roger Ebert
- **Best Actress:** Amy Poehler
- **Community:** Flickr
- **Music:** Pandora
- **Best Use of Animation or Motion Graphics:** The Pop Shoppe
- **Best Actor:** Zach Galifianakis
- **Celebrity/Fan:** Jim Carrey—Official Site
- **Charitable Organizations/Nonprofit:** Teenage Cancer Trust
- **Artist of the Year:** PS22 Chorus
- **Blog, Cultural:** Mashable
- **Film & Video Artist of the Year:** OK Go
- **News:** NYTimes.com
- **Family/Parenting:** SesameStreet.org
- **Social Networking:** Twitter
- **Green:** Love Letters to the Future
- **Movie and Film:** Mubi
- **Lifestyle:** All About Birds
- **Education:** We Choose the Moon
- **Sports:** Yahoo! Sports
- **Travel:** Iwannagothere.com
- **Youth:** National Geographic Kids
- **Science:** Mind Lab
- **Broadband:** Hulu
- **Best Practices:** Twitter

guess what? About 2.5 billion photos are uploaded to Facebook every month.

Computers and Communication

43

Internet Resource Sites for Kids

General

TIME For Kids **timeforkids.com**
4Kids.org **4kids.org**
Smithsonian Education **smithsonianeducation.org/students**
Brain Pop **brainpop.com**
Homework Help Yahoo! Kids **kids.yahoo.com/learn**
Internet Public Library **ipl.org/div/kidspace; ipl.org/div/teen**

Art

The Artist's Toolkit **artsconnected.org/toolkit**
MuseumKids **metmuseum.org/explore/museumkids.htm**
NGA (National Gallery of Art) Kids **nga.gov/kids**
The Renaissance Connection **renaissanceconnection.org**

Learn about art and make your own at nga.gov/kids.

Biography

Bio **biography.com**
Academy of Achievement **achievement.org/galleryachieve.html**

Environment

EekoWorld **pbskids.org/eekoworld**
National Institute of Environmental Health Sciences (NIEHS) Kids' Pages **kids.niehs.nih.gov**
National Wildlife Federation **nwf.org/kids**
EcoKids **ecokids.ca/pub/kids_home.cfm**
EPA Environmental Kids Club **epa.gov/kids**

Did you know that there are companies that make T-shirts from old soda bottles, and toothbrushes from the plastic in yogurt containers? Have you ever heard of creosote? It is a plant found in the desert. Its leaves close up during the hot days to keep from drying out, and unfurl at night to catch moisture. Eekoworld is full of fun environmental facts like these.

Geography

The CIA World Factbook **cia.gov/library/publications/the-world-factbook**
State Facts for Students **census.gov/schools/facts**
50states.com **50states.com**
National Geographic Kids **kids.nationalgeographic.com**

Can you match U.S. states or countries around the world to their locations on a map? Test your skills by playing USA States Map Match or Asia Map Match at kidsgeo.com.

Government and Politics

Congress for Kids **congressforkids.net**
KidsGeo.com **kidsgeo.com**
Kids.gov **kids.gov**
White House 101 **whitehouse.gov/kids**

"Andrew Carnegie's life was a true 'rags to riches' story. Born to a poor Scottish family that immigrated to the United States, Carnegie became a powerful businessman and a leading force in the American steel industry. Today, he is remembered as an industrialist, millionaire, and philanthropist. Carnegie believed that the wealthy had an obligation to give back to society, so he donated much of his fortune to causes like education and peace."

Health

KidsHealth **kidshealth.org/kid; kidshealth.org/teen**
BAM! Body and Mind **bam.gov**
Kidnetic.com **kidnetic.com**

History

History.com: This Day in History **history.com/this-day-in-history**
Women in World History **womeninworldhistory.com**
America's Story **americaslibrary.gov**
African American World for Kids **pbskids.org/aaworld**
NativeWeb **nativeweb.org/resources/history**

This entry is just one of the many profiles of people who changed the face of America. Read more at americaslibrary.gov.

14

Literature, Language, and Communication

FCC Kids Zone fcc.gov/cgb/kidszone
Aaron Shepard's Home Page aaronshep.com/index.html
Sylvan Book Adventure bookadventure.com
ABC's of the Writing Process angelfire.com/wi/writingprocess
RIF Reading Planet rif.org/readingplanet
The Blue Book of Grammar and Punctuation grammarbook.com

String instruments make up more than half of a traditional orchestra. The flared ends of brass instruments like French horns, trumpets, trombones, and tubas are called bells. Find facts like these at *sfskids.org*.

Music, Games, and Entertainment

Zoom: By Kids for Kids pbskids.org/zoom/games/index.html
Dallas Symphony Orchestra (DSO) Kids dsokids.com
AgameAday.com agameaday.com
PBS Kids Games pbskids.org/games/index.html
FunBrain.com funbrain.com/kidscenter.html
Club Penguin clubpenguin.com
San Francisco Symphony (SFS) Kids sfskids.org

Nature

Animal Corner animalcorner.co.uk
Field Trip Earth fieldtripearth.org
Kids' Planet kidsplanet.org
National Wildlife Federation nwf.org/kids

Learn about the bobcat, burrowing owl, arctic fox, killer whale, and other endangered species at *kidsplanet.org*.

News and Current Events

TIME For Kids News timeforkids.com/tfk/kids/news

Science, Technology, and Mathematics

The Exploratorium exploratorium.edu
The Yuckiest Site on the Internet yucky.discovery.com/flash
Discovery Kids kids.discovery.com
Coolmath.com coolmath.com
Webmath.com webmath.com
Ask Dr. Math mathforum.org/dr.math

What do you call a 14-sided figure? Find the answer at Ask Dr. Math.

Sports

SI Kids sikids.com
Major League Baseball mlb.com
Major League Soccer mlssoccer.com
National Basketball Association nba.com
Women's National Basketball Association wnba.com
National Football League nfl.com
National Hockey League nhl.com

Get up-to-date facts and stats on all your favorite hockey players at *nhl.com*.

going green

The Environmental Effects of Electronics

The increased use of e-mails, electronic billing, e-tickets, and digital newspapers all help to decrease the amount of paper that people use. That's great news for trees, but computers pose other threats to the environment. E-waste is the world's fastest growing type of solid waste. Discarded computers, cell phones, DVD players, and TV sets are filling up landfills, and they might be a threat to our safety, too. Some electronic waste can leak toxic materials into groundwater and endanger nearby communities. Visit *mygreenelectronics.org* to find more information about caring for and disposing of electronic equipment.

Computers and Communication

45

Countries

A Big Discovery in Egypt

By Alexandra DiPalma

Looking back at artwork from your early school days, you might find that the colors have faded or the paper has torn. Only a few years of sun and moisture can be damaging. But archaeologists have discovered a tomb in Saqqara, Egypt, with colorful paintings that have escaped the effects of time—even after 4,300 years!

"The colors of the [paintings] are fresh, as if they were painted yesterday," said archaeologist Abdel-Hakim Karar.

In May 2010, Egyptian archaeologists announced the discovery of a double tomb in an ancient cemetery near Cairo, Egypt's capital. The paintings found on the false doors helped archaeologists date the tomb to the Sixth Dynasty, the age of the pyramids.

SUPERVISORS OF THE MISSION

According to its inscriptions, the tomb held the remains of a father and son, Shendwas and Khonsu. They both served as heads of the royal scribes, a group that documented important

A worker helps to uncover tombs from the Old Kingdom period in Saqqara, Egypt.

events in Egypt's history. Most of what we know about ancient Egypt is due to the work of scribes.

Shendwas and Khonsu had other important jobs. The paintings on the tomb doors identified the two as "supervisors of the mission." According to Egypt's antiquities chief, Zahi Hawass, this means that the father and son oversaw the supply of materials used to build the pyramids.

MORE DISCOVERIES TO COME

Although the father's tomb was destroyed by humidity and the son's was robbed long ago, archaeologists found many ancient artifacts at the site. These included duck-shaped objects and a small limestone obelisk. An obelisk is a four-sided stone with a pyramid shape on top. Such statues were often buried with the dead in the Fifth and Sixth Dynasties to honor the sun god, Ra. Archaeologists say that the findings may lead to the discovery of the largest cemetery in ancient Egypt.

Zahi Hawass said the recent finds were "the most distinguished tombs ever found from the Old Kingdom."

THE WORLD'S NATIONS FROM A TO Z

On the following pages, you will find information about the world's nations. Here's an example.

This tells the main languages and the official languages (if any) spoken in a nation.

This is the type of currency, or money, used in the nation.

Life expectancy is the number of years a person can expect to live. It's affected by heredity, a person's health and nutrition, the health care and wealth of a nation, and a person's occupation.

This tells the percentage of people who can read and write.

This is an interesting fact about the country.

TAIWAN

LOCATION: Asia
CAPITAL: Taipei
AREA: 13,892 sq mi (35,980 sq km)
POPULATION ESTIMATE (2011): 23,071,779
GOVERNMENT: Multiparty democracy
LANGUAGES: Chinese (Mandarin), Taiwanese, Hakka dialects
MONEY: New Taiwan dollar
LIFE EXPECTANCY: 78
LITERACY RATE: 96%

 The national flower of Taiwan is the plum blossom.

AFGHANISTAN

LOCATION: Asia
CAPITAL: Kabul
AREA: 251,737 sq mi (652,230 sq km)
POPULATION ESTIMATE (2011): 29,835,392
GOVERNMENT: Islamic republic
LANGUAGES: Pashto and Dari (both official), others
MONEY: Afghani
LIFE EXPECTANCY: 45
LITERACY RATE: 28%

guess what? *The national sport of Afghanistan is buzkashi, or goat grabbing. During the game, riders on horseback compete to grab a goat or a calf and drop it off in a goal area.*

ALBANIA

LOCATION: Europe
CAPITAL: Tirana
AREA: 11,100 sq mi (28,748 sq km)
POPULATION ESTIMATE (2011): 2,994,667
GOVERNMENT: Parliamentary democracy
LANGUAGES: Albanian (Tosk is the official dialect), Greek, others
MONEY: Lek
LIFE EXPECTANCY: 77
LITERACY RATE: 99%

guess what? *Traditionally in Albania, if you nod your head up and down, it means no. And if you shake your head side to side, it means yes.*

ALGERIA

LOCATION: Africa
CAPITAL: Algiers
AREA: 919,590 sq mi (2,381,741 sq km)
POPULATION ESTIMATE (2011): 34,994,937
GOVERNMENT: Republic
LANGUAGES: Arabic (official), French, Berber dialects
MONEY: Dinar
LIFE EXPECTANCY: 75
LITERACY RATE: 70%

guess what? *In Algeria, most men have moustaches. Cursing a man's moustache is considered a great insult.*

ANDORRA

LOCATION: Europe
CAPITAL: Andorra la Vella
AREA: 181 sq mi (468 sq km)
POPULATION ESTIMATE (2011): 84,825
GOVERNMENT: Parliamentary democracy
LANGUAGES: Catalán (official), French, Castilian, Portuguese
MONEY: Euro (formerly French franc and Spanish peseta)
LIFE EXPECTANCY: 82
LITERACY RATE: 100%

guess what? *Andorra has no military. If the small nation were under attack, it would be up to France or Spain to defend it.*

Countries

47

ANGOLA

LOCATION: Africa
CAPITAL: Luanda
AREA: 481,350 sq mi
(1,246,700 sq km)
POPULATION ESTIMATE (2011): 13,338,541
GOVERNMENT: Republic
LANGUAGES: Portuguese (official), Bantu, others
MONEY: Kwanza
LIFE EXPECTANCY: 39
LITERACY RATE: 67%

guess what? *Angola is one of the most geographically diverse countries on the planet. It has tropical jungles, deserts, savannas, mountains, rivers, and waterfalls.*

ANTIGUA AND BARBUDA

LOCATION: Caribbean
CAPITAL: Saint John's
AREA: 171 sq mi (443 sq km)
POPULATION ESTIMATE (2011): 87,884
GOVERNMENT: Constitutional monarchy
LANGUAGE: English
MONEY: East Caribbean dollar
LIFE EXPECTANCY: 75
LITERACY RATE: 86%

guess what? *The widdy widdy is the national weed of Antigua and Barbuda. When cooked, it gets soft and sticky. There is a lot of protein in widdy widdy.*

ARGENTINA

LOCATION: South America
CAPITAL: Buenos Aires
AREA: 1,073,518 sq mi
(2,780,400 sq km)
POPULATION ESTIMATE (2011): 41,769,726
GOVERNMENT: Republic
LANGUAGES: Spanish (official), Italian, English, German, French
MONEY: Argentine peso
LIFE EXPECTANCY: 77
LITERACY RATE: 97%

guess what? *Argentinean law states that the president and vice president of the country must be Roman Catholic.*

ARMENIA

LOCATION: Asia
CAPITAL: Yerevan
AREA: 11,484 sq mi
(29,743 sq km)
POPULATION ESTIMATE (2011): 2,967,975
GOVERNMENT: Republic
LANGUAGES: Armenian, others
MONEY: Dram
LIFE EXPECTANCY: 73
LITERACY RATE: 99%

guess what? *In 301 A.D., Armenia became the first country to officially adopt Christianity as its national religion.*

AUSTRALIA

LOCATION: Oceania
CAPITAL: Canberra
AREA: 2,988,902 sq mi
(7,741,220 sq km)
POPULATION ESTIMATE (2011): 21,766,711
GOVERNMENT: Parliamentary democracy
LANGUAGE: English
MONEY: Australian dollar
LIFE EXPECTANCY: 82
LITERACY RATE: 99%

guess what? *The Tasmanian Devil is found only on the Australian island of Tasmania. It eats dead animals—even ones that have started to rot! It has powerful jaws and can eat every last scrap, including fur and bones!*

AUSTRIA

LOCATION: Europe
CAPITAL: Vienna
AREA: 32,382 sq mi
(83,871 sq km)
POPULATION ESTIMATE (2011): 8,217,280
GOVERNMENT: Federal republic
LANGUAGES: German (official), Croation (official in Burgenland), Turkish, Serbian, others
MONEY: Euro (formerly schilling)
LIFE EXPECTANCY: 80
LITERACY RATE: 98%

guess what? *In 1991, hikers found a body from the Stone Age in the mountains on the Austria–Italy border. Frozen in a glacier, the mummy was so well preserved that the hikers thought it was a modern skeleton.*

AZERBAIJAN

LOCATION: Asia
CAPITAL: Baku
AREA: 33,400 sq mi (86,600 sq km)
POPULATION ESTIMATE (2011): 8,372,373
GOVERNMENT: Republic
LANGUAGES: Azerbaijani, Lezgi, Russian, Armenian, others
MONEY: Azerbaijani manat
LIFE EXPECTANCY: 67
LITERACY RATE: 99%

guess what? *Novruz is the Azerbaijani celebration of the spring equinox. During Novruz, children run around banging spoons together and asking for treats.*

BAHAMAS

LOCATION: Caribbean
CAPITAL: Nassau
AREA: 5,359 sq mi (13,880 sq km)
POPULATION ESTIMATE (2011): 313,312
GOVERNMENT: Parliamentary democracy
LANGUAGES: English, Creole
MONEY: Bahamian dollar
LIFE EXPECTANCY: 71
LITERACY RATE: 96%

guess what? *Both Michael Jordan and Walt Disney World own islands in the Bahamas.*

BAHRAIN

LOCATION: Middle East
CAPITAL: Manama
AREA: 293 sq mi (760 sq km)
POPULATION ESTIMATE (2011): 1,214,705
GOVERNMENT: Constitutional monarchy
LANGUAGES: Arabic (official), English, Farsi, Urdu
MONEY: Bahraini dinar
LIFE EXPECTANCY: 78
LITERACY RATE: 87%

guess what? *Some researchers believe that the Garden of Eden written about in the Bible is based on an actual location on the island of Bahrain.*

BANGLADESH

LOCATION: Asia
CAPITAL: Dhaka
AREA: 55,598 sq mi (143,998 sq km)
POPULATION ESTIMATE (2011): 158,570,535
GOVERNMENT: Parliamentary democracy
LANGUAGES: Bangla (official), English
MONEY: Taka
LIFE EXPECTANCY: 70
LITERACY RATE: 48%

guess what? *The Sundarbans, a cluster of islands in the southwestern part of Bangladesh, is one of the largest unspoiled mangrove forests in the world, and home to the endangered Bengal tiger.*

BARBADOS

LOCATION: Caribbean
CAPITAL: Bridgetown
AREA: 166 sq mi (430 sq km)
POPULATION ESTIMATE (2011): 286,705
GOVERNMENT: Parliamentary democracy
LANGUAGE: English
MONEY: Barbadian dollar
LIFE EXPECTANCY: 74
LITERACY RATE: 100%

guess what? *The town of St. Andrew in Barbados was once believed to have healing properties. Many people traveled there and covered themselves in the sands of Cattlewash Beach in hopes of curing their health problems.*

BELARUS

LOCATION: Europe
CAPITAL: Minsk
AREA: 80,154 sq mi (207,600 sq km)
POPULATION ESTIMATE (2011): 9,577,552
GOVERNMENT: Republic
LANGUAGES: Belarusian, Russian
MONEY: Belarusian ruble
LIFE EXPECTANCY: 71
LITERACY RATE: 100%

guess what? *Marc Chagall, a famous painter, was born in Vitebsk, Belarus, in 1887. At the time, the country was part of the Russian Empire.*

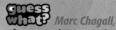

Countries

49

BELGIUM

LOCATION: Europe
CAPITAL: Brussels
AREA: 11,787 sq mi (30,528 sq km)
POPULATION ESTIMATE (2011): 10,431,477
GOVERNMENT: Parliamentary democracy under a constitutional monarchy
LANGUAGES: Dutch, French, and German (all official)
MONEY: Euro (formerly Belgian franc)
LIFE EXPECTANCY: 80
LITERACY RATE: 99%

Guess what? *Belgium is well known for its tasty chocolate. More chocolate is sold at the Brussels Airport than any other place in the world.*

BELIZE

LOCATION: Central America
CAPITAL: Belmopan
AREA: 8,867 sq mi (22,966 sq km)
POPULATION ESTIMATE (2011): 321,115
GOVERNMENT: Parliamentary democracy
LANGUAGES: Spanish, Creole, Mayan dialects, English (official), Garifuna, German
MONEY: Belizean dollar
LIFE EXPECTANCY: 68
LITERACY RATE: 77%

Guess what? *The endangered black howler monkey lives in Belize. Its roar can be heard as far as 2 miles (3.2 km) away.*

BENIN

LOCATION: Africa
CAPITAL: Porto-Novo
AREA: 43,483 sq mi (112,622 sq km)
POPULATION ESTIMATE (2011): 9,325,032
GOVERNMENT: Republic
LANGUAGES: French (official), Fon, Yoruba, other African languages
MONEY: CFA franc
LIFE EXPECTANCY: 60
LITERACY RATE: 35%

Guess what? *Benin was known as the Kingdom of Dahomey until 1975.*

BHUTAN

LOCATION: Asia
CAPITAL: Thimphu
AREA: 14,824 sq mi (38,394 sq km)
POPULATION ESTIMATE (2011): 708,427
GOVERNMENT: Constitutional monarchy
LANGUAGES: Dzongkha (official), various Tibetan and Nepalese dialects
MONEY: Ngultrum
LIFE EXPECTANCY: 67
LITERACY RATE: 47%

Guess what? *Bhutan is located at the eastern end of the Himalaya Mountains. Many Bhutanese call their country the Land of the Thunder Dragon because of the violent storms that often occur up in the mountains.*

BOLIVIA

LOCATION: South America
CAPITALS: La Paz (seat of government), Sucre (legislative capital)
AREA: 424,162 sq mi (1,098,581 sq km)
POPULATION ESTIMATE (2011): 10,118,683
GOVERNMENT: Republic
LANGUAGES: Spanish, Quechua, and Aymara (all official)
MONEY: Boliviano
LIFE EXPECTANCY: 68
LITERACY RATE: 87%

Guess what? *Around 5,000 footprints from more than 250 different dinosaurs can be found on a gigantic limestone slab in Sucre, Bolivia.*

BOSNIA AND HERZEGOVINA

LOCATION: Europe
CAPITAL: Sarajevo
AREA: 19,767 sq mi (51,197 sq km)
POPULATION ESTIMATE (2011): 4,622,163
GOVERNMENT: Emerging federal democratic republic
LANGUAGES: Bosnian and Croatian (both official), Serbian
MONEY: Convertible mark
LIFE EXPECTANCY: 79
LITERACY RATE: 97%

Guess what? *The land that is now Bosnia and Herzegovina was called Illyria in ancient times.*

BOTSWANA

LOCATION: Africa
CAPITAL: Gaborone
AREA: 224,607 sq mi (581,730 sq km)
POPULATION ESTIMATE (2011): 2,065,398
GOVERNMENT: Parliamentary republic
LANGUAGES: English (official), Setswana, Kalanga, Sekgalagadi
MONEY: Pula
LIFE EXPECTANCY: 58
LITERACY RATE: 81%

guess what? *The national animal of Botswana is the zebra.*

BRAZIL

LOCATION: South America
CAPITAL: Brasília
AREA: 3,287,612 sq mi (8,514,877 sq km)
POPULATION ESTIMATE (2011): 203,429,773
GOVERNMENT: Federal republic
LANGUAGES: Portuguese (official), Spanish, German, Italian, Japanese, English, various Amerindian languages
MONEY: Real
LIFE EXPECTANCY: 73
LITERACY RATE: 89%

guess what? *Rio de Janeiro's best-known monument is Christ the Redeemer. The statue is more than 100 feet (30.5 m) tall.*

BRUNEI

LOCATION: Asia
CAPITAL: Bandar Seri Begawan
AREA: 2,226 sq mi (5,765 sq km)
POPULATION ESTIMATE (2011): 401,890
GOVERNMENT: Constitutional sultanate
LANGUAGES: Malay (official), English, Chinese
MONEY: Bruneian dollar
LIFE EXPECTANCY: 76
LITERACY RATE: 93%

guess what? *Some of Brunei's most important agricultural products are rice, vegetables, fruits, chickens, and water buffalo.*

BULGARIA

LOCATION: Europe
CAPITAL: Sofia
AREA: 42,811 sq mi (110,879 sq km)
POPULATION ESTIMATE (2011): 7,093,635
GOVERNMENT: Parliamentary democracy
LANGUAGES: Bulgarian, Turkish, Roma, others
MONEY: Lev
LIFE EXPECTANCY: 74
LITERACY RATE: 98%

guess what? *Bulgarian inventor Peter Petroff developed the first digital wristwatch in 1969.*

BURKINA FASO

LOCATION: Africa
CAPITAL: Ouagadougou
AREA: 105,870 sq mi (274,200 sq km)
POPULATION ESTIMATE (2011): 16,751,455
GOVERNMENT: Parliamentary republic
LANGUAGES: French (official), tribal languages
MONEY: CFA franc
LIFE EXPECTANCY: 54
LITERACY RATE: 22%

guess what? *Burkina Faso means "land of honest people."*

BURUNDI

LOCATION: Africa
CAPITAL: Bujumbura
AREA: 10,745 sq mi (27,830 sq km)
POPULATION ESTIMATE (2011): 10,216,190
GOVERNMENT: Republic
LANGUAGES: Kirundi and French (both official), Swahili
MONEY: Burundi franc
LIFE EXPECTANCY: 59
LITERACY RATE: 59%

guess what? *Burundi is a landlocked country, but its southwest border falls on Lake Tanganyika, one of the largest lakes in the world.*

Countries

CAMBODIA

LOCATION: Asia
CAPITAL: Phnom Penh
AREA: 69,900 sq mi (181,035 sq km)
POPULATION ESTIMATE (2011): 14,701,717
GOVERNMENT: Multiparty democracy under a constitutional monarchy
LANGUAGES: Khmer (official), French, English
MONEY: Riel
LIFE EXPECTANCY: 63
LITERACY RATE: 74%

guess what? *Angkor in Cambodia is the site of ancient temples. Built between 802 and 1220, more than 100 stone temples are the only things that survive from the Khmer civilization.*

CAMEROON

LOCATION: Africa
CAPITAL: Yaoundé
AREA: 183,567 sq mi (475,440 sq km)
POPULATION ESTIMATE (2011): 19,711,291
GOVERNMENT: Republic
LANGUAGES: French and English (both official), various African languages
MONEY: CFA franc
LIFE EXPECTANCY: 54
LITERACY RATE: 68%

guess what? *The goliath frog, the world's biggest frog, comes from Cameroon. These amphibians can be more than 1 foot (30 cm) long and weigh as much as a house cat, about 7.2 pounds (3.3 kg).*

CANADA

LOCATION: North America
CAPITAL: Ottawa
AREA: 3,855,081 sq mi (9,984,670 sq km)
POPULATION ESTIMATE (2011): 34,030,589
GOVERNMENT: Parliamentary democracy
LANGUAGES: English and French (both official)
MONEY: Canadian dollar
LIFE EXPECTANCY: 81
LITERACY RATE: 99%

guess what? *Poutine (poo-teen) is a popular dish in Quebec. It is made with layers of french fries, cheese curds, and beef gravy.*

CAPE VERDE

LOCATION: Africa
CAPITAL: Praia
AREA: 1,557 sq mi (4,033 sq km)
POPULATION ESTIMATE (2011): 516,100
GOVERNMENT: Republic
LANGUAGES: Portuguese, Crioulo
MONEY: Cape Verdean escudo
LIFE EXPECTANCY: 71
LITERACY RATE: 77%

guess what? *Cape Verde is an island nation off the west coast of Africa. The islands were formed by volcanoes.*

CENTRAL AFRICAN REPUBLIC

LOCATION: Africa
CAPITAL: Bangui
AREA: 240,534 sq mi (622,984 sq km)
POPULATION ESTIMATE (2011): 4,950,027
GOVERNMENT: Republic
LANGUAGES: French (official), Sangho, other African languages
MONEY: CFA franc
LIFE EXPECTANCY: 50
LITERACY RATE: 49%

guess what? *This country was known as Ubangi-Shari before gaining its independence from France in 1960.*

CHAD

LOCATION: Africa
CAPITAL: N'Djamena
AREA: 495,752 sq mi (1,284,000 sq km)
POPULATION ESTIMATE (2011): 10,758,945
GOVERNMENT: Republic
LANGUAGES: French and Arabic (both official), Sara, others
MONEY: CFA franc
LIFE EXPECTANCY: 48
LITERACY RATE: 26%

guess what? *The blue stripe on Chad's flag represents the sky and hope. The yellow stripe is for the sun and desert, and the red stripe stands for progress, unity, and sacrifice.*

CHILE

LOCATION: South America
CAPITAL: Santiago
AREA: 291,933 sq mi
(756,102 sq km)
POPULATION ESTIMATE (2011):
16,888,760
GOVERNMENT: Republic
LANGUAGES: Spanish (official),
Mapudungun, German, English
MONEY: Chilean peso
LIFE EXPECTANCY: 78
LITERACY RATE: 96%

guess what? *Chile's San Alfonso del Mar is the world's biggest swimming pool. It is more than 3,324 feet (1,013 m) long and holds 66 million gallons (250 million L) of water. This gigantic pool is only a few steps away from the Pacific Ocean.*

CHINA

LOCATION: Asia
CAPITAL: Beijing
AREA: 3,705,386 sq mi
(9,596,961 sq km)
POPULATION ESTIMATE (2011):
1,336,718,015
GOVERNMENT: Communist state
LANGUAGES: Chinese (Mandarin; official), Yue (Cantonese), local dialects
MONEY: Renminbi yuan
LIFE EXPECTANCY: 75
LITERACY RATE: 92%

guess what? *In 1974, peasants digging a well near Xi'an (shee-an) discovered more than 6,000 life-size statues of warriors and horses. Made of terra-cotta clay, they were part of a tomb built in 246 B.C.*

COLOMBIA

LOCATION: South America
CAPITAL: Bogotá
AREA: 439,733 sq mi
(1,138,914 sq km)
POPULATION ESTIMATE (2011):
44,725,543
GOVERNMENT: Republic
LANGUAGE: Spanish
MONEY: Colombian peso
LIFE EXPECTANCY: 75
LITERACY RATE: 90%

guess what? *Colombia is the world's leading exporter of emeralds.*

COMOROS

LOCATION: Africa
CAPITAL: Moroni
AREA: 863 sq mi (2,235 sq km)
POPULATION ESTIMATE (2011): 794,683
GOVERNMENT: Republic
LANGUAGES: French and Arabic (both official), Shikomoro
MONEY: Comoran franc
LIFE EXPECTANCY: 64
LITERACY RATE: 57%

guess what? *In 1938, a fisherman captured the first live coelacanth, a fish known only from fossils. It had a large body, armor-like scales, and more fins than most fish. Because some of these fins look like stumpy legs, some scientists think it may be related to the first four-legged land animals.*

CONGO, DEMOCRATIC REPUBLIC OF THE

LOCATION: Africa
CAPITAL: Kinshasa
AREA: 905,355 sq mi
(2,344,858 sq km)
POPULATION ESTIMATE (2011):
71,712,867
GOVERNMENT: Republic
LANGUAGES: French (official), Lingala, Kingwana, others
MONEY: Congolese franc
LIFE EXPECTANCY: 55
LITERACY RATE: 67%

guess what? *This country is almost landlocked, except for 25 miles (40 km) of coastline along the Atlantic Ocean.*

CONGO, REPUBLIC OF THE

LOCATION: Africa
CAPITAL: Brazzaville
AREA: 132,046 sq mi
(342,000 sq km)
POPULATION ESTIMATE (2011):
4,243,929
GOVERNMENT: Republic
LANGUAGES: French (official), Lingala, Monokutuba, Kikongo, others
MONEY: CFA franc
LIFE EXPECTANCY: 55
LITERACY RATE: 84%

guess what? *The Republic of the Congo gained independence from France in 1960.*

Countries

COSTA RICA

LOCATION: Central America
CAPITAL: San José
AREA: 19,730 sq mi (51,100 sq km)
POPULATION ESTIMATE (2011): 4,576,562
GOVERNMENT: Democratic republic
LANGUAGES: Spanish (official), English
MONEY: Costa Rican colón
LIFE EXPECTANCY: 78
LITERACY RATE: 95%

Guess what? *At 7:00 a.m. each day, all of the radio stations in Costa Rica play the country's national anthem, "Noble patria, tu hermosa bandera." In English, the song title is "Noble Homeland, Beautiful Flag."*

COTE D'IVOIRE (IVORY COAST)

LOCATION: Africa
CAPITAL: Yamoussoukro
AREA: 124,502 sq mi (322,463 sq km)
POPULATION ESTIMATE (2011): 21,504,162
GOVERNMENT: Republic
LANGUAGES: French (official), various African languages
MONEY: CFA franc
LIFE EXPECTANCY: 57
LITERACY RATE: 49%

Guess what? *The Ivory Coast produces 40% of the world's cocoa crop.*

CROATIA

LOCATION: Europe
CAPITAL: Zagreb
AREA: 21,851 sq mi (56,594 sq km)
POPULATION ESTIMATE (2011): 4,483,804
GOVERNMENT: Presidential parliamentary democracy
LANGUAGES: Croatian, Serbian
MONEY: Kuna
LIFE EXPECTANCY: 76
LITERACY RATE: 98%

Guess what? *Croatia was part of Yugoslavia until it declared independence in 1991.*

CUBA

LOCATION: Caribbean
CAPITAL: Havana
AREA: 42,803 sq mi (110,860 sq km)
POPULATION ESTIMATE (2011): 11,087,330
GOVERNMENT: Communist state
LANGUAGE: Spanish
MONEY: Cuban peso
LIFE EXPECTANCY: 78
LITERACY RATE: 100%

Guess what? *The island of Cuba is shaped like a crocodile. That is why some Cubans refer to their country as El Cocodrilo.*

CYPRUS

LOCATION: Europe
CAPITAL: Nicosia
AREA: 3,571 sq mi (9,250 sq km)
POPULATION ESTIMATE (2011): 1,120,489
GOVERNMENT: Republic
LANGUAGES: Greek and Turkish (both official), English
MONEY: Euro (formerly Cyprus pound), Turkish new lira
LIFE EXPECTANCY: 77.5
LITERACY RATE: 98%

Guess what? *The national animal of Cyprus is the mouflon, a type of wild sheep.*

CZECH REPUBLIC

LOCATION: Europe
CAPITAL: Prague
AREA: 30,450 sq mi (78,866 sq km)
POPULATION ESTIMATE (2011): 10,190,213
GOVERNMENT: Parliamentary democracy
LANGUAGES: Czech, Slovak, others
MONEY: Koruna
LIFE EXPECTANCY: 77
LITERACY RATE: 99%

Guess what? *According to legend, the villagers who built the Charles Bridge in Prague mixed egg yolks into the mortar, believing it would make the bridge stronger. Built in the 1350s, it is one of the oldest structures in Europe.*

DENMARK

LOCATION: Europe
CAPITAL: Copenhagen
AREA: 16,639 sq mi (43,094 sq km)
POPULATION ESTIMATE (2011): 5,529,888
GOVERNMENT: Constitutional monarchy
LANGUAGES: Danish, Faroese, Greenlandic, German
MONEY: Krone
LIFE EXPECTANCY: 79
LITERACY RATE: 99%

guess what? *Tivoli opened in 1843 in Copenhagen. It is home to roller coasters and rides for all ages, including the world's tallest carousel, which is 262 feet (80 m) tall.*

DJIBOUTI

LOCATION: Africa
CAPITAL: Djibouti
AREA: 8,958 sq mi (23,200 sq km)
POPULATION ESTIMATE (2011): 757,074
GOVERNMENT: Republic
LANGUAGES: Arabic and French (both official), Somali, Afar
MONEY: Djiboutian franc
LIFE EXPECTANCY: 61
LITERACY RATE: 68%

guess what? *Lake Abbe, a lake on the Ethiopia–Djibouti border, has lots of chimney rock formations that were created by hot springs.*

DOMINICA

LOCATION: Caribbean
CAPITAL: Roseau
AREA: 291 sq mi (754 sq km)
POPULATION ESTIMATE (2011): 72,969
GOVERNMENT: Parliamentary democracy
LANGUAGES: English (official), French patois
MONEY: East Caribbean dollar
LIFE EXPECTANCY: 76
LITERACY RATE: 94%

guess what? *Some scenes from* Pirates of the Caribbean: Dead Man's Chest *and* Pirates of the Caribbean: At World's End *were filmed in Dominica.*

DOMINICAN REPUBLIC

LOCATION: Caribbean
CAPITAL: Santo Domingo
AREA: 18,792 sq mi (48,670 sq km)
POPULATION ESTIMATE (2011): 9,956,648
GOVERNMENT: Democratic republic
LANGUAGE: Spanish
MONEY: Dominican peso
LIFE EXPECTANCY: 77
LITERACY RATE: 87%

guess what? *The Dominican Republic held its first bull run in 2001, but instead of chasing the runners, the bulls had to be pushed through the streets.*

EAST TIMOR (TIMOR-LESTE)

LOCATION: Asia
CAPITAL: Dili
AREA: 5,743 sq mi (14,874 sq km)
POPULATION ESTIMATE (2011): 1,177,834
GOVERNMENT: Republic
LANGUAGES: Tetum and Portuguese (both official), Indonesian, English
MONEY: U.S. dollar
LIFE EXPECTANCY: 68
LITERACY RATE: 59%

guess what? *East Timor gained independence from Indonesia in 2002.*

ECUADOR

LOCATION: South America
CAPITAL: Quito
AREA: 109,483 sq mi (283,560 sq km)
POPULATION ESTIMATE (2011): 15,007,343
GOVERNMENT: Republic
LANGUAGES: Spanish (official), Quechua
MONEY: U.S. dollar
LIFE EXPECTANCY: 76
LITERACY RATE: 91%

guess what? *The giant tortoise, which can weigh more than 500 pounds (267 kg) and live more than 100 years, lives in the Galápagos Islands.*

EGYPT

LOCATION: Africa
CAPITAL: Cairo
AREA: 386,660 sq mi (1,001,450 sq km)
POPULATION ESTIMATE (2011): 82,079,636
GOVERNMENT: Republic
LANGUAGE: Arabic
MONEY: Egyptian pound
LIFE EXPECTANCY: 73
LITERACY RATE: 71%

guess what? *The ancient Egyptians believed in preserving a body after death, a process called mummification. King Tut is Egypt's most famous mummy.*

EL SALVADOR

LOCATION: Central America
CAPITAL: San Salvador
AREA: 8,124 sq mi (21,040 sq km)
POPULATION ESTIMATE (2011): 6,071,774
GOVERNMENT: Republic
LANGUAGES: Spanish, Nahua
MONEY: U.S. dollar
LIFE EXPECTANCY: 73
LITERACY RATE: 81%

guess what? *El Salvador is a popular surfing destination because of the regularly occurring riptides, which are strong surface currents that flow away from the shore and create giant waves.*

EQUATORIAL GUINEA

LOCATION: Africa
CAPITAL: Malabo
AREA: 10,830 sq mi (28,051 sq km)
POPULATION ESTIMATE (2011): 668,225
GOVERNMENT: Republic
LANGUAGES: Spanish and French (both official), Fang, Bubi
MONEY: CFA franc
LIFE EXPECTANCY: 62
LITERACY RATE: 87%

guess what? *Equatorial Guinea is the only African country with Spanish as its official language.*

ERITREA

LOCATION: Africa
CAPITAL: Asmara
AREA: 45,406 sq mi (117,600 sq km)
POPULATION ESTIMATE (2011): 5,939,484
GOVERNMENT: Transitional
LANGUAGES: Afar, Arabic, Tigre, Kunama, Tigrinya, others
MONEY: Nakfa
LIFE EXPECTANCY: 63
LITERACY RATE: 59%

guess what? *The Danakil Depression in Eritrea is one of the hottest places on Earth. Temperatures can reach as high as 145°F (63°C).*

ESTONIA

LOCATION: Europe
CAPITAL: Tallinn
AREA: 17,463 sq mi (45,228 sq km)
POPULATION ESTIMATE (2011): 1,282,963
GOVERNMENT: Parliamentary republic
LANGUAGES: Estonian (official), Russian
MONEY: Kroon
LIFE EXPECTANCY: 73
LITERACY RATE: 100%

guess what? *The Kadriorg Palace in Tallinn was built by Russian czar Peter I (Peter the Great).*

ETHIOPIA

LOCATION: Africa
CAPITAL: Addis Ababa
AREA: 426,373 sq mi (1,104,300 sq km)
POPULATION ESTIMATE (2011): 90,873,739
GOVERNMENT: Federal republic
LANGUAGES: Amarigna, English, and Arabic (all official), Oromigna and Tigrigna (both regional official), others
MONEY: Birr
LIFE EXPECTANCY: 56
LITERACY RATE: 43%

guess what? *In 1974, parts of a 3.2-million-year-old skeleton, known as Lucy, were found near Hadar, Ethiopia.*

FIJI

LOCATION: Oceania
CAPITAL: Suva
AREA: 7,057 sq mi (18,274 sq km)
POPULATION ESTIMATE (2011): 883,125
GOVERNMENT: Republic
LANGUAGES: Fijian and English (both official), Hindustani
MONEY: Fijian dollar
LIFE EXPECTANCY: 71
LITERACY RATE: 94%

guess what? *Some Fijians used to engage in cannibalism, or the eating of human flesh. A boot with teeth marks that supposedly belonged to the country's last victim can be seen in the Fiji Museum.*

FINLAND

LOCATION: Europe
CAPITAL: Helsinki
AREA: 130,559 sq mi (338,145 sq km)
POPULATION ESTIMATE (2011): 5,259,250
GOVERNMENT: Republic
LANGUAGES: Finnish and Swedish (both official), others
MONEY: Euro (formerly markka)
LIFE EXPECTANCY: 79
LITERACY RATE: 100%

guess what? *A group in Finland hosts a mosquito swatting competition every year. Contestants try to squash as many mosquitoes as they can in five minutes.*

FRANCE

LOCATION: Europe
CAPITAL: Paris
AREA: 248,429 sq mi (643,427 sq km)
POPULATION ESTIMATE (2011): 65,102,719
GOVERNMENT: Republic
LANGUAGE: French
MONEY: Euro (formerly franc)
LIFE EXPECTANCY: 81
LITERACY RATE: 99%

guess what? *When Paris hosted the 1900 Olympic Games, athletes did not compete for medals. Instead, winners received valuable pieces of art.*

GABON

LOCATION: Africa
CAPITAL: Libreville
AREA: 103,346 sq mi (267,667 sq km)
POPULATION ESTIMATE (2011): 1,576,665
GOVERNMENT: Republic
LANGUAGES: French (official), Fang, Myene, Nzebi, Bapounou/Eschira, Bandjabi
MONEY: CFA franc
LIFE EXPECTANCY: 53
LITERACY RATE: 63%

guess what? *President Omar Bongo was Gabon's head of state from 1967 to 2009, when he died. He was the longest-serving leader in African history.*

THE GAMBIA

LOCATION: Africa
CAPITAL: Banjul
AREA: 4,361 sq mi (11,295 sq km)
POPULATION ESTIMATE (2011): 1,779,860
GOVERNMENT: Republic
LANGUAGES: English (official), Mandinka, Wolof, Fula, others
MONEY: Dalasi
LIFE EXPECTANCY: 64
LITERACY RATE: 40%

guess what? *Except for a small area along the Atlantic Ocean, The Gambia is almost entirely surrounded by Senegal.*

GEORGIA

LOCATION: Asia
CAPITAL: Tbilisi
AREA: 26,911 sq mi (69,700 sq km)
POPULATION ESTIMATE (2011): 4,585,874
GOVERNMENT: Republic
LANGUAGES: Georgian (official), Russian, Armenian, Azeri
MONEY: Lari
LIFE EXPECTANCY: 77
LITERACY RATE: 100%

guess what? *The medieval cave city of Vardzia, complete with a monastery and a water system, is built into the side of a mountain in southern Georgia.*

Countries

57

GERMANY

LOCATION: Europe
CAPITAL: Berlin
AREA: 137,847 sq mi
(357,022 sq km)
POPULATION ESTIMATE (2011):
81,471,834
GOVERNMENT: Federal republic
LANGUAGE: German
MONEY: Euro (formerly
deutsche mark)
LIFE EXPECTANCY: 80
LITERACY RATE: 99%

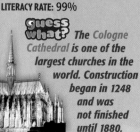

guess what? *The Cologne Cathedral is one of the largest churches in the world. Construction began in 1248 and was not finished until 1880.*

GHANA

LOCATION: Africa
CAPITAL: Accra
AREA: 92,098 sq mi
(238,533 sq km)
POPULATION ESTIMATE (2011):
24,791,073
GOVERNMENT: Constitutional
democracy
LANGUAGES: English (official),
Asante, Ewe, Fante, Boron,
Dagomba, Dagarte, others
MONEY: Cedi
LIFE EXPECTANCY: 61
LITERACY RATE: 58%

guess what? *In Ghana, the first Friday in December is Farmers' Day, a day to honor the nation's growers.*

GREECE

LOCATION: Europe
CAPITAL: Athens
AREA: 50,949 sq mi
(131,957 sq km)
POPULATION ESTIMATE (2011):
10,760,136
GOVERNMENT: Parliamentary
republic
LANGUAGE: Greek
MONEY: Euro (formerly drachma)
LIFE EXPECTANCY: 80
LITERACY RATE: 96%

guess what? *According to ancient mythology, Greek gods, such as Zeus, Athena, and Aphrodite, lived atop Mt. Olympus, the highest mountain in Greece.*

GRENADA

LOCATION: Caribbean
CAPITAL: Saint George's
AREA: 133 sq mi (344 sq km)
POPULATION ESTIMATE (2011): 108,419
GOVERNMENT: Parliamentary
democracy
LANGUAGES: English (official),
French patois
MONEY: East Caribbean dollar
LIFE EXPECTANCY: 73
LITERACY RATE: 96%

guess what? *Grenada is known as a tri-island state because it is made up of three islands: Grenada, Carriacou, and Petite Martinique.*

GUATEMALA

LOCATION: Central America
CAPITAL: Guatemala City
AREA: 42,042 sq mi
(108,889 sq km)
POPULATION ESTIMATE (2011):
13,824,463
GOVERNMENT: Republic
LANGUAGES: Spanish, Amerindian
languages
MONEY: Quetzal
LIFE EXPECTANCY: 71
LITERACY RATE: 69%

guess what? *The longest civil war in Latin-American history was the Guatemalan civil war. It lasted 36 years, finally ending in 1996.*

GUINEA

LOCATION: Africa
CAPITAL: Conakry
AREA: 94,925 sq mi
(245,860 sq km)
POPULATION ESTIMATE (2011):
10,601,009
GOVERNMENT: Republic
LANGUAGES: French (official),
native languages
MONEY: Guinean franc
LIFE EXPECTANCY: 58
LITERACY RATE: 30%

guess what? *Together, Guinea and Australia possess almost half of the world's bauxite reserves. Bauxite is used in items such as makeup, soda cans, cement, and house siding, and can be recycled.*

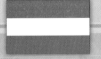

GUINEA-BISSAU

LOCATION: Africa
CAPITAL: Bissau
AREA: 13,948 sq mi
(36,125 sq km)
POPULATION ESTIMATE (2011):
1,596,677
GOVERNMENT: Republic
LANGUAGES: Portuguese (official),
Crioulo, African languages
MONEY: CFA franc
LIFE EXPECTANCY: 49
LITERACY RATE: 42%

guess what? *The cashew nut is this country's biggest export.*

GUYANA

LOCATION: South America
CAPITAL: Georgetown
AREA: 83,000 sq mi
(214,969 sq km)
POPULATION ESTIMATE (2011): 744,768
GOVERNMENT: Republic
LANGUAGES: English (official),
Amerindian dialects, Creole,
Caribbean Hindustani, Urdu
MONEY: Guyanese dollar
LIFE EXPECTANCY: 67
LITERACY RATE: 92%

guess what? *Kaieteur Falls in Guyana is 741 feet (226 m) high. That is more than four times taller than Niagara Falls!*

HAITI

LOCATION: Caribbean
CAPITAL: Port-au-Prince
AREA: 10,714 sq mi
(27,750 sq km)
POPULATION ESTIMATE (2011):
9,719,932
GOVERNMENT: Republic
LANGUAGES: Creole and French
(both official)
MONEY: Gourde
LIFE EXPECTANCY: 62
LITERACY RATE: 53%

guess what? *A devastating earthquake hit Haiti in January 2010. It registered 7.0 on the Richter scale, which is the scale scientists use to measure the strength of an earthquake. The strongest earthquake recorded was a 9.5 on the Richter scale.*

HONDURAS

LOCATION: Central America
CAPITAL: Tegucigalpa
AREA: 43,278 sq mi
(112,090 sq km)
POPULATION ESTIMATE (2011):
8,143,564
GOVERNMENT: Democratic
constitutional republic
LANGUAGES: Spanish, Amerindian
dialects
MONEY: Lempira
LIFE EXPECTANCY: 71
LITERACY RATE: 80%

guess what? *The orchid is the national flower of Honduras.*

HUNGARY

LOCATION: Europe
CAPITAL: Budapest
AREA: 35,918 sq mi
(93,028 sq km)
POPULATION ESTIMATE (2011):
9,976,062
GOVERNMENT: Parliamentary
democracy
LANGUAGE: Hungarian
MONEY: Forint
LIFE EXPECTANCY: 75
LITERACY RATE: 99%

guess what? *Franz Liszt, a famous Hungarian composer, was one of the greatest pianists of all time. He was taught to play by his father, beginning at the age of 6 or 7.*

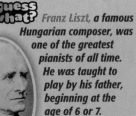

ICELAND

LOCATION: Europe
CAPITAL: Reykjavík
AREA: 39,768 sq mi
(103,000 sq km)
POPULATION ESTIMATE (2011): 311,058
GOVERNMENT: Constitutional
republic
LANGUAGES: Icelandic, English
MONEY: Icelandic krona
LIFE EXPECTANCY: 81
LITERACY RATE: 99%

guess what? *Iceland's Ring Road is an 830-mile (1,335 km) loop around the island. It passes glaciers, lava fields, fishing villages, waterfalls, hot springs, and more.*

Countries

59

INDIA

LOCATION: Asia
CAPITAL: New Delhi
AREA: 1,269,219 sq mi
(3,287,263 sq km)
POPULATION ESTIMATE (2011):
1,189,172,906
GOVERNMENT: Federal republic
LANGUAGES: Hindi (national),
English, 14 other official
languages
MONEY: Indian rupee
LIFE EXPECTANCY: 67
LITERACY RATE: 61%

guess what? *Indira Gandhi became prime minister of India in 1966. She was one of the first women elected to lead a nation.*

INDONESIA

LOCATION: Asia
CAPITAL: Jakarta
AREA: 735,358 sq mi
(1,904,569 sq km)
POPULATION ESTIMATE (2011):
245,613,043
GOVERNMENT: Republic
LANGUAGES: Bahasa Indonesia
(official), Dutch, English,
many local dialects
MONEY: Rupiah
LIFE EXPECTANCY: 71
LITERACY RATE: 90%

guess what? *The Taman Sari Water Castle in Yogyakarta, Indonesia, was built in 1758. Now a popular tourist destination, it includes a mosque, meditation chambers, pools, canals, and lakes.*

IRAN

LOCATION: Middle East
CAPITAL: Tehran
AREA: 636,372 sq mi
(1,648,195 sq km)
POPULATION ESTIMATE (2011):
77,891,220
GOVERNMENT: Theocratic republic
LANGUAGES: Persian, Turkic,
Kurdish, others
MONEY: Rial
LIFE EXPECTANCY: 70
LITERACY RATE: 77%

guess what? *Iran was known as Persia until 1935.*

IRAQ

LOCATION: Middle East
CAPITAL: Baghdad
AREA: 169,235 sq mi
(438,317 sq km)
POPULATION ESTIMATE (2011):
30,399,572
GOVERNMENT: Parliamentary
democracy
LANGUAGES: Arabic (official),
Kurdish, Turkoman, Assyrian
MONEY: Iraqi dinar
LIFE EXPECTANCY: 71
LITERACY RATE: 74%

guess what? *The ancient civilization of Mesopotamia was founded in what is today called Iraq.*

IRELAND

LOCATION: Europe
CAPITAL: Dublin
AREA: 27,132 sq mi
(70,273 sq km)
POPULATION ESTIMATE (2011):
4,670,976
GOVERNMENT: Republic
LANGUAGES: Irish (Gaelic) and
English (both official)
MONEY: Euro (formerly Irish
pound, or punt)
LIFE EXPECTANCY: 80
LITERACY RATE: 99%

guess what? *Irish writer James Joyce's famous 1922 novel Ulysses recounts the events of a single day (June 16, 1904). Fans gather in Dublin every June to celebrate by staging performances and readings.*

ISRAEL

LOCATION: Middle East
CAPITAL: Jerusalem
AREA: 8,019 sq mi (20,770 sq km)
POPULATION ESTIMATE (2011):
7,473,052
GOVERNMENT: Parliamentary
democracy
LANGUAGES: Hebrew (official),
Arabic, English
MONEY: New Israeli shekel
LIFE EXPECTANCY: 81
LITERACY RATE: 97%

guess what? *The lowest point on Earth is the Dead Sea, in Israel, at 1,312 feet (400 m) below sea level. The Dead Sea is one of the saltiest bodies of water in the world.*

ITALY

LOCATION: Europe
CAPITAL: Rome
AREA: 116,348 sq mi (301,340 sq km)
POPULATION ESTIMATE (2011): 61,016,804
GOVERNMENT: Republic
LANGUAGES: Italian (official), German, French, Slovene
MONEY: Euro (formerly lira)
LIFE EXPECTANCY: 82
LITERACY RATE: 98%

guess what? *William Shakespeare's famous play Romeo and Juliet is set in Verona, Italy.*

JAMAICA

LOCATION: Caribbean
CAPITAL: Kingston
AREA: 4,244 sq mi (10,991 sq km)
POPULATION ESTIMATE (2011): 2,868,380
GOVERNMENT: Parliamentary democracy
LANGUAGES: English, English patois
MONEY: Jamaican dollar
LIFE EXPECTANCY: 73
LITERACY RATE: 88%

guess what? *Famous reggae singer Bob Marley was born in Jamaica.*

JAPAN

LOCATION: Asia
CAPITAL: Tokyo
AREA: 145,914 sq mi (377,915 sq km)
POPULATION ESTIMATE (2011): 126,475,664
GOVERNMENT: Parliamentary government with a constitutional monarchy
LANGUAGE: Japanese
MONEY: Yen
LIFE EXPECTANCY: 82
LITERACY RATE: 99%

guess what? *Yoshino Mountain, near Tokyo, is covered with tens of thousands of white mountain cherry trees. The famous trees are hundreds of years old, and bloom in the spring.*

JORDAN

LOCATION: Middle East
CAPITAL: Amman
AREA: 34,495 sq mi (89,342 sq km)
POPULATION ESTIMATE (2011): 6,508,271
GOVERNMENT: Constitutional monarchy
LANGUAGE: Arabic (official)
MONEY: Jordanian dinar
LIFE EXPECTANCY: 80
LITERACY RATE: 90%

guess what? *Petra, a city in Jordan carved into the canyon walls, was rediscovered in 1812. It is one of the new seven wonders of the world.*

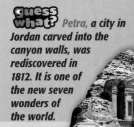

KAZAKHSTAN

LOCATION: Asia
CAPITAL: Astana
AREA: 1,052,090 sq mi (2,724,900 sq km)
POPULATION ESTIMATE (2011): 15,522,373
GOVERNMENT: Republic
LANGUAGES: Kazakh, Russian (official)
MONEY: Tenge
LIFE EXPECTANCY: 69
LITERACY RATE: 100%

guess what? *The first manned space flight was launched from the Baikonur space center in Kazakhstan in 1961.*

KENYA

LOCATION: Africa
CAPITAL: Nairobi
AREA: 224,081 sq mi (580,367 sq km)
POPULATION ESTIMATE (2011): 41,070,934
GOVERNMENT: Republic
LANGUAGES: English and Kiswahili (both official), others
MONEY: Kenyan shilling
LIFE EXPECTANCY: 60
LITERACY RATE: 85%

guess what? *Every year in Kenya, hundreds of thousands of wildebeests travel from the Serengeti Plains to the Masai Mara game reserve and back again, crossing crocodile-filled rivers along the way.*

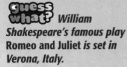

Countries

61

KIRIBATI

LOCATION: Oceania
CAPITAL: Tarawa
AREA: 313 sq mi (811 sq km)
POPULATION ESTIMATE (2011): 110,743
GOVERNMENT: Republic
LANGUAGES: English (official), I-Kiribati (Gilbertese)
MONEY: Australian dollar
LIFE EXPECTANCY: 64
LITERACY RATE: Not available

guess what? *Before achieving independence in 1979, Kiribati was known as the Gilbert Islands, a British colony since 1915.*

KOREA, NORTH

LOCATION: Asia
CAPITAL: Pyongyang
AREA: 46,540 sq mi (120,538 sq km)
POPULATION ESTIMATE (2011): 24,457,492
GOVERNMENT: Communist dictatorship
LANGUAGE: Korean
MONEY: North Korean won
LIFE EXPECTANCY: 69
LITERACY RATE: 99%

guess what? *North Korea has one of the largest militaries in the world.*

KOREA, SOUTH

LOCATION: Asia
CAPITAL: Seoul
AREA: 38,541 sq mi (99,720 sq km)
POPULATION ESTIMATE (2011): 48,754,657
GOVERNMENT: Republic
LANGUAGE: Korean
MONEY: South Korean won
LIFE EXPECTANCY: 79
LITERACY RATE: 98%

guess what? *Currently, the only way to get in or out of South Korea is by boat or plane because the country's only land border, with North Korea, is closed to travelers.*

KOSOVO

LOCATION: Europe
CAPITAL: Pristina
AREA: 4,203 sq mi (10,887 sq km)
POPULATION ESTIMATE (2011): 1,825,632
GOVERNMENT: Republic
LANGUAGES: Albanian and Serbian (both official), Bosnian, Turkish, Roma
MONEY: Euro (formerly deutsche mark)
LIFE EXPECTANCY: Not available
LITERACY RATE: 92%

guess what? *Former President Bill Clinton is a beloved figure in Kosovo. There is an 11-foot (3.4 m) statue of the U.S. President on Bill Clinton Boulevard in Pristina.*

KUWAIT

LOCATION: Middle East
CAPITAL: Kuwait City
AREA: 6,880 sq mi (17,820 sq km)
POPULATION ESTIMATE (2011): 2,595,628
GOVERNMENT: Constitutional emirate
LANGUAGES: Arabic (official), English
MONEY: Kuwaiti dinar
LIFE EXPECTANCY: 77
LITERACY RATE: 93%

guess what? *The falcon is a national symbol of Kuwait. It is featured on stamps and on the Kuwaiti dinar.*

KYRGYZSTAN

LOCATION: Asia
CAPITAL: Bishkek
AREA: 77,202 sq mi (199,951 sq km)
POPULATION ESTIMATE (2011): 5,587,443
GOVERNMENT: Republic
LANGUAGES: Kyrgyz and Russian (both official), Uzbek, others
MONEY: Som
LIFE EXPECTANCY: 70
LITERACY RATE: 99%

guess what? *Making shyrdaks, or colorful felt carpets, is a popular craft for the nomadic people of Kyrgyzstan.*

LAOS

LOCATION: Asia
CAPITAL: Vientiane
AREA: 91,429 sq mi
(236,800 sq km)
POPULATION ESTIMATE (2011):
6,477,211
GOVERNMENT: Communist state
LANGUAGES: Lao (official), French, English
MONEY: Kip
LIFE EXPECTANCY: 62
LITERACY RATE: 73%

guess what? *Designed in 1958, Vientiane's Xieng Khuan (also called Buddha Park) is a sculpture garden filled with hundreds of Hindu and Buddhist statues.*

LATVIA

LOCATION: Europe
CAPITAL: Riga
AREA: 24,938 sq mi
(64,589 sq km)
POPULATION ESTIMATE (2011):
2,204,708
GOVERNMENT: Parliamentary democracy
LANGUAGES: Latvian, Russian
MONEY: Lat
LIFE EXPECTANCY: 73
LITERACY RATE: 100%

guess what? *Latvia, Lithuania, and Estonia are known as the Baltic states. The Baltic Sea is to the west of the Baltic states.*

LEBANON

LOCATION: Middle East
CAPITAL: Beirut
AREA: 4,015 sq mi
(10,400 sq km)
POPULATION ESTIMATE (2011):
4,143,101
GOVERNMENT: Republic
LANGUAGES: Arabic (official), French, English, Armenian
MONEY: Lebanese pound
LIFE EXPECTANCY: 75
LITERACY RATE: 87%

guess what? *The national tree of Lebanon is the cedar tree. Because of its strength, cedar was often used for building ships and sturdy furniture. Demand for the wood has greatly reduced the number of cedar trees in the country.*

LESOTHO

LOCATION: Africa
CAPITAL: Maseru
AREA: 11,720 sq mi
(30,355 sq km)
POPULATION ESTIMATE (2011):
1,924,886
GOVERNMENT: Parliamentary constitutional monarchy
LANGUAGES: English (official), Sesotho, Zulu, Xhosa
MONEY: Loti
LIFE EXPECTANCY: 52
LITERACY RATE: 85%

guess what? *The image in the center of Lesotho's flag is a Basotho hat. Often worn by tribesmen in this mountainous country, these hats are made of straw.*

LIBERIA

LOCATION: Africa
CAPITAL: Monrovia
AREA: 43,000 sq mi
(111,369 sq km)
POPULATION ESTIMATE (2011):
3,786,764
GOVERNMENT: Republic
LANGUAGES: English (official), ethnic dialects
MONEY: Liberian dollar
LIFE EXPECTANCY: 57
LITERACY RATE: 58%

guess what? *Liberia has had two female Presidents: Ruth Perry and Ellen Johnson Sirleaf, the country's current leader.*

LIBYA

LOCATION: Africa
CAPITAL: Tripoli
AREA: 679,358 sq mi
(1,759,540 sq km)
POPULATION ESTIMATE (2011):
6,597,960
GOVERNMENT: Authoritarian state
LANGUAGES: Arabic, Italian, English
MONEY: Libyan dinar
LIFE EXPECTANCY: 78
LITERACY RATE: 83%

guess what? *To supply its people with water, Libya has built the Great Man-Made River, a huge system of pipes that draws water from beneath the Sahara Desert.*

Countries

LIECHTENSTEIN

LOCATION: Europe
CAPITAL: Vaduz
AREA: 62 sq mi (160 sq km)
POPULATION ESTIMATE (2011): 35,236
GOVERNMENT: Constitutional monarchy
LANGUAGES: German (official), Alemannic dialect
MONEY: Swiss franc
LIFE EXPECTANCY: 80
LITERACY RATE: 100%

guess what? *Liechtenstein is famous worldwide for its stamps. The Postage Stamp Museum in Vaduz has some rare examples that date back to 1912.*

LITHUANIA

LOCATION: Europe
CAPITAL: Vilnius
AREA: 25,212 sq mi (65,300 sq km)
POPULATION ESTIMATE (2011): 3,535,547
GOVERNMENT: Parliamentary democracy
LANGUAGES: Lithuanian (official), Polish, Russian
MONEY: Litas
LIFE EXPECTANCY: 75
LITERACY RATE: 100%

guess what? *Lithuania was the first country to declare its independence from the Soviet Union, but was not recognized until nearly one and a half years later. Lithuania and 14 other countries gained independence in 1991.*

LUXEMBOURG

LOCATION: Europe
CAPITAL: Luxembourg
AREA: 998 sq mi (2,586 sq km)
POPULATION ESTIMATE (2011): 503,302
GOVERNMENT: Constitutional monarchy
LANGUAGES: Luxembourgish, German, French
MONEY: Euro (formerly Luxembourg franc)
LIFE EXPECTANCY: 80
LITERACY RATE: 100%

guess what? *The Ardennes region covers nearly half of Luxembourg. The historic Battle of the Bulge took place in the Ardennes during World War II.*

MACEDONIA

LOCATION: Europe
CAPITAL: Skopje
AREA: 9,928 sq mi (25,713 sq km)
POPULATION ESTIMATE (2011): 2,077,328
GOVERNMENT: Parliamentary democracy
LANGUAGES: Macedonian and Albanian (official), others
MONEY: Macedonian denar
LIFE EXPECTANCY: 75
LITERACY RATE: 96%

guess what? *Mother Teresa, a Roman Catholic nun who helped the poor, was born in Skopje. She won the Nobel Prize for Peace in 1979.*

MADAGASCAR

LOCATION: Africa
CAPITAL: Antananarivo
AREA: 226,658 sq mi (587,041 sq km)
POPULATION ESTIMATE (2011): 21,926,221
GOVERNMENT: Republic
LANGUAGES: Malagasy, French, and English (all official)
MONEY: Malagasy ariary
LIFE EXPECTANCY: 64
LITERACY RATE: 69%

guess what? *Hissing cockroaches come from the island of Madagascar. They are about 3 inches (7.5 cm) long and hiss during fights. A small colony can eat a large carrot in one day.*

MALAWI

LOCATION: Africa
CAPITAL: Lilongwe
AREA: 45,747 sq mi (118,484 sq km)
POPULATION ESTIMATE (2011): 15,879,252
GOVERNMENT: Multiparty democracy
LANGUAGES: Chichewa (official), Chinyanja, Chiyao, Chitumbuka
MONEY: Kwacha
LIFE EXPECTANCY: 52
LITERACY RATE: 63%

guess what? *Lake Malawi is home to 600 species of cichlid that are not found anywhere else in the world. Cichlids are spiny-finned freshwater fish.*

MALAYSIA

LOCATION: Asia
CAPITAL: Kuala Lumpur
AREA: 127,355 sq mi (329,847 sq km)
POPULATION ESTIMATE (2011): 28,728,607
GOVERNMENT: Constitutional monarchy
LANGUAGES: Bahasa Malay (official), Chinese, Tamil, English, others
MONEY: Ringgit
LIFE EXPECTANCY: 74
LITERACY RATE: 89%

Guess what? *Rafflesias, the largest flowers in the world, grow in the forests of Sabah, Malaysia. They can grow to be 3 feet (91 cm) in diameter and weigh up to 15 pounds (7 kg).*

MALDIVES

LOCATION: Asia
CAPITAL: Male
AREA: 116 sq mi (300 sq km)
POPULATION ESTIMATE (2011): 394,999
GOVERNMENT: Republic
LANGUAGES: Dhivehi (official), English
MONEY: Rufiyaa
LIFE EXPECTANCY: 75
LITERACY RATE: 94%

Guess what? *About 80% of Maldives sits less than 3.3 feet (1 m) above sea level.*

MALI

LOCATION: Africa
CAPITAL: Bamako
AREA: 478,841 sq mi (1,240,192 sq km)
POPULATION ESTIMATE (2011): 14,159,904
GOVERNMENT: Republic
LANGUAGES: French (official), Bambara, African languages
MONEY: CFA franc
LIFE EXPECTANCY: 53
LITERACY RATE: 46%

Guess what? *The Great Mosque of Djenné in Mali is made completely from mud.*

MALTA

LOCATION: Europe
CAPITAL: Valletta
AREA: 122 sq mi (316 sq km)
POPULATION ESTIMATE (2011): 408,333
GOVERNMENT: Republic
LANGUAGES: Maltese and English (both official)
MONEY: Euro (formerly Maltese lira)
LIFE EXPECTANCY: 80
LITERACY RATE: 93%

Guess what? *Ancient Greeks and Romans knew Malta as "Melita," the land of honey.*

MARSHALL ISLANDS

LOCATION: Oceania
CAPITAL: Majuro
AREA: 70 sq mi (181 sq km)
POPULATION ESTIMATE (2011): 67,182
GOVERNMENT: Constitutional government
LANGUAGES: Marshallese and English (both official)
MONEY: U.S. dollar
LIFE EXPECTANCY: 72
LITERACY RATE: 94%

Guess what? *The four main plants of the Marshall Islands are the pandanus plant, breadfruit tree, coconut palm, and swamp taro, which are all edible.*

MAURITANIA

LOCATION: Africa
CAPITAL: Nouakchott
AREA: 397,953 sq mi (1,030,700 sq km)
POPULATION ESTIMATE (2011): 3,281,634
GOVERNMENT: Military junta
LANGUAGES: Arabic (official), French, Pulaar, Soninke, others
MONEY: Ouguiya
LIFE EXPECTANCY: 61
LITERACY RATE: 51%

Guess what? *Half of Mauritania's land area is covered by desert sand dunes.*

Countries

65

MAURITIUS

LOCATION: Africa
CAPITAL: Port Louis
AREA: 788 sq mi (2,040 sq km)
POPULATION ESTIMATE (2011): 1,303,717
GOVERNMENT: Parliamentary democracy
LANGUAGES: English (official), Creole, Bhojpuri, French
MONEY: Mauritian rupee
LIFE EXPECTANCY: 75
LITERACY RATE: 84%

guess what? *The dodo, an extinct flightless bird, lived only on the island of Mauritius. It was the inspiration for the character of the Dodo in Lewis Carroll's Alice in Wonderland.*

MEXICO

LOCATION: North America
CAPITAL: Mexico City
AREA: 758,449 sq mi (1,964,375 sq km)
POPULATION ESTIMATE (2011): 113,724,226
GOVERNMENT: Republic
LANGUAGES: Spanish, indigenous languages
MONEY: Peso
LIFE EXPECTANCY: 77
LITERACY RATE: 86%

guess what? *Mariachi is a type of music that originated in Mexico. Mariachi ensembles can feature as many as eight violins, two trumpets, a Mexican folk harp, guitarrón (a type of bass), and several types of guitars.*

MICRONESIA, FEDERATED STATES OF

LOCATION: Oceania
CAPITAL: Palikir
AREA: 271 sq mi (702 sq km)
POPULATION ESTIMATE (2011): 106,836
GOVERNMENT: Constitutional government
LANGUAGES: English (official), Chuukese, Kosrean, Pohnpeian, Yapese, Ulithian, others
MONEY: U.S. dollar
LIFE EXPECTANCY: 72
LITERACY RATE: 89%

guess what? *At almost 40 miles (64 km) wide and 300 feet (91 m) deep, Micronesia's Chuuk Lagoon holds more than 100 wrecked ships, planes, and submarines from World War II.*

MOLDOVA

LOCATION: Europe
CAPITAL: Chisinau
AREA: 13,070 sq mi (33,851 sq km)
POPULATION ESTIMATE (2011): 4,314,377
GOVERNMENT: Republic
LANGUAGES: Moldovan (official), Russian, Gagauz
MONEY: Leu
LIFE EXPECTANCY: 71
LITERACY RATE: 99%

guess what? *Moldova was part of an area known as Bessarabia, which was part of Romania before the Soviet Union took control of the region in the 1940s.*

MONACO

LOCATION: Europe
CAPITAL: Monaco
AREA: 0.75 sq mi (1.95 sq km)
POPULATION ESTIMATE (2011): 30,539
GOVERNMENT: Constitutional monarchy
LANGUAGES: French (official), English, Italian, Monégasque
MONEY: Euro (formerly French franc)
LIFE EXPECTANCY: 90
LITERACY RATE: 99%

guess what? *The average person could walk across Monaco in 56 minutes.*

MONGOLIA

LOCATION: Asia
CAPITAL: Ulaanbaatar
AREA: 603,909 sq mi (1,564,116 sq km)
POPULATION ESTIMATE (2011): 3,133,318
GOVERNMENT: Parliamentary republic
LANGUAGES: Khalkha Mongol, Turkic, Russian
MONEY: Togrog/tugrik
LIFE EXPECTANCY: 68
LITERACY RATE: 98%

guess what? *The Mongol empire was the largest empire in history. It included much of Asia and extended into Europe as far as modern-day Hungary. It was ruled by Genghis Khan.*

MONTENEGRO

LOCATION: Europe
CAPITAL: Podgorica
AREA: 5,333 sq mi (13,812 sq km)
POPULATION ESTIMATE (2011): 661,807
GOVERNMENT: Republic
LANGUAGES: Montenegrin (official), Serbian, Bosnian, Albanian
MONEY: Euro (formerly deutsche mark)
LIFE EXPECTANCY: 72.8
LITERACY RATE: 94%

guess what? *The gusle is a traditional Montenegrin musical instrument. It has only one string.*

MOROCCO

LOCATION: Africa
CAPITAL: Rabat
AREA: 172,413 sq mi (446,550 sq km)
POPULATION ESTIMATE (2011): 31,968,361
GOVERNMENT: Constitutional monarchy
LANGUAGES: Arabic (official), French, Berber dialects
MONEY: Dirham
LIFE EXPECTANCY: 76
LITERACY RATE: 52%

guess what? *Date palms grow throughout Morocco. Their fruit, the date, is an important source of food for families. At different times in Morocco's past, it has been unlawful to sell a date tree.*

MOZAMBIQUE

LOCATION: Africa
CAPITAL: Maputo
AREA: 308,642 sq mi (799,380 sq km)
POPULATION ESTIMATE (2011): 22,948,858
GOVERNMENT: Republic
LANGUAGES: Portuguese (official), Emakhuwa, Xichangana, others
MONEY: Metical
LIFE EXPECTANCY: 52
LITERACY RATE: 48%

guess what? *Mozambique's tropical climate can result in dangerous flooding of the nation's rivers. In 2001, flooding of the Zambezi River valley forced the evacuation of 80,000 people from their homes.*

MYANMAR (BURMA)

LOCATION: Asia
CAPITAL: Nay Pyi Taw
AREA: 261,228 sq mi (676,578 sq km)
POPULATION ESTIMATE (2011): 53,999,804
GOVERNMENT: Military regime
LANGUAGES: Burmese, minority languages
MONEY: Kyat
LIFE EXPECTANCY: 65
LITERACY RATE: 90%

guess what? *Thousands of pagodas are found throughout Bagan, the ancient Buddhist capital of Myanmar. The temples were built between the 11th and 13th centuries, many to honor Buddha.*

NAMIBIA

LOCATION: Africa
CAPITAL: Windhoek
AREA: 318,261 sq mi (824,292 sq km)
POPULATION ESTIMATE (2011): 2,147,585
GOVERNMENT: Republic
LANGUAGES: English (official), Afrikaans, German, native languages
MONEY: Namibian dollar
LIFE EXPECTANCY: 52
LITERACY RATE: 85%

guess what? *The Namibian fog beetle survives in the dry desert by "fog basking." To get drinking water, it will do a handstand in fog. Mist droplets gather on its body and slide down to its mouth.*

NAURU

LOCATION: Oceania
CAPITAL: Yaren District (unofficial)
AREA: 8.11 sq mi (21 sq km)
POPULATION ESTIMATE (2011): 9,322
GOVERNMENT: Republic
LANGUAGES: Nauruan (official), English
MONEY: Australian dollar
LIFE EXPECTANCY: 65
LITERACY RATE: Not available

guess what? *A traditional sport in Nauru is catching the national bird, the frigate, in mid-flight. People keep the birds, tame them, and use them to attract other wild frigates for the next round of games.*

Countries

NEPAL
LOCATION: Asia
CAPITAL: Kathmandu
AREA: 56,827 sq mi
(147,181 sq km)
POPULATION ESTIMATE (2011):
29,391,883
GOVERNMENT: Republic
LANGUAGES: Nepali (official),
Maithali, Bhojpuri, Tharu,
Tamang
MONEY: Nepalese rupee
LIFE EXPECTANCY: 66
LITERACY RATE: 49%

guess what? *Mt. Everest, the tallest mountain in the world, is in Nepal, along the Tibetan border. Part of the Himalaya range, Mt. Everest is about 29,035 feet (8,850 m) tall.*

THE NETHERLANDS
LOCATION: Europe
CAPITAL: Amsterdam
AREA: 16,040 sq mi
(41,543 sq km)
POPULATION ESTIMATE (2011):
16,847,007
GOVERNMENT: Constitutional
monarchy
LANGUAGES: Dutch and Frisian
(both official)
MONEY: Euro (formerly guilder)
LIFE EXPECTANCY: 80
LITERACY RATE: 99%

guess what? *In Amsterdam, many people travel around the city in boats on canals. For foot traffic, there are more than 1,200 bridges in the city.*

NEW ZEALAND
LOCATION: Oceania
CAPITAL: Wellington
AREA: 103,363 sq mi
(267,710 sq km)
POPULATION ESTIMATE (2011):
4,290,347
GOVERNMENT: Parliamentary
democracy
LANGUAGES: English, Maori, and
sign language (all official)
MONEY: New Zealand dollar
LIFE EXPECTANCY: 81
LITERACY RATE: 99%

guess what? *In 1953, New Zealander Edmund Hillary, along with his guide Tenzing Norgay, were the first people to reach the summit of Mt. Everest, the tallest peak in the world.*

NICARAGUA
LOCATION: Central America
CAPITAL: Managua
AREA: 50,336 sq mi
(130,370 sq km)
POPULATION ESTIMATE (2011):
5,666,301
GOVERNMENT: Republic
LANGUAGE: Spanish (official)
MONEY: Cordoba
LIFE EXPECTANCY: 72
LITERACY RATE: 68%

guess what? *Gallo pinto is a traditional dish in Nicaragua. It consists of rice, onions, sweet peppers, and beans, and is eaten with most meals.*

NIGER
LOCATION: Africa
CAPITAL: Niamey
AREA: 489,189 sq mi
(1,267,000 sq km)
POPULATION ESTIMATE (2011):
16,468,886
GOVERNMENT: Republic
LANGUAGES: French (official),
Hausa, Djerma
MONEY: CFA franc
LIFE EXPECTANCY: 53
LITERACY RATE: 29%

guess what? *Most of Niger is in the Sahara desert.*

NIGERIA
LOCATION: Africa
CAPITAL: Abuja
AREA: 356,667 sq mi
(923,768 sq km)
POPULATION ESTIMATE (2011):
155,215,573
GOVERNMENT: Republic
LANGUAGES: English (official),
Hausa, Yoruba, Igbo, Fulani
MONEY: Naira
LIFE EXPECTANCY: 48
LITERACY RATE: 68%

guess what? *One of Nigeria's best-known foods is spicy pepper soup, which is made with onions, hot chili peppers, and either meat or fish.*

NORWAY
LOCATION: Europe
CAPITAL: Oslo
AREA: 125,021 sq mi (323,802 sq km)
POPULATION ESTIMATE (2011): 4,691,849
GOVERNMENT: Constitutional monarchy
LANGUAGES: Two official forms of Norwegian: Bokmal and Nynorsk
MONEY: Krone
LIFE EXPECTANCY: 80
LITERACY RATE: 100%

Guess what? *Many Norwegians love to ski. Some even buy roller skis so they can ski along the roads in the summertime.*

OMAN
LOCATION: Middle East
CAPITAL: Muscat
AREA: 119,499 sq mi (309,500 sq km)
POPULATION ESTIMATE (2011): 3,027,959
GOVERNMENT: Monarchy
LANGUAGES: Arabic (official), English, Baluchi, Urdu, Indian dialects
MONEY: Omani rial
LIFE EXPECTANCY: 74
LITERACY RATE: 81%

Guess what? *Some Omani women wear a heavy silver necklace called a hirz. The necklaces hold verses from the Koran (the Muslim holy book) and are said to protect the wearer against evil.*

PAKISTAN
LOCATION: Asia
CAPITAL: Islamabad
AREA: 307,374 sq mi (790,095 sq km)
POPULATION ESTIMATE (2011): 187,342,721
GOVERNMENT: Republic
LANGUAGES: Punjabi, Sindhi, Siraiki, Pashtu, Urdu (official), others
MONEY: Pakistani rupee
LIFE EXPECTANCY: 66
LITERACY RATE: 50%

Guess what? *Similar to Hollywood in the United States and Bollywood in India, Lollywood is the name used for Pakistan's film industry. It is headquartered in the city of Lahore.*

PALAU
LOCATION: Oceania
CAPITAL: Melekeok
AREA: 177 sq mi (458 sq km)
POPULATION ESTIMATE (2011): 20,956
GOVERNMENT: Constitutional government
LANGUAGES: Palauan, English, Sonsoralese, Tobi, Anguar, Filipino, Chinese
MONEY: U.S. dollar
LIFE EXPECTANCY: 72
LITERACY RATE: 92%

Guess what? *Thousands of jellyfish live in Jellyfish Lake in Palau. Unlike many other jellyfish, the ones living there do not harm people.*

PANAMA
LOCATION: Central America
CAPITAL: Panama City
AREA: 29,120 sq mi (75,420 sq km)
POPULATION ESTIMATE (2011): 3,460,462
GOVERNMENT: Constitutional democracy
LANGUAGES: Spanish (official), English
MONEY: Balboa, U.S. dollar
LIFE EXPECTANCY: 78
LITERACY RATE: 92%

Guess what? *In Panama, you can see the sun rise over the Pacific and set over the Atlantic.*

PAPUA NEW GUINEA
LOCATION: Oceania
CAPITAL: Port Moresby
AREA: 178,703 sq mi (462,840 sq km)
POPULATION ESTIMATE (2011): 6,187,591
GOVERNMENT: Constitutional parliamentary democracy
LANGUAGES: Tok Pisin, English, and Hiri (all official), about 860 native languages
MONEY: Kina
LIFE EXPECTANCY: 66
LITERACY RATE: 57%

Guess what? *The largest butterfly in the world is the Queen Alexandra birdwing. Found only in Papua New Guinea, its wingspan can be as big as 12 inches (30.5 cm).*

Countries

69

PARAGUAY

LOCATION: South America
CAPITAL: Asunción
AREA: 157,046 sq mi (406,750 sq km)
POPULATION ESTIMATE (2011): 6,459,058
GOVERNMENT: Republic
LANGUAGES: Spanish and Guaraní (both official)
MONEY: Guaraní
LIFE EXPECTANCY: 76
LITERACY RATE: 94%

Guess what? *It is legal to duel in Paraguay as long as both duelers are registered blood donors.*

PERU

LOCATION: South America
CAPITAL: Lima
AREA: 496,223 sq mi (1,285,220 sq km)
POPULATION ESTIMATE (2011): 29,248,943
GOVERNMENT: Republic
LANGUAGES: Spanish and Quechua (both official), Aymara, other native languages
MONEY: Nuevo sol
LIFE EXPECTANCY: 73
LITERACY RATE: 93%

Guess what? *The Incan city of Machu Picchu in the mountains of southeastern Peru was built between 1460 and 1470. It had been empty for nearly 400 years when Hiram Bingham rediscovered it in 1911.*

PHILIPPINES

LOCATION: Asia
CAPITAL: Manila
AREA: 115,830 sq mi (300,000 sq km)
POPULATION ESTIMATE (2011): 101,833,938
GOVERNMENT: Republic
LANGUAGES: Filipino (based on Tagalog) and English (both official), regional languages
MONEY: Philippine peso
LIFE EXPECTANCY: 72
LITERACY RATE: 93%

Guess what? *The Pacific Ring of Fire is an area well known for earthquakes and volcanic eruptions. One of the most recent eruptions was the Mayon Volcano, in the Philippines, in December 2009.*

POLAND

LOCATION: Europe
CAPITAL: Warsaw
AREA: 120,728 sq mi (312,685 sq km)
POPULATION ESTIMATE (2011): 38,441,588
GOVERNMENT: Republic
LANGUAGE: Polish
MONEY: Zloty
LIFE EXPECTANCY: 76
LITERACY RATE: 100%

Guess what? *Astronomer Nicolaus Copernicus was born in Poland. He was the first to suggest that the sun, not Earth, was the center of the universe.*

PORTUGAL

LOCATION: Europe
CAPITAL: Lisbon
AREA: 35,556 sq mi (92,090 sq km)
POPULATION ESTIMATE (2011): 10,760,305
GOVERNMENT: Republic
LANGUAGES: Portuguese and Mirandese (both official)
MONEY: Euro (formerly escudo)
LIFE EXPECTANCY: 79
LITERACY RATE: 93%

Guess what? *Lisbon, Portugal's capital, is known as the City of Seven Hills. These hills are São Jorge, São Vicente, Sant'Ana, Santo Andre, Chagas, Santa Catarina, and São Roque.*

QATAR

LOCATION: Middle East
CAPITAL: Doha
AREA: 4,473 sq mi (11,586 sq km)
POPULATION ESTIMATE (2011): 848,016
GOVERNMENT: Traditional monarchy (emirate)
LANGUAGES: Arabic (official), English
MONEY: Qatari rial
LIFE EXPECTANCY: 76
LITERACY RATE: 89%

Guess what? *March begins the month-long Doha Cultural Festival, which presents music, poetry, theater, and dance performances.*

70

ROMANIA

LOCATION: Europe
CAPITAL: Bucharest
AREA: 92,043 sq mi (238,391 sq km)
POPULATION ESTIMATE (2011): 21,904,551
GOVERNMENT: Republic
LANGUAGES: Romanian (official), Hungarian, Romany
MONEY: Leu
LIFE EXPECTANCY: 74
LITERACY RATE: 97%

Guess what? *Bram Stoker based his novel Dracula on Vlad Tepes, a cruel 15th-century Wallachian prince. Wallachia merged with Moldavia in 1859 to become Romania.*

RUSSIA

LOCATION: Europe and Asia
CAPITAL: Moscow
AREA: 6,601,668 sq mi (17,098,242 sq km)
POPULATION ESTIMATE (2011): 138,739,892
GOVERNMENT: Federation
LANGUAGES: Russian, others
MONEY: Ruble
LIFE EXPECTANCY: 66
LITERACY RATE: 99%

Guess what? *Moscow's subway system is known for its decoration. The marble stations were built in the 1930s, and feature chandeliers and art deco designs.*

RWANDA

LOCATION: Africa
CAPITAL: Kigali
AREA: 10,169 sq mi (26,338 sq km)
POPULATION ESTIMATE (2011): 11,370,425
GOVERNMENT: Republic
LANGUAGES: Kinyarwanda, French, and English (all official)
MONEY: Rwandan franc
LIFE EXPECTANCY: 58
LITERACY RATE: 70%

Guess what? *The mountain gorillas that make their home in Volcanoes National Park, Rwanda, were the basis for the book Gorillas in the Mist, which was made into a movie starring Sigourney Weaver.*

SAINT KITTS AND NEVIS

LOCATION: Caribbean
CAPITAL: Basseterre
AREA: 101 sq mi (261 sq km)
POPULATION ESTIMATE (2011): 50,314
GOVERNMENT: Parliamentary democracy
LANGUAGE: English
MONEY: East Caribbean dollar
LIFE EXPECTANCY: 75
LITERACY RATE: 98%

Guess what? *The island of Nevis is made up almost entirely of a single mountain called Nevis Peak.*

SAINT LUCIA

LOCATION: Caribbean
CAPITAL: Castries
AREA: 238 sq mi (616 sq km)
POPULATION ESTIMATE (2011): 161,557
GOVERNMENT: Parliamentary democracy
LANGUAGES: English (official), French patois
MONEY: East Caribbean dollar
LIFE EXPECTANCY: 77
LITERACY RATE: 90%

Guess what? *The island of Saint Lucia, which is only 27 miles (43.5 km) long and 14 miles (22.5 km) wide, was formed as the result of volcanic activity.*

SAINT VINCENT AND THE GRENADINES

LOCATION: Caribbean
CAPITAL: Kingstown
AREA: 150 sq mi (389 sq km)
POPULATION ESTIMATE (2011): 103,869
GOVERNMENT: Parliamentary democracy
LANGUAGES: English, French patois
MONEY: East Caribbean dollar
LIFE EXPECTANCY: 74
LITERACY RATE: 96%

Guess what? *Saint Vincent and the Grenadines is a nation located in the Lesser Antilles archipelago. Dominica, Barbados, and Grenada are some of the other islands in that archipelago, or island chain.*

Countries

SAMOA

LOCATION: Oceania
CAPITAL: Apia
AREA: 1,093 sq mi (2,831 sq km)
POPULATION ESTIMATE (2011): 193,161
GOVERNMENT: Parliamentary democracy
LANGUAGES: Samoan, English
MONEY: Tala
LIFE EXPECTANCY: 72
LITERACY RATE: 100%

guess what? When French explorer Louis-Antoine de Bougainville first spotted Samoa in 1768, he called it the Navigators Islands because of the many canoes he saw moving around the shores.

SAN MARINO

LOCATION: Europe
CAPITAL: San Marino
AREA: 24 sq mi (61 sq km)
POPULATION ESTIMATE (2011): 31,817
GOVERNMENT: Republic
LANGUAGE: Italian
MONEY: Euro (formerly Italian lira)
LIFE EXPECTANCY: 83
LITERACY RATE: 96%

guess what? San Marino, founded around 301 A.D., is the world's oldest republic.

SAO TOME AND PRINCIPE

LOCATION: Africa
CAPITAL: São Tomé
AREA: 372 sq mi (964 sq km)
POPULATION ESTIMATE (2011): 179,506
GOVERNMENT: Republic
LANGUAGE: Portuguese (official)
MONEY: Dobra
LIFE EXPECTANCY: 63
LITERACY RATE: 85%

guess what? The two stars on São Tomé and Príncipe's flag represent the two main islands. The red triangle symbolizes the struggle for independence. The green, yellow, and black colors represent unity among African nations.

SAUDI ARABIA

LOCATION: Middle East
CAPITAL: Riyadh
AREA: 830,000 sq mi (2,149,690 sq km)
POPULATION ESTIMATE (2011): 26,131,703
GOVERNMENT: Monarchy
LANGUAGE: Arabic
MONEY: Saudi riyal
LIFE EXPECTANCY: 74
LITERACY RATE: 79%

guess what? King Fahd's Fountain in Jeddah, Saudi Arabia, is the tallest in the world. It spews water as high up as 1,023 feet (312 m). That's almost as high as the top of the Eiffel Tower!

SENEGAL

LOCATION: Africa
CAPITAL: Dakar
AREA: 75,955 sq mi (196,722 sq km)
POPULATION ESTIMATE (2011): 12,643,799
GOVERNMENT: Republic
LANGUAGES: French (official), Wolof, Pulaar, Jola, Mandinka
MONEY: CFA franc
LIFE EXPECTANCY: 60
LITERACY RATE: 39%

guess what? The Pink Lake, just outside Dakar, is actually pink! Deposits of feldspar, a kind of crystalline mineral, reflect sunlight through the salty water, making it appear pink.

SERBIA

LOCATION: Europe
CAPITAL: Belgrade
AREA: 29,913 sq mi (77,474 sq km)
POPULATION ESTIMATE (2011): 7,310,555
GOVERNMENT: Republic
LANGUAGES: Serbian, Hungarian, others
MONEY: Serbian dinar
LIFE EXPECTANCY: 74
LITERACY RATE: 96%

guess what? Belgrade was first settled by the Celts in the 3rd century B.C., making it one of the oldest cities in Europe.

SEYCHELLES
LOCATION: Africa
CAPITAL: Victoria
AREA: 176 sq mi (455 sq km)
POPULATION ESTIMATE (2011): 89,188
GOVERNMENT: Republic
LANGUAGES: Creole, English (official), other
MONEY: Seychelles rupee
LIFE EXPECTANCY: 74
LITERACY RATE: 92%

guess what? *The Indian Ocean's only flightless bird, the white-throated rail, lives on the Aldabra group of islands in Seychelles.*

SIERRA LEONE
LOCATION: Africa
CAPITAL: Freetown
AREA: 27,699 sq mi (71,740 sq km)
POPULATION ESTIMATE (2011): 5,363,669
GOVERNMENT: Constitutional democracy
LANGUAGES: English (official), Mende, Temne, Krio
MONEY: Leone
LIFE EXPECTANCY: 56
LITERACY RATE: 35%

guess what? *Sierra Leone is one of Africa's major producers of diamonds.*

SINGAPORE
LOCATION: Asia
CAPITAL: Singapore
AREA: 269 sq mi (697 sq km)
POPULATION ESTIMATE (2011): 4,740,737
GOVERNMENT: Parliamentary republic
LANGUAGES: Chinese (Mandarin), English, Malay, Hokkien, Cantonese, others
MONEY: Singapore dollar
LIFE EXPECTANCY: 82
LITERACY RATE: 93%

guess what? *Singapore has banned the import and sale of chewing gum.*

SLOVAKIA
LOCATION: Europe
CAPITAL: Bratislava
AREA: 18,933 sq mi (49,035 sq km)
POPULATION ESTIMATE (2011): 5,477,038
GOVERNMENT: Parliamentary democracy
LANGUAGES: Slovak (official), Hungarian, Roma, Ukranian
MONEY: Koruna
LIFE EXPECTANCY: 76
LITERACY RATE: 100%

guess what? *Slovakia is famous for its caves. Of the thousands of caves around the country, fewer than 20 are open to the public.*

SLOVENIA
LOCATION: Europe
CAPITAL: Ljubljana
AREA: 7,827 sq mi (20,273 sq km)
POPULATION ESTIMATE (2011): 2,000,092
GOVERNMENT: Parliamentary republic
LANGUAGES: Slovenian, Serbo-Croatian
MONEY: Euro (formerly Slovenian tolar)
LIFE EXPECTANCY: 77
LITERACY RATE: 100%

guess what? *Predjamski Grad, a castle in Slovenia, was built into the mouth of a cave between the 12th and 16th centuries.*

SOLOMON ISLANDS
LOCATION: Oceania
CAPITAL: Honiara
AREA: 111,517 sq mi (28,896 sq km)
POPULATION ESTIMATE (2011): 571,890
GOVERNMENT: Parliamentary democracy
LANGUAGES: Melanesian pidgin, English (official), more than 120 local languages
MONEY: Solomon Islands dollar
LIFE EXPECTANCY: 74
LITERACY RATE: Not available

guess what? *Marovo Lagoon in New Georgia, Solomon Islands, is the world's largest saltwater lagoon. Lagoons are shallow bodies of water cut off from larger bodies, often by coral reefs.*

Countries

SOMALIA

LOCATION: Africa
CAPITAL: Mogadishu
AREA: 246,199 sq mi (637,657 sq km)
POPULATION ESTIMATE (2011): 9,925,640
GOVERNMENT: Transitional government
LANGUAGES: Somali (official), Arabic, English, Italian
MONEY: Somali shilling
LIFE EXPECTANCY: 50
LITERACY RATE: 38%

guess what? *Somali pirates are a growing problem in the waters off East Africa. They take over boats, oil tankers, and freighters, and force people or companies to pay to get their boats or merchandise back.*

SOUTH AFRICA

LOCATION: Africa
CAPITALS: Pretoria (administrative), Cape Town (legislative), Bloemfontein (judicial)
AREA: 471,008 sq mi (1,219,090 sq km)
POPULATION ESTIMATE (2011): 49,004,031
GOVERNMENT: Republic
LANGUAGES: Zulu, Xhosa, Afrikaans, Sepedi, English, Setswana, Sesotho, Tsonga, others
MONEY: Rand
LIFE EXPECTANCY: 49
LITERACY RATE: 86%

guess what? *Actress Charlize Theron is from South Africa.*

SPAIN

LOCATION: Europe
CAPITAL: Madrid
AREA: 195,124 sq mi (505,370 sq km)
POPULATION ESTIMATE (2011): 46,754,784
GOVERNMENT: Parliamentary monarchy
LANGUAGES: Castilian Spanish (official), Catalan, Galician, Basque
MONEY: Euro (formerly peseta)
LIFE EXPECTANCY: 81
LITERACY RATE: 98%

guess what? *Spanish children are not visited by the tooth fairy. Instead, there is a mouse named Ratoncito Pérez who will take the tooth and leave a treasure.*

SRI LANKA

LOCATION: Asia
CAPITAL: Colombo
AREA: 25,332 sq mi (65,610 sq km)
POPULATION ESTIMATE (2011): 21,283,913
GOVERNMENT: Republic
LANGUAGES: Sinhala (official), Tamil, English
MONEY: Sri Lankan rupee
LIFE EXPECTANCY: 76
LITERACY RATE: 91%

guess what? *The Pinnawela Elephant Orphanage, near Colombo, was established in 1975 to care for rescued motherless baby elephants.*

SUDAN

LOCATION: Africa
CAPITAL: Khartoum
AREA: 967,493 sq mi (2,505,810 sq km)
POPULATION ESTIMATE (2011): 45,074,502
GOVERNMENT: Authoritarian regime
LANGUAGES: Arabic and English (both official), Nubian, Ta Bedawie, others
MONEY: Sudanese pound
LIFE EXPECTANCY: 55
LITERACY RATE: 61%

guess what? *The White Nile, which flows from Uganda, and the Blue Nile, which flows from Ethiopia, join together in Sudan to form the main Nile River.*

SURINAME

LOCATION: South America
CAPITAL: Paramaribo
AREA: 63,251 sq mi (163,820 sq km)
POPULATION ESTIMATE (2011): 491,989
GOVERNMENT: Constitutional democracy
LANGUAGES: Dutch (official), Surinamese, English, others
MONEY: Surinamese dollar
LIFE EXPECTANCY: 74
LITERACY RATE: 90%

guess what? *Rain forests cover 80% of Suriname.*

74

SWAZILAND

LOCATION: Africa
CAPITAL: Mbabane
AREA: 6,704 sq mi (17,360 sq km)
POPULATION ESTIMATE (2011): 1,370,424
GOVERNMENT: Monarchy
LANGUAGES: Swati and English (both official)
MONEY: Emalangeni
LIFE EXPECTANCY: 49
LITERACY RATE: 82%

Guess what? *At the end of every summer, some Swazi women and girls participate in the Umhlanga, or "reed dance," an eight-day festival filled with parades, dancing, and feasts.*

SWEDEN

LOCATION: Europe
CAPITAL: Stockholm
AREA: 173,860 sq mi (450,295 sq km)
POPULATION ESTIMATE (2011): 9,088,728
GOVERNMENT: Constitutional monarchy
LANGUAGE: Swedish
MONEY: Krona
LIFE EXPECTANCY: 81
LITERACY RATE: 99%

Guess what? *Gamla Stan, a small island in the middle of Stockholm, was built in the 13th century and has many tiny medieval streets. The narrowest is just 35 inches (89 cm) wide. Some people need to turn sideways to fit through it.*

SWITZERLAND

LOCATION: Europe
CAPITAL: Bern
AREA: 15,937 sq mi (41,277 sq km)
POPULATION ESTIMATE (2011): 7,639,961
GOVERNMENT: Federal republic
LANGUAGES: German, French, Italian, and Romansh (all official), others
MONEY: Swiss franc
LIFE EXPECTANCY: 81
LITERACY RATE: 99%

Guess what? *According to legend, yodeling was developed in the Swiss Alps as a form of long-distance communication. The high mountains allowed for clear echoes.*

SYRIA

LOCATION: Middle East
CAPITAL: Damascus
AREA: 71,498 sq mi (185,180 sq km)
POPULATION ESTIMATE (2011): 22,517,750
GOVERNMENT: Republic under an authoritarian regime
LANGUAGES: Arabic (official), Kurdish, Armenian, Aramaic, Circassian
MONEY: Syrian pound
LIFE EXPECTANCY: 75
LITERACY RATE: 80%

Guess what? *Damascus is one of the oldest cities in the world.*

TAIWAN

LOCATION: Asia
CAPITAL: Taipei
AREA: 13,892 sq mi (35,980 sq km)
POPULATION ESTIMATE (2011): 23,071,779
GOVERNMENT: Multiparty democracy
LANGUAGES: Chinese (Mandarin), Taiwanese, Hakka dialects
MONEY: New Taiwan dollar
LIFE EXPECTANCY: 78
LITERACY RATE: 96%

Guess what? *The national flower of Taiwan is the plum blossom.*

TAJIKISTAN

LOCATION: Asia
CAPITAL: Dushanbe
AREA: 55,251 sq mi (143,100 sq km)
POPULATION ESTIMATE (2011): 7,627,200
GOVERNMENT: Republic
LANGUAGES: Tajik (official), Russian
MONEY: Somoni
LIFE EXPECTANCY: 66
LITERACY RATE: 100%

Guess what? *The Nurek Dam, in Tajikistan, is the tallest completed dam in the world. Its walls are 984 feet (300 m) high.*

Countries

TANZANIA
LOCATION: Africa
CAPITAL: Dar es Salaam
AREA: 365,755 sq mi
(947,300 sq km)
POPULATION ESTIMATE (2011):
42,746,620
GOVERNMENT: Republic
LANGUAGES: Swahili and English
(both official), Arabic, local
languages
MONEY: Tanzanian shilling
LIFE EXPECTANCY: 53
LITERACY RATE: 69%

guess what? *Lake Natron, in Tanzania, is the breeding ground for lesser flamingos. Every year, more than 1 million flamingos go there from all over Africa.*

THAILAND
LOCATION: Asia
CAPITAL: Bangkok
AREA: 198,117 sq mi
(513,120 sq km)
POPULATION ESTIMATE (2011):
66,720,153
GOVERNMENT: Constitutional
monarchy
LANGUAGES: Thai (Siamese),
English, regional dialects
MONEY: Baht
LIFE EXPECTANCY: 74
LITERACY RATE: 93%

guess what? *The official ceremonial name of the capital city, Bangkok, is more than 20 words long.*

TOGO
LOCATION: Africa
CAPITAL: Lomé
AREA: 21,925 sq mi
(56,785 sq km)
POPULATION ESTIMATE (2011):
6,771,993
GOVERNMENT: Republic, under
transition to multiparty
democratic rule
LANGUAGES: French (official), Ewe,
Mina, Kabye, Dagomba
MONEY: CFA franc
LIFE EXPECTANCY: 63
LITERACY RATE: 61%

guess what? *Togolese vendors carry their wares on their heads—whether it is a small bunch of bananas or a big basket of chickens.*

TONGA
LOCATION: Oceania
CAPITAL: Nuku'alofa
AREA: 289 sq mi (748 sq km)
POPULATION ESTIMATE (2011): 105,916
GOVERNMENT: Constitutional
monarchy
LANGUAGES: Tongan, English
MONEY: Pa'anga
LIFE EXPECTANCY: 76
LITERACY RATE: 99%

guess what? *Tonga is made up of about 170 islands, but fewer than 50 are inhabited.*

TRINIDAD AND TOBAGO
LOCATION: Caribbean
CAPITAL: Port-of-Spain
AREA: 1,980 sq mi (5,128 sq km)
POPULATION ESTIMATE (2011):
1,227,505
GOVERNMENT: Parliamentary
democracy
LANGUAGES: English (official),
Hindi, French, Spanish, Chinese
MONEY: Trinidad and
Tobago dollar
LIFE EXPECTANCY: 71
LITERACY RATE: 99%

guess what? *Calypso is a popular type of music in Trinidad and Tobago. The Caribbean steel pan, a type of drum often used in calypso music, was invented there in the 1930s.*

TUNISIA
LOCATION: Africa
CAPITAL: Tunis
AREA: 63,170 sq mi
(163,610 sq km)
POPULATION ESTIMATE (2011):
10,629,186
GOVERNMENT: Republic
LANGUAGES: Arabic (official),
French
MONEY: Tunisian dinar
LIFE EXPECTANCY: 75
LITERACY RATE: 74%

guess what? *Harissa is a spicy chili paste or sauce used in North African cooking, especially in Tunisian cuisine.*

TURKEY

LOCATION: Europe and Asia
CAPITAL: Ankara
AREA: 302,535 sq mi
(783,562 sq km)
POPULATION ESTIMATE (2011):
78,785,548
GOVERNMENT: Parliamentary
democracy
LANGUAGES: Turkish (official),
Kurdish, others
MONEY: New
Turkish lira
LIFE EXPECTANCY: 73
LITERACY RATE: 87%

 guess what? Istanbul's *Grand Bazaar is* famous for its tiled arches and decorations, and for its hundreds of shops.

TURKMENISTAN

LOCATION: Asia
CAPITAL: Ashgabat
AREA: 188,455 sq mi
(488,100 sq km)
POPULATION ESTIMATE (2011):
4,997,503
GOVERNMENT: Republic
LANGUAGES: Turkmen, Russian,
Uzbek, others
MONEY: Manat
LIFE EXPECTANCY: 69
LITERACY RATE: 99%

guess what? *The Arvana dromedary camel is bred only in Turkmenistan. These camels produce lots of milk, and are good for carrying packs and even for riding.*

TUVALU

LOCATION: Oceania
CAPITAL: Funafuti
AREA: 10 sq mi (26 sq km)
POPULATION ESTIMATE (2011): 10,544
GOVERNMENT: Parliamentary
democracy
LANGUAGES: Tuvaluan, English,
Samoan, Kiribati
MONEY: Australian dollar,
Tuvaluan dollar
LIFE EXPECTANCY: 65
LITERACY RATE: Not available

guess what? *Tuvalu consists of nine atolls, which are groups of coral islands often made up of a reef surrounding a lagoon.*

UGANDA

LOCATION: Africa
CAPITAL: Kampala
AREA: 93,065 sq mi
(241,038 sq km)
POPULATION ESTIMATE (2011):
34,612,250
GOVERNMENT: Republic
LANGUAGES: English (official),
Luganda, Swahili, others
MONEY: Ugandan shilling
LIFE EXPECTANCY: 53
LITERACY RATE: 67%

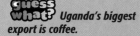 **guess what?** *Uganda's biggest export is coffee.*

UKRAINE

LOCATION: Europe
CAPITAL: Kiev
AREA: 233,032 sq mi
(603,550 sq km)
POPULATION ESTIMATE (2011):
45,134,707
GOVERNMENT: Republic
LANGUAGES: Ukrainian, Russian
MONEY: Hryvnia
LIFE EXPECTANCY: 69
LITERACY RATE: 99%

guess what? *Ukraine's flag was adopted in 1992. The blue represents the country's sky, streams, and mountains. The yellow symbolizes the golden wheat that flourishes there.*

UNITED ARAB EMIRATES

LOCATION: Middle East
CAPITAL: Abu Dhabi
AREA: 32,278 sq mi
(83,600 sq km)
POPULATION ESTIMATE (2011):
5,148,664
GOVERNMENT: Federation
LANGUAGES: Arabic (official),
Persian, English, Hindi, Urdu
MONEY: U.A.E. dirham
LIFE EXPECTANCY: 77
LITERACY RATE: 78%

guess what? *Man-made islands are being developed in Dubai. The Palm Islands were created in the shape of palm trees.*

Countries

UNITED KINGDOM

LOCATION: Europe
CAPITAL: London
AREA: 94,058 sq mi (243,610 sq km)
POPULATION ESTIMATE (2011): 62,698,362
GOVERNMENT: Constitutional monarchy
LANGUAGES: English, Scots, Scottish Gaelic, Welsh, Irish
MONEY: British pound
LIFE EXPECTANCY: 80
LITERACY RATE: 99%

guess what? *The flag of the United Kingdom is known as the Union Jack. The three crosses on the flag represent England, Scotland, and Ireland. Wales is not represented.*

UNITED STATES

LOCATION: North America
CAPITAL: Washington, D.C.
AREA: 3,794,100 sq mi (9,826,675 sq km)
POPULATION ESTIMATE (2011): 313,232,044
GOVERNMENT: Republic
LANGUAGES: English, Spanish (spoken by a sizable minority)
MONEY: U.S. dollar
LIFE EXPECTANCY: 78
LITERACY RATE: 99%

guess what? *Iced tea was first commercially served at the 1904 World's Fair in St. Louis, Missouri.*

URUGUAY

LOCATION: South America
CAPITAL: Montevideo
AREA: 68,039 sq mi (176,220 sq km)
POPULATION ESTIMATE (2011): 3,308,535
GOVERNMENT: Republic
LANGUAGES: Spanish, Portunol, Brazilero
MONEY: Uruguayan peso
LIFE EXPECTANCY: 76
LITERACY RATE: 98%

guess what? *Uruguay hosted the first World Cup soccer tournament in 1930.*

UZBEKISTAN

LOCATION: Asia
CAPITAL: Tashkent
AREA: 172,741 sq mi (447,400 sq km)
POPULATION ESTIMATE (2011): 28,128,600
GOVERNMENT: Republic
LANGUAGES: Uzbek, Russian, Tajik, others
MONEY: Uzbekistani soum
LIFE EXPECTANCY: 73
LITERACY RATE: 99%

guess what? *Uzbekistan is one of two doubly landlocked countries in the world, which means it is entirely surrounded by other landlocked countries. The other is Liechtenstein.*

VANUATU

LOCATION: Oceania
CAPITAL: Port-Vila
AREA: 4,710 sq mi (12,200 sq km)
POPULATION ESTIMATE (2011): 224,564
GOVERNMENT: Republic
LANGUAGES: Most people speak one of more than 100 local languages; Bislama, English
MONEY: Vatu
LIFE EXPECTANCY: 65
LITERACY RATE: 74%

guess what? *When France and Great Britain controlled the 83 islands of Vanuatu, they were known as the New Hebrides.*

VATICAN CITY (HOLY SEE)

LOCATION: Europe
CAPITAL: Vatican City
AREA: 0.17 sq mi (0.44 sq km)
POPULATION ESTIMATE (2011): 832
GOVERNMENT: Ecclesiastical
LANGUAGES: Italian, Latin, French
MONEY: Euro
LIFE EXPECTANCY: Not available
LITERACY RATE: 100%

guess what? *St. Peter's Basilica, in Vatican City, is the largest church in the world. The nave, which is the long, narrow central hall, is 715 feet (218 m) long and can hold 60,000 people.*

VENEZUELA
LOCATION: South America
CAPITAL: Caracas
AREA: 352,143 sq mi
(912,050 sq km)
POPULATION ESTIMATE (2011):
27,635,743
GOVERNMENT: Republic
LANGUAGES: Spanish (official),
native languages
MONEY: Bolivar
LIFE EXPECTANCY: 74
LITERACY RATE: 93%

Guess what? *Because of its proximity to the equator, Venezuela experiences only two seasons, dry and wet.*

VIETNAM
LOCATION: Asia
CAPITAL: Hanoi
AREA: 127,881 sq mi
(331,210 sq km)
POPULATION ESTIMATE (2011):
90,549,390
GOVERNMENT: Communist state
LANGUAGES: Vietnamese (official),
French, English, Khmer, Chinese
MONEY: Dong
LIFE EXPECTANCY: 72
LITERACY RATE: 90%

Guess what? *At the Cai Rang Floating Market, in Can Thao City, Vietnam, vendors in small boats float along the Mekong River selling bananas, papayas, pineapples, and other food and goods.*

YEMEN
LOCATION: Middle East
CAPITAL: Sanaa
AREA: 203,849 sq mi
(527,970 sq km)
POPULATION ESTIMATE (2011)
24,133,492
GOVERNMENT: Republic
LANGUAGE: Arabic
MONEY: Yemeni rial
LIFE EXPECTANCY: 64
LITERACY RATE: 50%

Guess what? *Yemen is part of the Arabian Peninsula, along with Bahrain, Kuwait, Oman, Qatar, Saudi Arabia, and United Arab Emirates. It is the area's only republic.*

ZAMBIA
LOCATION: Africa
CAPITAL: Lusaka
AREA: 290,584 sq mi
(752,614 sq km)
POPULATION ESTIMATE (2011):
13,881,336
GOVERNMENT: Republic
LANGUAGES: Bemba, Nyanja, Tonga, Lozi, Lunda, Kaonde, Luvale, and English (all official), others
MONEY: Kwacha
LIFE EXPECTANCY: 52
LITERACY RATE: 81%

Guess what? *Zambia was known as Northern Rhodesia until its independence from Britain in 1964.*

ZIMBABWE
LOCATION: Africa
CAPITAL: Harare
AREA: 150,872 sq mi
(390,757 sq km)
POPULATION ESTIMATE (2011):
12,084,304
GOVERNMENT: Parliamentary democracy
LANGUAGES: English (official), Shona, Ndebele (Sindebele)
MONEY: Zimbabwean dollar
LIFE EXPECTANCY: 50
LITERACY RATE: 91%

Guess what? *Shoppers can find just about anything they need at the Mbare Market, in Harare, including food, plumbing supplies, ceremonial herbs, and musical instruments such as thumb pianos.*

I was born in 1254 in Venice, Italy. I was a merchant and an explorer. I traveled the Silk Road east from Italy to China. Nearly 200 years later, my journey inspired Christopher Columbus to find a western route to China.

WHO AM I?

Answer on page 242.

Countries

79

COOL LANDMARKS AROUND THE WORLD

La Sagrada Família, Spain

Golden Gate Bridge, United States

Statue of Liberty, United States

Teotihuacán, Mexico

Machu Picchu, Peru

Iguazú Falls, Argentina/Brazil

Leptis Magna, Libya

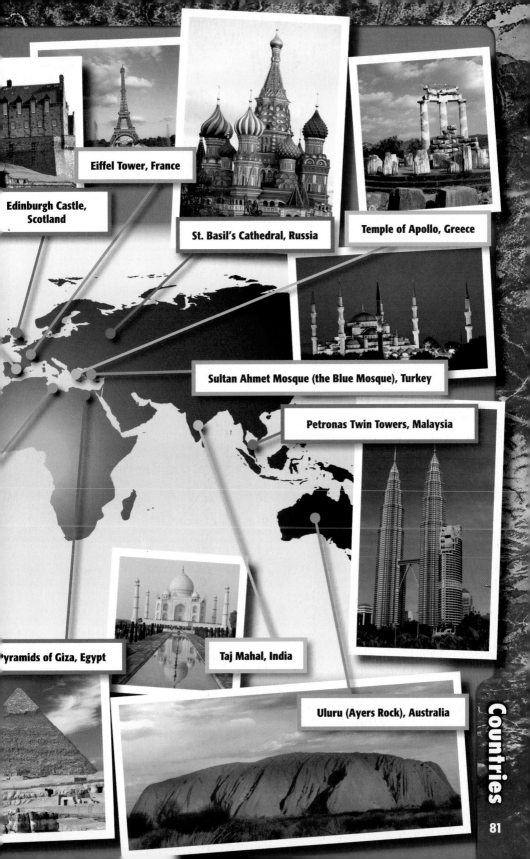

Eiffel Tower, France

Edinburgh Castle, Scotland

St. Basil's Cathedral, Russia

Temple of Apollo, Greece

Sultan Ahmet Mosque (the Blue Mosque), Turkey

Petronas Twin Towers, Malaysia

Pyramids of Giza, Egypt

Taj Mahal, India

Uluru (Ayers Rock), Australia

Countries

81

FROM
TIME
FOR KIDS
MAGAZINE

Coral Crisis

By Suzanne Zimbler

Imagine a beautiful underwater scene. Do you see schools of striped fish darting in and out of colorful rocklike formations? If so, then you are picturing a coral reef.

Coral

Though it is often mistaken for rock, coral is made up of tiny animals called coral polyps. Millions of the creatures stick together and form a hard outer shell. When coral die, their skeletons are left behind, and new coral build on top. Over the years, the Great Barrier Reef, off Australia's east coast, has grown to be 1,240 miles (1,996 km) long. Made up of 2,900 connected reefs, the area is home to thousands of plant and animal species. Much of the reef system is protected, but conservationists have long worried that not enough was being done to safeguard the area. On April 3, 2010, their concerns came true. A large ship veered off course and slammed into a protected section of Australia's Great Barrier Reef. Part of the fragile ecosystem is now damaged.

A SHIP THAT STRAYED

Shen Neng I left Australia for China carrying 65,000 tons (58,967 m tons) of coal. Five hours into its journey, the vessel strayed from its shipping lane. It plowed through a protected reef, destroying everything in its path.

The damage covers an area as large as five football fields. "It's a white, flat plane of sand and crushed coral rubble," says David Wachenfeld of the Great Barrier Reef Marine Park Authority.

With more and more ships passing through the Great Barrier Reef, experts fear an even bigger accident is bound to happen. Tougher rules are expected to take effect in July 2011. For Richard Leck of the environmental group WWF-Australia, the changes cannot come soon enough. "Every time an incident like this happens," he says, "we hope that this isn't going to be the time when there is a massive oil spill."

Great Barrier Reef

The crash also caused between 2 and 4 tons (1.8 and 3.6 m tons) of fuel oil to seep into the water.

ENVIRONMENTAL THREATS

Earth is always changing. Volcanoes, earthquakes, floods, erosion, and other natural occurrences constantly alter the planet. Humans also leave their mark on the environment. Industrial development, over-farming, deforestation, and generating trash are just a few of the ways that people can damage the world around them. Here are some forms of pollution that threaten the health of the planet.

SMOG

The word *smog* is a combination of *smoke* and *fog*. Exhaust from cars and trucks, factory emissions, smoke from burning wood, and some chemical processes release particles into the air. These particles can get trapped in the air near the ground, resulting in smog. This "dirty air" can be especially harmful to the elderly and people with asthma or other breathing troubles.

OIL SPILLS

Oil spills are particularly devastating to the oceans because of their widespread effects on marine life. Birds cannot fly when their wings are soaked in oil, so many drown or get poisoned when they try to clean themselves. Oil sticks to furry marine animals such as seals, otters, and walruses. When this happens, they can no longer keep themselves warm and may freeze to death. The blowholes of whales, porpoises, and dolphins can be blocked up with oil, so they cannot breathe.

ACID RAIN

Today, Earth's air contains many pollutants. Sulfur dioxide (SO_2) and nitrogen dioxide (NO_2) are two of the most common. These gases are released when fossil fuels such as coal and petroleum are burned by factories, vehicles, and power plants. Acid rain is formed when water vapor in the air combines with SO_2 and NO_2 to form sulfuric and nitric acids.

TRASH

More trash is produced in the United States every year than in any other country. In fact, 5% of the people on the planet generate 40% of the world's waste. All of this garbage poses a serious threat to wildlife. If it is not properly disposed of, it can end up clogging waterways and damaging habitats, or it may be mistaken for food by animals.

Inorganic items like plastics, metal, Styrofoam™, and glass do not decompose quickly. They may take months, years, or even centuries to break down. Some trash is collected and tossed into enormous landfills, which are carefully designed to contain the waste and any dangerous particles that may be released as items break down. When garbage contaminates groundwater, it can ruin water sources and harm humans and wildlife in the area.

On average, every person in the United States produces about 4.6 pounds (2 kg) of trash per day. Write down a list of what you throw away for a week. How can you toss less?

Energy and the Environment

83

NONRENEWABLE ENERGY SOURCES

Nonrenewable energy sources are in limited supply, and will eventually be used up entirely. Coal, petroleum, and natural gas were formed in the Earth over millions of years, and are known as fossil fuels.

COAL is a hard rock made of carbon. It started out as decaying plant matter that was covered with many layers of dirt. Over the course of millions of years, the pressure of all this dirt, as well as Earth's heat, transformed the matter into coal. Because coal takes so long to form, it cannot be manufactured. Coal is the largest source of fossil fuel in the United States.

NATURAL GAS was formed in the same way and over the same amount of time as coal and petroleum, except that it is the odorless byproduct of decaying matter. Bubbles of gas are trapped underground and can be piped to the surface. Natural gas is used as a source of home heating as well as for cooking.

PETROLEUM is found deep within the Earth, and has to be drilled and piped to the surface. It is made of decaying plant and animal remains that were trapped or covered with mud. Like coal, it was formed from pressure and heat over millions of years. In its crude state—before it is refined—it is known as petroleum. Petroleum can be refined into **oil, gasoline,** and **diesel fuel,** which are used to power engines in vehicles, machines in factories, and furnaces in homes.

NUCLEAR ENERGY was developed in the 20th century. It relies on the heat given off when an atom is split during a process known as **nuclear fission.** In nuclear fission, the nucleus of a uranium-235 atom is hit with an atomic particle called a neutron. The uranium atom splits and gives off a lot of heat, which is used to boil water. The steam from this water powers electrical generators. The waste created during nuclear fission is extremely dangerous and must be stored for thousands of years away from people.

guess what? Many everyday household products include petroleum, such as deodorant, crayons, bubble gum, CDs and DVDs, sunglasses, shower curtains, nail polish, and footballs.

The Dangers of FOSSIL FUELS

About 85% of the energy used in the United States today is supplied by fossil fuels, but fossil fuels can have negative effects on humans, animals, and the environment. For example, burning fossil fuels contributes to global warming, can cause acid rain, and can make water dirty and air unhealthy. Mining coal damages the land, destroys water supplies, and harms the health of miners.

The Greenhouse Effect

Burning fossil fuels creates the energy that can be used to power manufacturing plants, enable you to ride in a car, and keep the lights on in your home. But it also releases carbon dioxide (CO_2) and other gases into Earth's atmosphere, which is made up of layers of gases that surround the planet and protect it from extreme heat and cold.

Gases such as CO_2 and methane trap the heat of the sun in the atmosphere just like the walls of a greenhouse trap heat and moisture inside. In this way, gases like CO_2 and methane help keep the temperature of the planet warm enough for living things. But scientists believe that humans are producing far more CO_2 and methane than the atmosphere needs. As a result, the world is getting warmer.

Global Warming

Earth has gotten more than 1°F (0.6°C) warmer over the past century. That may not seem like a big difference, but even the difference of a single degree can affect the patterns of the Earth's winds and the temperature of the oceans. Hurricanes become stronger and more numerous as the oceans heat up. Glaciers melt, destroying habitat that was previously home to polar bears and other animals, and causing an increase in sea levels. Tropical diseases also spread further into temperate climates as they get warmer.

going green Trees combat global warming by removing carbon dioxide from the air and releasing oxygen into the atmosphere. To help offset the negative effects of the energy you use each day, plant a tree or donate time or money to an organization that plants trees and forests around the world.

85

RENEWABLE ENERGY SOURCES

Renewable energy sources are created continually by nature.

SUNLIGHT can be converted into heat and electricity.
- Solar cells absorb the heat from the sun and convert it into energy. They are used in calculators, watches, and some highway signs.
- Solar power plants collect the sun's heat on huge **solar panels**, which then heat water to produce steam. The steam, in turn, powers electrical generators. A similar system is used on a smaller scale in solar-powered homes.

WATER can produce energy called **hydropower**. Water pressure can turn the shafts of powerful electrical generators, making electricity. Waterfalls and fast-running rivers are major sources of hydropower because their natural flow creates pressure. Another way to harness hydropower is the storage method, in which dams are used to trap water in large reservoirs. When power is needed, the dams are opened and the water flows out. The water pressure created is then converted into energy.

WIND has been used as an energy source for centuries. For example, windmills were used to help grind grain. Today, wind towers much taller than those windmills—usually about 20 stories high—are used to capture the power of wind. The wind turns giant blades connected to a long shaft that moves up and down to power electrical generators.

Wind Power on the Rise

As of 2009, energy derived from wind power accounted for nearly 2% of U.S. electricity. But the use of wind power is increasing by about 25 to 40% each year. In 2010, the U.S. government approved the first offshore wind energy project in the country. Cape Wind is planned for a windy spot in the calm waters off the coast of Massachusetts. Each of the 130 turbines that make up the wind farm will stand taller than the Statue of Liberty and help generate clean energy for use by homes and businesses in the area.

GEOTHERMAL ENERGY uses the heat that rises from Earth's core, which is located 3,000 to 4,000 miles (4,800 to 6,400 km) under the planet's surface. The most common way of harnessing geothermal energy involves capturing steam that comes from deep in the Earth and emerges in volcanoes, hot springs, fumaroles (vents in Earth's surface that give off steam), and geysers (fountainlike bursts of hot water). This steam, heat, or hot water can be trapped in pipes that lead directly to electrical power plants and even to homes.

HYDROGEN is the most common element in the universe. It is everywhere, but it doesn't exist on its own. Instead, hydrogen atoms bind with the atoms of other elements to form such compounds as water (hydrogen and oxygen), methane (hydrogen and carbon), and ammonia (hydrogen and nitrogen). Up-to-date technology is being used to separate hydrogen molecules and turn the hydrogen gas into a liquid that can be used in fuel cells. These fuel cells can power vehicles and electrical generators.

BIOMASS is an energy source found in plants and animals. It can be found in such natural products as wood, corn, sugarcane, manure, and plant and animal fats, and also in organic trash. Biomass energy can be used in three ways:

- When burned, it creates steam that can be converted into electricity or captured to heat homes.
- Sources such as manure and organic trash give off a gas called methane, which can be used as fuel.
- Plant crops and plant and animal fats can be made into ethanol and biodiesel, two fuels used to power cars and trucks.

Energy Use in the United States

Here's a breakdown of how energy is used throughout the country.

Industry 30%
(including manufacturing, agriculture, mining, and construction)

Transportation 29%
(cars, trucks, buses, motorcycles, trains, subways, aircraft, boats)

Residential 22%
(houses and apartments)

Commercial Spaces 19%
(offices, malls, stores, schools, hotels, hospitals, and other buildings)

Energy and the Environment

87

The Three Rs

REDUCING, REUSING, and RECYCLING are important actions every person can take to lessen his or her **carbon footprint**. Here are a few simple tips to help you generate less garbage.

PLASTIC

Fix broken furniture and appliances rather than immediately replacing them.

Avoid single-use products. For example, wipe down the kitchen counter with a fabric towel rather than a paper towel or moist towelette.

Pick products that do not come with lots of extra packaging.

Get crafty with your leftovers. Soft, worn T-shirts can be turned into warm quilts or scarves. Used bottles, cans, and jars can be turned into one-of-a-kind vases, art caddies, and jewelry boxes.

Try not to buy more than you need.

Donate gently used clothes and toys to a charity or community organization.

Ask your parents to build a compost pile for your organic trash (fruit and vegetable stems and peels, used tea bags and coffee grounds, eggshells, leaves, and even shredded newspaper). It will fertilize soil and create mulch that helps plants to grow strong and healthy.

The term **carbon footprint** refers to the total amount of greenhouse gas emissions that result from your activities. There is a growing trend of people trying to combat their personal negative environmental impact by investing in carbon offsets. For example, an international flight releases a lot of CO_2 into the atmosphere, so a traveler might purchase solar power or wind power to offset the impact of the flight.

guess what? A round-trip flight from New York City to Paris releases approximately 1,696 pounds (769 kg) of CO_2 into the air.

Recycling by the Numbers

650 pounds (295 kg): Amount of paper each American uses in a year

2,000 pounds (907 kg): Amount of paper that needs to be recycled in order to save 17 trees

2.5 million: Number of plastic bottles Americans use each hour

40 million tons: Electronics waste thrown out each year around the world

25 billion: Approximate number of Styrofoam™ cups Americans throw away every year

guess what? Five recycled plastic soda bottles provide enough fiber to make an extra-large T-shirt. The material could also be used to fill the inside of a ski jacket or create a square foot (929 sq cm) of carpeting.

88

Energy Use at Home

The average U.S. household produces more than 26,000 pounds (12,000 kg) of carbon dioxide per year. Here are the activities and objects that use the most energy in the home, along with a few tips on cutting down your energy use.

Heating the home: 46%
Instead of turning up the heat in the winter, put on a sweater.

Heating water: 14%
Take shorter showers.

Other: 12%
Switch off power strips at night when you go to sleep.

Cooling the home: 7%
Close the curtains or blinds on a hot day to keep the sun's heat out.

Computers: 1%
Turn off your computer monitor if you are walking away from your computer for short periods, and turn off your computer if you will be gone longer.

Electronics (such as TVs): 3%
Spend one night a week electronics-free. Read a book or play a board game with your family.

Lighting: 6%
Turn off lights when you leave a room.

Washing machines: 4%
Wait until you have a full load of laundry before running the washing machine.

Cooking/Clean-up: 3%
Allow dishes to air dry rather than using the dishwasher's drying cycle.

Refrigeration: 4%
Only open the refrigerator door to get something. Don't let the door hang open while you think about a snack.

Energy and the Environment

89

Habitats and Wildlife

The landmasses on Earth can be grouped into large regions called biomes. The environment of each biome reflects the climate, temperature, and geographical features that exist there. Within a biome are many smaller areas called habitats. Wildlife thrives in its own habitat. For example, thick-furred animals live in the Arctic Circle, and color-changing chameleons thrive in lush forests filled with colorful plants. The relationship between various species of plants, insects, and other animals within a habitat is called an ecosystem. Here are the six major biomes.

TROPICAL RAIN FOREST

Tropical rain forests are hot, humid, and rainy. More kinds of trees exist in rain forests than anywhere else in the world. Rain forests are lush, with tall, densely growing trees and thick undergrowth. Rain forests in Africa, Asia, and South America have different species of wildlife, but include monkeys, jaguars, anteaters, toucans, snakes, frogs, and parrots. Many insects thrive in tropical rain forests, including colorful butterflies, ants, and camouflaged stick insects.

DESERT

Deserts, both hot and cold, receive very little rain. The Sahara and the Mojave Desert are examples of hot, dry deserts. They are filled with sandy dunes and have little plant life. Cacti, low shrubs, and short woody trees such as sweet acacia can survive in the harsh climate. Snakes, fennec foxes, scorpions, and camels are some animals found in hot deserts. The Gobi Desert and the Patagonian Desert are examples of cold deserts. Shrubs, sagebrush, gazelles, hawks, wolves, mice, arctic foxes, and jackrabbits are some examples of plants and animals found in cold deserts.

90

TAIGA

Winter in the taiga is long, snowy, and cold. The summers are short and wet. Many evergreen, or coniferous, trees live there. The rocky soil of the taiga is covered with twigs and evergreen needles. Elk, grizzly bears, moose, caribou, lynx, wolverines, rabbits, sparrows, and reindeer are some examples of taiga wildlife.

TEMPERATE FOREST

In temperate forests, also known as deciduous forests, there are four seasons and a moderate amount of rain. Many hardwood trees, such as maple, oak, birch, and hickory, are found in this climate. Mushrooms, shrubs, moss, and lichen grow in temperate forests. Some pine trees and coniferous trees are also found in temperate forests, though they thrive in the taiga. Most trees lose their leaves in winter in temperate forests. Animals include deer, foxes, squirrels, frogs, rabbits, eagles, sparrows, cardinals, and black bears.

TUNDRA

It is very cold year-round in the tundra biome. Tundra covers much of the land between the North Pole and the taiga below it. There is hardly any precipitation—rain or snow—in the tundra. Underneath a rocky layer of topsoil is a layer of permafrost, which is permanently frozen soil that never gets soft or warm enough to cultivate plant life. The tundra is a treeless area where moss, lichen, grasses, and low shrubs can be found. During the short, cool summers, some flowering plants flourish. Tundra animals include polar bears, foxes, seals, wolves, falcons, owls, and salmon.

GRASSLAND

There are several types of grassland. Savannas are warm year-round, with rainy and dry seasons. They have dusty soil and some scattered trees. Trees and shrubs are largely absent from temperate grassland, such as prairies and steppes. In a prairie, there are hot summers and cold winters. The soil is rich and grows wildflowers and grasses, but no trees. In the steppes, the winters are cool and the summers are hot. Steppe soil is dry. Grassland animals include zebras, elephants, lions, tigers, giraffes, buffalo, ostriches, cattle, sheep, horses, meerkats, and coyotes.

Energy and the Environment

91

Food and Nutrition

What's Eating Michael Pollan?

By TFK Kid Reporter Erin Wiens St. John

Food writer Michael Pollan spoke with TFK Kid Reporter Erin Wiens St. John about the young-readers' edition of his book, *The Omnivore's Dilemma.*

Pollan thinks that a person who eats both plants and animals (an omnivore) faces a difficult choice when it comes to choosing the right food. Supermarkets are jam-packed with shelves upon shelves of cheap, packaged foods—anything from frozen dinners to fruit roll-ups. But how are these foods made, and what's in them? Pollan's book tells the story of where our food comes from and how kids can make more healthful eating choices.

TFK: What inspired you to write the young-readers' edition of *The Omnivore's Dilemma?*

POLLAN: We need to change the way we think about food. We're going to need kids involved in that change, because they're the next generation. Their choices can change the way Americans eat for the better.

TFK: What do you think needs to change first, the food industry or people's eating habits?

POLLAN: People's eating habits need to change first…. We like snack foods, so we buy snack foods, and the industry, of course, keeps producing snack foods. We will see change when we start buying real foods, real ingredients, and cooking those foods ourselves. We can't count on the farmers to change things. We can't count on the food industry to change things. We have to change first.

TFK: I read that your family doesn't eat meat on Mondays. Why not?

POLLAN: Eating meat takes a huge toll on the environment. It represents about 25% of your carbon footprint, the amount of greenhouse gases that you're directly responsible for. [For more information

Michael Pollan

LOCAL FARE

A locavore is a person who eats food that has been produced locally, usually within an area of 100 miles (161 km). Local food is fresher and less damaging to the environment (transporting food long distances means more carbon emissions, which contribute to global warming). When you buy from a nearby farmer, you are also helping your community.

guess what? The average food item travels 1,500 miles (2,414 km) before it reaches the consumer!

on greenhouse gases, see page 85.] But many people like meat and don't want to give it up entirely. A reasonable step is to avoid meat one day a week. You can eat pasta and vegetables on that day. If everybody went without meat one day a week, it would be the equivalent of taking 20 million cars off the road.

TFK: It takes a lot of time and effort to eat healthful, local foods. How do you manage this in your own life?

POLLAN: My advice is to share the work with others. My wife and I cook together. My son helps us cook when he doesn't have too much homework.

TFK: Do you have additional eating tips for our readers?

POLLAN: If you really like junk food, cook it yourself. For example, if you love french fries, make french fries. You won't do it that often, because it's a lot of work. You'll do it about once a month, which is probably as often as you should eat french fries.

TFK: What would you say to people who think they can't cook?

POLLAN: It's easier than it looks. If you've got some olive oil and some garlic, you can cook just about anything. It's not rocket science.

TFK: Many people love foods such as chocolate or pineapple or bananas that can't be grown locally. How do you recommend solving that problem?

POLLAN: I don't think that everything we eat has to be local. The key is to grow what we can where we live, or nearby, and import the other things. I'm not against eating chocolate or kiwis or any number of things. We've been trading food around the world for hundreds and hundreds of years, and there's nothing wrong with that. I just think it's gotten out of hand. We grow really good garlic in California, but we're bringing in most of our garlic from China now. That doesn't seem to be a good use of fossil fuel.

Pollan says that the best-tasting, freshest food you can eat is from the garden.

SUPERFOODS *TO THE* RESCUE

Whether you include them in your main meals, snack on them, or sip them, there are some foods that provide amazing health benefits. These are known as superfoods.

 BLUEBERRIES are chock-full of vitamin C, potassium, and antioxidants. They are great for your heart and circulation.

SOYBEANS are packed with protein, B vitamins, iron, and calcium. You can eat soy in the form of tofu, edamame, and soy milk.

WALNUTS have a lot of antioxidants and disease-fighting omega-3 fatty acids, which means they lower the risk of heart disease and might help improve memory.

 AVOCADOS are rich in potassium, antioxidants, and vitamins A, E, B, and C. They are excellent for your heart and especially good for your skin.

 DARK CHOCOLATE helps your heart, gives you energy, lowers blood pressure, and may improve memory. Try chocolate with 70% or higher cocoa content—the darker it is, the better it is for you. Just remember that chocolate often has a high fat and sugar content and can be bad for your teeth.

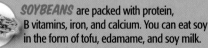

93

NUTRITION BASICS

Food provides the human body with the nutrients it needs to grow, repair itself, and keep fit and healthy. These nutrients include carbohydrates, proteins, fats, vitamins, and minerals.

CARBOHYDRATES

Carbohydrates are the body's main source of fuel. Your body breaks down carbohydrates into glucose (blood sugar), which travels through your bloodstream and supplies your cells with energy. Simple carbohydrates, which are found in fruits, soda, candy, and table sugar, are digested quickly. Complex carbohydrates (fiber and starches), which are found in rice, bread, whole grains, pasta, and vegetables, take longer for the body to digest.

EAT THE RAINBOW!
Consuming many different-colored foods in a day helps ensure that you get lots of different vitamins and minerals.

PROTEINS

Proteins, found in fish, meat, poultry, eggs, nuts, dairy products, and legumes (such as peanuts, lentils, and beans), keep us strong. They help the body build new cells and repair damaged ones. Most Americans eat much more protein than they actually need. Excess protein is often stored in our bodies as fat.

FATS

Not only do fats help your body grow, but they also help protect your internal organs and your skin. They should be eaten only in small quantities. There are different types of fats, and some are better for you than others. Saturated fats are considered "bad" fats, as they increase your risk for diseases. Saturated fats are most often found in foods that come from animals, including meat, cheese, and butter. Monounsaturated fats and polyunsaturated fats are considered "good" fats. They lower your risk for disease. These fats are found in olive, safflower, and canola oils, among others. They are also found in fish and nuts.

KEEP MOVING!
In addition to eating healthfully, exercise regularly to stay fit. Playing basketball, tennis, and soccer are great ways to get your heart rate up.

94

CALORIES

Calories measure how much energy we get from food. You can tell how many calories a food has by looking at the nutrition facts label. Girls ages 9 through 13 need between 1,600 and 2,200 calories a day, while boys of the same age need between 1,800 and 2,600. Eating too many calories can lead to weight gain.

A LITTLE SWEET GOES A LONG WAY
Avoid eating too many sugary sweets and fried foods.

VITAMINS AND MINERALS

Vitamins and minerals are micronutrients that help regulate body processes.

VITAMIN A, found in milk, many greens, carrots, and egg yolks, benefits your skin and eyes.

VITAMIN C, found in many fruits and vegetables, is good for skin, teeth, gums, and the immune system.

VITAMIN D, found in fish, eggs, milk, yogurt, and cheese, helps promote strong bones and teeth, and regulates cell growth.

VITAMIN E, found in spinach, nuts, and olives, has great antioxidant properties, and it may lower your risk for heart disease.

MINERALS such as potassium, calcium, iron, and magnesium are necessary for healthy bones, blood, and muscle. Minerals are found naturally in many foods. For example, milk, yogurt, broccoli, and leafy greens like spinach are good sources of calcium, and red meat is high in iron. Minerals are sometimes added to foods to make them more nutritious. You may see calcium-fortified orange juice at the grocery store.

WHAT ARE ANTIOXIDANTS?
Antioxidants are substances in foods that prevent or repair damage to your cells.

STAY HYDRATED!
Make sure to drink lots of water every day.

MYSTERY PERSON

I was born in Pasadena, California, in 1912. While living in Paris, France, I studied at a famous cooking school. In 1961, I moved to Massachusetts. That year, I published my cookbook *Mastering the Art of French Cooking*. It led to a long-running television show called *The French Chef*. It introduced many Americans to the foods of France.

WHO AM I? _____

Answer on page 242.

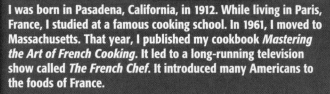

Food and Nutrition

95

Geography

THE SEVEN CONTINENTS

NORTH AMERICA
(including Central America and the Caribbean)
How big is it? 9,449,460 square miles (24,474,000 sq km)
Highest point Mount McKinley, 20,322 feet (6,194 m)
Lowest point Death Valley, 282 feet (86 m) below sea level

EUROPE
How big is it? 3,837,000 square miles (9,938,000 sq km)
Highest point Mount Elbrus, 18,481 feet (5,642 m)
Lowest point Caspian Sea, 92 feet (28 m) below sea level

ASIA
(including the Middle East)
How big is it? 17,212,000 square miles (44,579,000 sq km)
Highest point Mount Everest, 29,035 feet (8,850 m)
Lowest point Dead Sea, 1,286 feet (392 m) below sea level

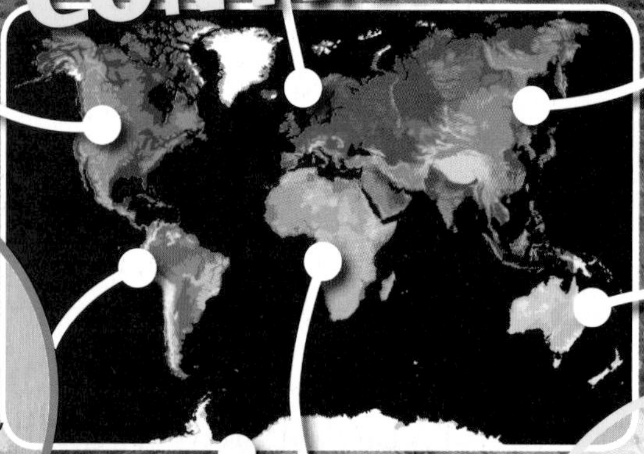

SOUTH AMERICA
How big is it? 6,879,000 square miles (17,819,000 sq km)
Highest point Mount Aconcagua, 22,834 feet (6,960 m)
Lowest point Valdés Peninsula, 131 feet (40 m) below sea level

AUSTRALIA/ OCEANIA
How big is it? 3,132,000 square miles (8,112,000 sq km)
Highest point Mount Wilhelm, 14,794 feet (4,509 m)
Lowest point Lake Eyre, 52 feet (16 m) below sea level

ANTARCTICA
How big is it? 5,100,000 square miles (13,209,000 sq km)
Highest point Vinson Massif, 16,066 feet (4,897 m)
Lowest point Bentley Subglacial Trench, 8,383 feet (2,555 m) below sea level

AFRICA
How big is it? 11,608,000 square miles (30,065,000 sq km)
Highest point Mount Kilimanjaro, 19,340 feet (5,895 m)
Lowest point Lake Assal, 512 feet (156 m) below sea level

OUR CHANGING PLANET

Earth is approximately 4.5 billion years old. In its lifetime, it has changed a lot. The ground that we walk on is the outer layer of the Earth, or the Earth's crust. On the continents, the crust averages about 20 miles (32 km) thick, but beneath the oceans, it may be only a few miles (kms) thick. Beneath the crust is the mantle, a rocky layer that makes up about two-thirds of the weight of the planet. The center, or the core, of the Earth consists of a liquid layer of molten rock and lava and a solid ball of mostly iron and nickel. Although we do not feel the land shifting beneath our feet, it is moving.

Sometimes, events like erupting volcanoes and earthquakes occur and quickly change the face of the planet, but most of the time, the changes happen very slowly.

During a volcanic eruption, the molten rock from deep in the Earth leaks or shoots out from the crust.

PLATE TECTONICS

The Earth's crust is broken up into seven major plates: the African, North American, South American, Eurasian, Australian, Antarctic, and Pacific plates. There are other, smaller plates, including the Arabian, Nazca, and Philippine plates. Volcanoes form where plates meet—both above ground and deep underwater. In areas where plates frequently move alongside one another, earthquakes occur more often. The San Andreas Fault in California is one of these places.

The word *Pangaea* (pan-*jee*-uh) means "all lands" in Greek.

PANGAEA

Many scientists believe that the seven continents we have today were once part of a single gigantic supercontinent, which they call Pangaea. According to this theory, Pangaea began to break apart about 200 million to 225 million years ago, and the continents have been slowly drifting ever since. Valleys and rifts were formed by plates moving away from one another, and mountains were formed when plates crashed together.

Due to the slow movement of two of Earth's plates, the Atlantic Ocean actually becomes about 1 inch (2.5 cm) wider each year.

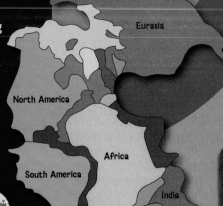

This is how the continents may have once fit together.

Geography

97

THE FIVE OCEANS

More than 70% of Earth's surface is water. Here are the five oceans that cover much of the planet.

ARCTIC OCEAN

Area: 5,427,000 square miles (14,056,000 sq km)
Average depth: 3,953 feet (1,205 m)

The Portland Head Lighthouse sits on the Maine coast of the Atlantic Ocean.

Glaciers flow into the Arctic Ocean.

ATLANTIC OCEAN

Area: 29,637,900 square miles (76,762,000 sq km)
Average depth: 12,880 feet (3,926 m)

INDIAN OCEAN

Area: 26,469,500 square miles (68,556,000 sq km)
Average depth: 13,002 feet (3,963 m)

PACIFIC OCEAN

Area: 60,060,700 square miles (155,557,000 sq km)
Average depth: 15,215 feet (4,638 m)

RECORD BREAKER
The Pacific Ocean covers about one-third of Earth's surface.

Fish swim by a coral reef in the Indian Ocean.

At a luxury resort in French Polynesia, rooms are built just above the Pacific Ocean.

SOUTHERN OCEAN

Area: 7,848,300 square miles (20,327,000 sq km)
Average depth: 13,100–16,400 feet (4,000–5,000 m)*

*Official depths of the Southern Ocean are in dispute.

guess what? The average depth of Earth's oceans is more than 2.5 miles (4 km). The average temperature of ocean water is 38.3°F (3.5°C).

Penguins walk along the ice next to the Southern Ocean.

98

One Salty Place

It may sound scary, but the Dead Sea is a popular place. This huge lake is in the Middle East, bordering Jordan and Israel. It has the world's saltiest water. People can float in it without even trying. How come? It's because of the salt. Salt water can support more weight than freshwater. The saltier the water, the easier it is to float on.

guess what? You can test out the difference between salt water and freshwater by performing a simple experiment. Grab two glasses and fill them both halfway with water. Add four to five tablespoons of salt to one of the glasses and stir until the salt has dissolved. Place an egg in each glass and see the difference.

Baku, the capital of Azerbaijan, sits on the western edge of the Caspian Sea.

TOP 10 Largest Lakes in the World

LAKE	CONTINENT	SIZE
1. Caspian Sea	Asia	152,239 square miles (394,299 sq km)
2. Lake Superior	North America	31,820 square miles (82,414 sq km)
3. Lake Victoria	Africa	26,828 square miles (69,485 sq km)
4. Lake Huron	North America	23,010 square miles (59,596 sq km)
5. Lake Michigan	North America	22,400 square miles (58,016 sq km)
6. Aral Sea	Asia	13,000 square miles (33,800 sq km)
7. Lake Tanganyika	Africa	12,700 square miles (32,893 sq km)
8. Lake Baikal	Asia	12,162 square miles (31,500 sq km)
9. Great Bear Lake	North America	12,000 square miles (31,080 sq km)
10. Lake Nyasa	Africa	11,600 square miles (30,044 sq km)

Lake Baikal is the deepest lake in the world. Found in Siberia, a region in Russia, Lake Baikal has a depth of 5,371 feet (1,637 m). Though it freezes over for several months a year, it is home to some unique wildlife, including a freshwater seal called a **nerpa,** the largest flatworm on Earth (it is so big it hunts fish for food), and the golomyanka, or Baikal oil fish, which actually melts in the sunlight.

Geography

99

WHAT'S THAT?

Here are some terms that you might come across when looking at a map or a globe.

A group of scattered islands is called an ARCHIPELAGO. Many archipelagoes have formed in isolated parts of the ocean. Examples include Hawaii, Indonesia, and Fiji.

A BAY is a section of an ocean or lake that fills an indentation in the coastline. Large bays are usually called GULFS. Examples include San Francisco Bay and the Gulf of Mexico.

A CANAL is a man-made waterway. The Suez and Panama Canals are two well-known examples built to provide shorter passageways for people and goods. Venice, Italy (pictured), is famous for its canals.

A CANYON is a deep, narrow valley with steep sides. The Grand Canyon in the United States and the Copper Canyon (pictured) in Mexico are well-known examples.

The EQUATOR is an imaginary line drawn all the way around the world. It is located halfway between the North and South Poles. Above the equator, you will find the Northern Hemisphere, and below, the Southern Hemisphere.

The state of Florida is an example of a PENINSULA, which is a piece of land that juts into the water.

A STRAIT, sometimes called a channel, is a narrow strip of water connecting two larger bodies of water. The Bering Strait is between Alaska and Russia. The English Channel separates Great Britain and France.

MYSTERY PERSON

I was born in 1866 in Charles County, Maryland. I was an African-American explorer who joined Robert Peary on expeditions to the Arctic. I was an expert at handling dog teams. On April 6, 1909, we became the first explorers to reach the North Pole. I placed the American flag there.

WHO AM I? _____

Answer on page 242.

TOP 5 Largest Deserts

Deserts are the driest places on the planet, getting only about 10 inches (25 cm) of rain a year. Some are hot, like the Sahara. Others are cold, like the Gobi. Here are the largest deserts.

DESERT	CONTINENT	SIZE
1. Sahara	Africa	3.5 million square miles (9 million sq km)
2. Arabian	Asia	1 million square miles (2.6 million sq km)
3. Australian	Australia	570,000 square miles (1.5 million sq km)
4. Gobi	Asia	500,000 square miles (1.3 million sq km)
5. Kalahari	Africa	225,000 square miles (580,000 sq km)

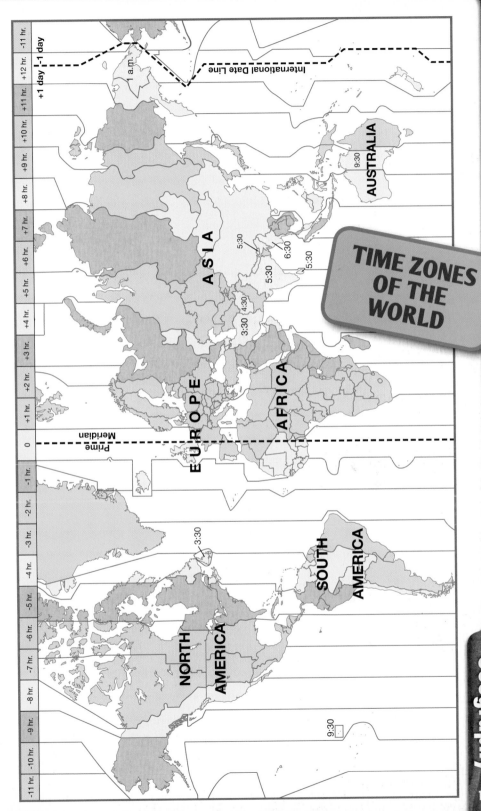

TIME ZONES OF THE WORLD

AFRICA

ATLANTIC OCEAN
E U R O P E
MEDITERRANEAN SEA
BLACK SEA
RED SEA
S A H A R A
Nile River
Niger River
Benue River
Congo River
Madeira Islands
Canary Is.
Corsica
Sardinia
Majorca
Sicily
Crete
PORTUGAL
SPAIN
FRANCE
SWITZERLAND
ITALY
AUSTRIA
SLOVENIA
CROATIA
BOSNIA AND HERZEGOVINA
MONTENEGRO
HUNGARY
ALBANIA
GREECE
MACEDONIA
KOSOVO
BULGARIA
ROMANIA
MOLDOVA
MALTA
TURKEY
CYPRUS
LEBANON
ISRAEL
JORDAN
SYRIA
IRAQ
IRAN
KUWAIT
BAHRAIN
QATAR
SAUDI ARABIA
YEMEN
GEORGIA
ARMENIA
AZERBAIJAN
MOROCCO
Tangier
Fès
Rabat
Casablanca
Marrakech
Erfoud
ALGERIA
Oran
Algiers
Constantine
TUNISIA
Tunis
Qafsah
LIBYA
Tripoli
Banghazi
Al Jawf
EGYPT
Alexandria
Cairo
Suez
Luxor
Aswan
SUDAN
Port Sudan
Khartoum
Juba
ERITREA
Asmara
DJIBOUTI
Djibouti
ETHIOPIA
Addis Ababa
Harer
Gore
Hargeysa
SOMALIA
UGANDA
WESTERN SAHARA
Layoune (El Aaiún)
MAURITANIA
Nouakchott
SENEGAL
Dakar
THE GAMBIA
Banjul
GUINEA-BISSAU
Bissau
GUINEA
Conakry
SIERRA LEONE
Freetown
LIBERIA
Monrovia
CÔTE D'IVOIRE
Yamoussoukro
Abidjan
MALI
Timbuktu
Bamako
BURKINA FASO
Ouagadougou
Gaoua
GHANA
Accra
TOGO
Lome
BENIN
Porto-Novo
NIGER
Niamey
Agadez
Zinder
NIGERIA
Lagos
Ibadan
Abuja
Kano
CHAD
N'Djamena
CAMEROON
Yaoundé
Douala
CENTRAL AFRICAN REPUBLIC
Bangui
Malabo
EQUATORIAL GUINEA

INDIAN OCEAN

ATLANTIC OCEAN

MADAGASCAR

Antananarivo

COMOROS

Moroni

Mozambique Channel

Mombasa

Dar es Salaam

Zanzibar

TANZANIA

Kigoma

Lake Tanganyika

BURUNDI

Bujumbura

REPUBLIC OF THE CONGO

Kinshasa

Brazzaville

Pointe-Noire

Kananga

Lubumbashi

Kitwe

Luanda

Lubango

Namibe

ANGOLA

ZAMBIA

Lusaka

MALAWI

Lake Nyasa

Lilongwe

Blantyre

MOZAMBIQUE

Cidade de Nacala

Beira

ZIMBABWE

Harare

BOTSWANA

Gaborone

NAMIBIA

Windhoek

Walvis Bay

Maputo

SWAZILAND

Mbabane

Pretoria

Johannesburg

LESOTHO

Maseru

SOUTH AFRICA

Durban

Port Elizabeth

Cape Town

1,000 mi.

500 mi.

0 mi.

1,000 km

500 km

0 km

Geography

103

MIDDLE EAST AND ASIA

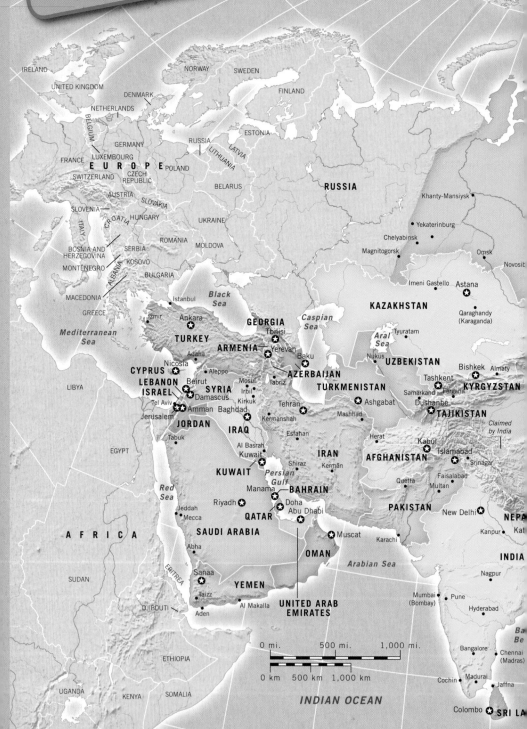

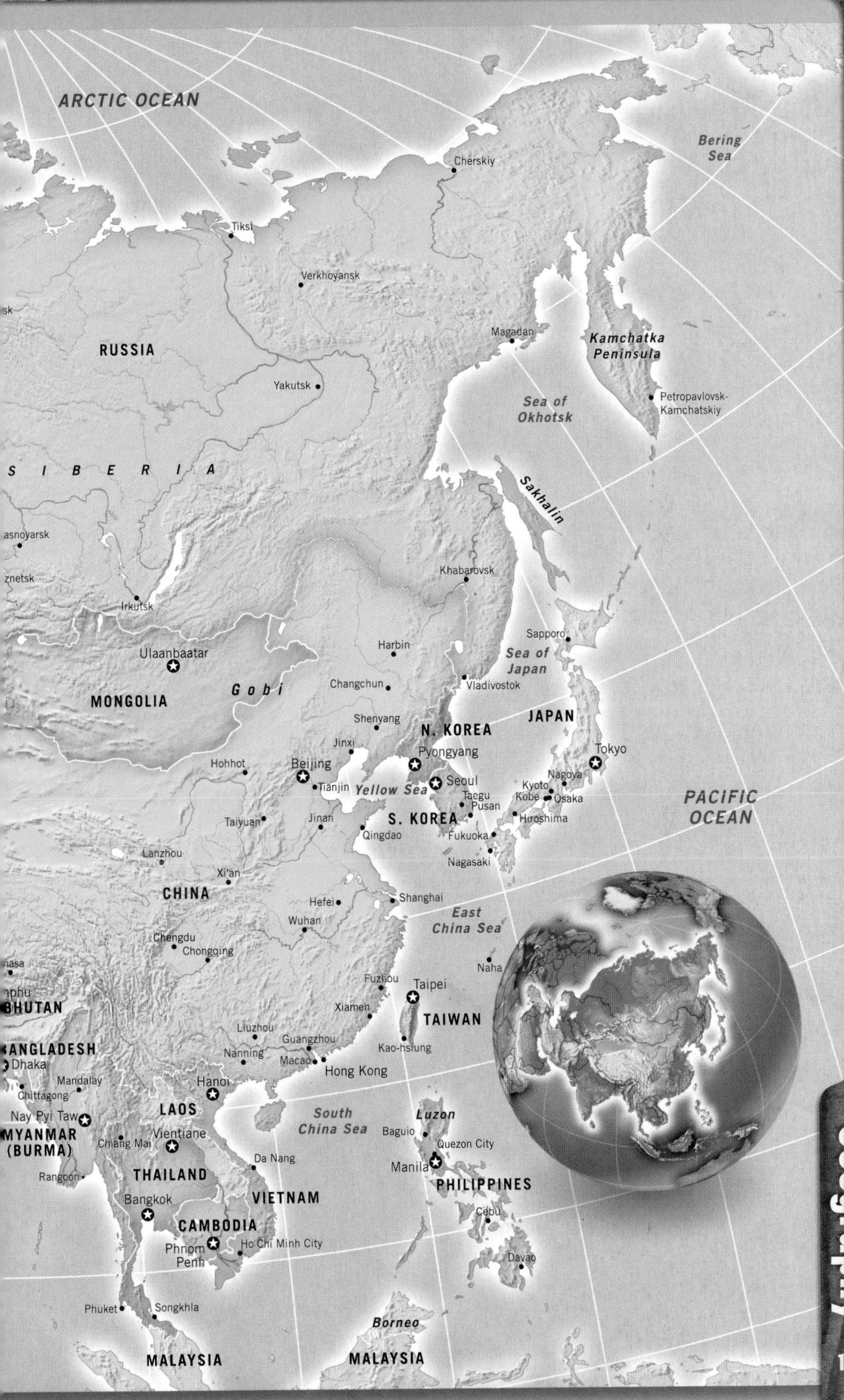

ARCTIC OCEAN

Bering
Sea

Cherskiy

Tiksi

Verkhoyansk

RUSSIA

Magadan

Kamchatka
Peninsula

Yakutsk

Sea of
Okhotsk

Petropavlovsk-
Kamchatskiy

S I B E R I A

asnoyarsk

Khabarovsk

znetsk

Sakhalin

Irkutsk

Sapporo

Harbin

Sea of
Japan

Ulaanbaatar

Gobi

Changchun

Vladivostok

JAPAN

MONGOLIA

Shenyang

N. KOREA

Tokyo

Jinxi

Pyongyang

Nagoya

Hohhot

Beijing

Seoul

Kyoto

Taiyuan

Tianjin

Yellow Sea

Taegu

Kobe

Osaka

Jinan

Pusan

PACIFIC
OCEAN

S. KOREA

Hiroshima

Lanzhou

Qingdao

Fukuoka

Xi'an

Nagasaki

CHINA

Hefei

Shanghai

Chengdu

Wuhan

East
China Sea

nasa

Chongqing

phu

Naha

Fuzhou

BHUTAN

Taipei

Xiamen

ANGLADESH

Liuzhou

TAIWAN

Dhaka

Guangzhou

Kao-hsiung

Mandalay

Nanning

Macao

Chittagong

Hanoi

Hong Kong

Luzon

Nay Pyi Taw

LAOS

Baguio

MYANMAR
(BURMA)

Chiang Mai

Vientiane

South
China Sea

Quezon City

Da Nang

Manila

Rangoon

PHILIPPINES

THAILAND

VIETNAM

Cebu

Bangkok

CAMBODIA

Phnom
Penh

Ho Chi Minh City

Davao

Phuket

Songkhla

Borneo

MALAYSIA

MALAYSIA

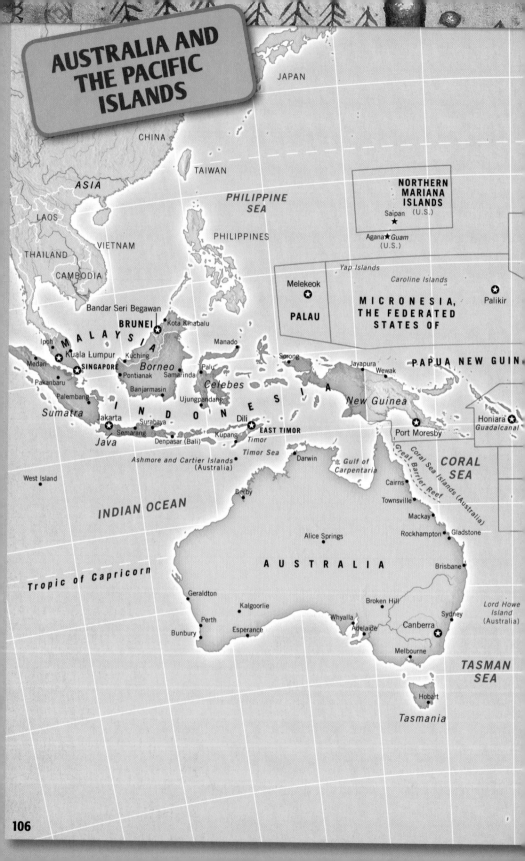

AUSTRALIA AND THE PACIFIC ISLANDS

JAPAN

CHINA

ASIA

TAIWAN

PHILIPPINE SEA

LAOS

VIETNAM

PHILIPPINES

THAILAND

CAMBODIA

NORTHERN MARIANA ISLANDS (U.S.)

Saipan

Agana ★ Guam (U.S.)

Yap Islands

Caroline Islands

Melekeok

MICRONESIA, THE FEDERATED STATES OF

Palikir

PALAU

Bandar Seri Begawan

BRUNEI

Kota Kinabalu

Manado

Sorong

Jayapura

Wewak

PAPUA NEW GUIN

MALAYSIA

Ipoh

Medan

Kuala Lumpur

Kuching

SINGAPORE

Pontianak

Samarinda

Palu

Borneo

Pakanbaru

Banjarmasin

Celebes

New Guinea

Palembang

Ujungpandang

INDONESIA

Honiara

Guadalcanal

Sumatra

Jakarta

Surabaya

Dili

Semarang

Port Moresby

Java

Denpasar (Bali)

Kupang

EAST TIMOR

Timor

Ashmore and Cartier Islands (Australia)

Timor Sea

Darwin

Gulf of Carpentaria

Coral Sea Islands (Australia)

Great Barrier Reef

CORAL SEA

West Island

INDIAN OCEAN

Derby

Cairns

Townsville

Mackay

Alice Springs

Rockhampton

Gladstone

Tropic of Capricorn

AUSTRALIA

Brisbane

Geraldton

Broken Hill

Lord Howe Island (Australia)

Kalgoorlie

Whyalla

Sydney

Perth

Esperance

Adelaide

Canberra

Bunbury

Melbourne

TASMAN SEA

Hobart

Tasmania

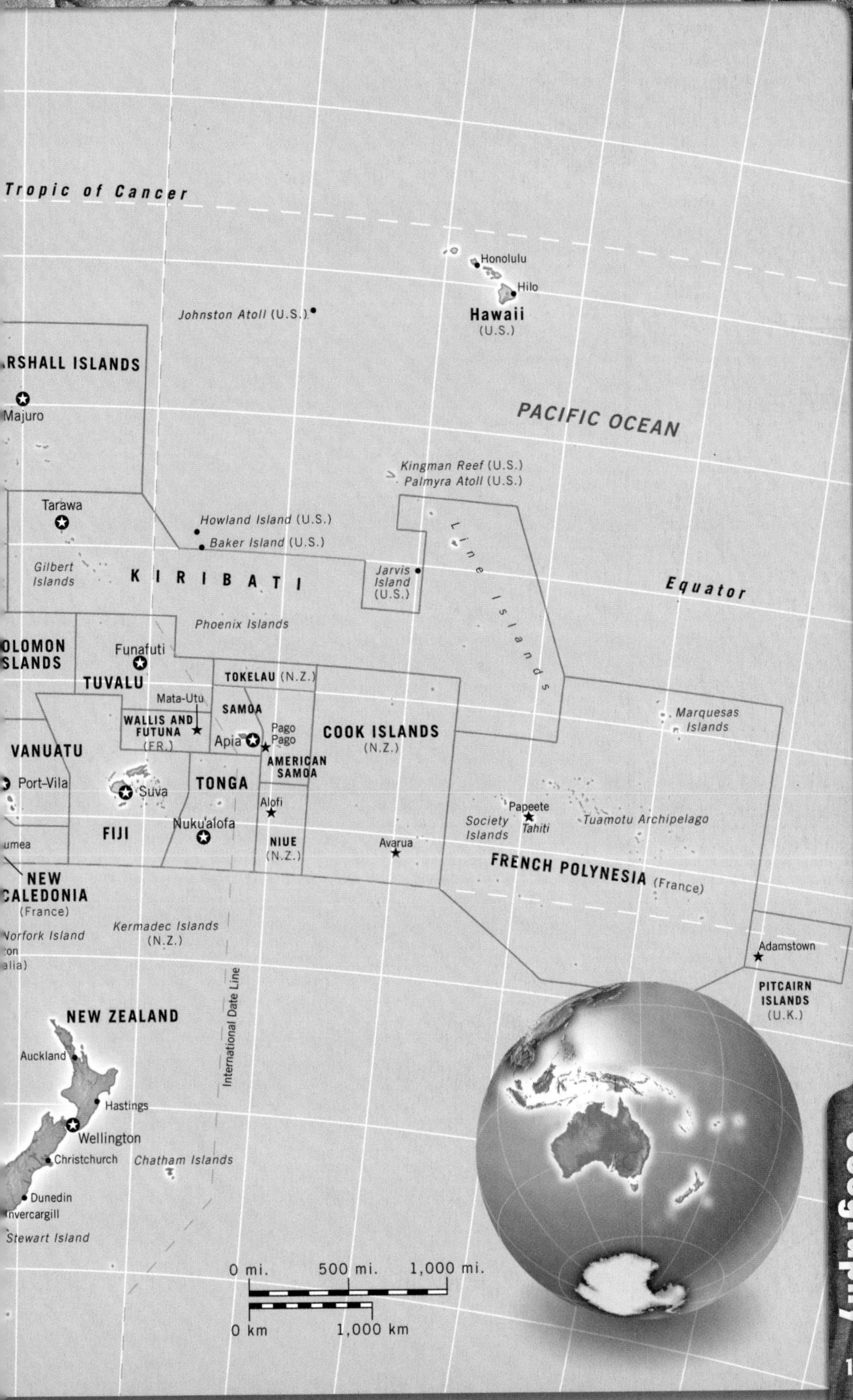

Tropic of Cancer

Honolulu
Hilo
Hawaii
(U.S.)

Johnston Atoll (U.S.)

PACIFIC OCEAN

RSHALL ISLANDS

Majuro

Kingman Reef (U.S.)
Palmyra Atoll (U.S.)

Tarawa

Howland Island (U.S.)
Baker Island (U.S.)

Jarvis
Island
(U.S.)

*Gilbert
Islands*

K I R I B A T I

Line Islands

Equator

Phoenix Islands

OLOMON
SLANDS

Funafuti

TUVALU

TOKELAU (N.Z.)

Mata-Utu

SAMOA

**WALLIS AND
FUTUNA**
(FR.)

Apia
Pago
Pago

COOK ISLANDS
(N.Z.)

Marquesas
Islands

VANUATU

Port-Vila

Suva

TONGA

**AMERICAN
SAMOA**

Alofi

Papeete
Tahiti

Tuamotu Archipelago

*Society
Islands*

umea

FIJI

Nuku'alofa

NIUE
(N.Z.)

Avarua

FRENCH POLYNESIA (France)

**NEW
CALEDONIA**
(France)

*Norfork Island
ton
alia)*

Kermadec Islands
(N.Z.)

Adamstown

**PITCAIRN
ISLANDS**
(U.K.)

NEW ZEALAND

Auckland

Hastings

Wellington
Christchurch

Chatham Islands

Dunedin

nvercargill

Stewart Island

International Date Line

0 mi.   500 mi.   1,000 mi.

0 km   1,000 km

EUROPE

Reykjavik
ICELAND

Arctic Circle

NORWEGIAN SEA

FAROE ISLANDS (Denmark)
Tórshavn

Trondheim

SHETLAND ISLANDS

HEBRIDES

ORKNEY ISLANDS

NORWAY

Bergen
Oslo

Stavanger

SWEDEN

0 mi.   300 mi.   600 mi.
0 km   300 km   600 km

Aberdeen
Glasgow
Edinburgh
Belfast

DENMARK
Ålborg
Göteborg

Copenhagen
Malmö

Dublin
IRELAND

UNITED KINGDOM

Liverpool   Leeds
Manchester
Sheffield

Birmingham

London

NORTH SEA

NETHERLANDS
Amsterdam
The Hague
Rotterdam

Hamburg
Bremen

Berlin
Po

GERMANY

ATLANTIC OCEAN

GUERNSEY (U.K.)
JERSEY (U.K.)

Calais
Lille
Le Havre
Brussels
BELGIUM

Antwerp
Essen
Dusseldorf
Cologne
Bonn
Frankfurt

LUXEMBOURG

Paris
Luxembourg

Nantes

Strasbourg
Stuttgart

Dijon

FRANCE

LIECHTENSTEIN
Zürich   Vaduz
Bern
SWITZERLAND

Munich

Prag
CZECH REPUBLIC
Brat

Vienna
AUSTRIA

BAY OF BISCAY

Bordeaux
Geneva
Lyon

SLOVEN
Ljubljana
Trieste

Porto
Bilbao
Toulouse

Turin
Milan

CROATIA

Genoa

SAN MARINO
BOSN
HERZI
Sara

Lisbon
PORTUGAL
Madrid
Andorra la Vella
Marseille
MONACO
ANDORRA
Bastia
Florence
ITALY
ADRIATI
MO

Faro
Seville
SPAIN
Barcelona
CORSICA
Rome
VATICAN CITY

Málaga
Valencia
MAJORCA
Palma
SARDINIA
Naples
Bari

Gibraltar
MEDITERRANEAN SEA
Cagliari

MOROCCO
ALGERIA

Palermo   Messina
SICILY

AFRICA
TUNISIA
Valletta
MALTA

108

ASIA

Murmansk
Pachora

Arkhangel'sk

FINLAND

Tampere
Turku Helsinki
St. Petersburg

Tallinn
ESTONIA

RUSSIA

Izhevsk

Nizhniy Novgorod
Kazan

Riga LATVIA
Moscow
Samara

LITHUANIA
Vilnius
Smolensk

RUSSIA
Minsk
Saratov

POLAND
BELARUS
Homyel'
Lipetsk
Voronezh

KAZAKHSTAN

Brest

Kiev
Kharkiv
Volgograd

L'viv
Voroshilovgrad

Derazhnya
Gorlovka

UKRAINE
Makeyevka

Zhdanov
Rostov

Chisinau
Iasi
Odessa
Mykolavia
Kerch

Groznyy

MOLDOVA
Simferopol'

Arad
ROMANIA
Sevastopol'

Craiova
Bucharest

Constanta
BLACK SEA

Varna

Nis
Sofia

Pristina
BULGARIA

Skopje
Istanbul

MACEDONIA
Thessaloniki

T U R K E Y

Volos

GREECE
Izmir

Athens

SYRIA

CRETE
CYPRUS
IRAQ
LEBANON

Geography

109

NORTH AMERICA AND CENTRAL AMERICA

GREENLAND (Denmark)

Narsarsuaq

Nuuk (Godthab)

Labrador Sea

St. John's

Island of Newfoundland

Happy Valley Goose Bay

CANADA

Davis Strait

Baffin Bay

Qaanaaq (Thule)

Iqaluit

Baffin Island

Chisasibi (Fort George)

Moosonee

HUDSON BAY

Alert

Queen Elizabeth Islands

Kangiqtuq (Resolute)

Arctic Circle

Churchill

Winnipeg

ARCTIC OCEAN

Banks Island

Victoria Island

Bismarck

Beaufort Sea

Echo Bay

Yellowknife

Saskatoon

Regina

Inuvik

Edmonton

Barrow

Prudhoe Bay

Calgary

Helena

RUSSIA

Alaska (U.S.)

Fairbanks

Anchorage

Valdez

Whitehorse

Juneau

Vancouver

Victoria

Seattle

Olympia

Portland

Salem

Boise

Nome

Bethel

Kodiak

Bering Sea

Aleutian Islands

110

ATLANTIC OCEAN

BERMUDA (U.K.)
★ Hamilton

1,000 mi.
500 mi.
0 mi.
1,000 km
500 km
0 km

BAHAMAS
Freeport
Nassau

TURKS AND CAICOS ISLANDS (U.K.)
Grand ★ Turk

DOMINICAN REPUBLIC
PUERTO RICO (U.S.)
San Juan
Santiago
Santo Domingo

VIRGIN ISLANDS (U.S., U.K.)
ANGUILLA (U.K.)
SAINT MAARTEN/ SAINT MARTIN (Neth. Antilles)/(Fr.)
SAINT BARTHÉLEMY (Guad.)
ANTIGUA AND BARBUDA
SAINT KITTS AND NEVIS
MONTSERRAT (U.K.)
GUADELOUPE (Fr.)
DOMINICA
MARTINIQUE (Fr.)
SAINT LUCIA
BARBADOS
SAINT VINCENT AND THE GRENADINES
GRENADA
TRINIDAD AND TOBAGO

NETHERLANDS ANTILLES (Neth.)
ARUBA (Neth.)

HAITI
Port-au-Prince

CARIBBEAN SEA

VENEZUELA
GUYANA
COLOMBIA

Miami
Jacksonville
Savannah

Columbia
Raleigh
Charleston
Richmond
Frankfort
Charlotte
Nashville
Atlanta
Tallahassee
Montgomery
Birmingham
Memphis
Jackson
Baton Rouge
New Orleans

CUBA
Havana
★
Camaguey
Guantánamo Bay
Montego Bay
Kingston
JAMAICA
CAYMAN ISLANDS (U.K.)
George Town ★

Washington, D.C.
Baltimore
Dover
Philadelphia
Harrisburg
Norfolk
Pittsburgh
Cleveland
Buffalo
Detroit
Toledo
Cincinnati
Indianapolis
Louisville
Springfield
Saint Louis

Boston
Providence
Hartford
New York
Albany
New Haven

United STATES

GULF OF MEXICO

Cancun
Merida
Belize City
BELIZE
Belmopan
HONDURAS
Tegucigalpa
Guatemala City
GUATEMALA
San Salvador
EL SALVADOR
NICARAGUA
Managua
COSTA RICA
San José
PANAMA
Panama City

Chicago
Des Moines
Omaha
Lincoln
Kansas City
Topeka
Jefferson City
Little Rock
Dallas
Oklahoma City
Austin
Houston
San Antonio

Tampico
Veracruz
Puebla
Oaxaca
Mexico City ★
León
MEXICO
Monterrey
Acapulco
Guadalajara

Denver
Santa Fe
El Paso
Ciudad Juárez
Hermosillo

Phoenix

Los Angeles
San Diego
Tijuana

Mazatlán
Puerto Vallarta
La Paz
Gulf of California

PACIFIC OCEAN

Tropic of Cancer

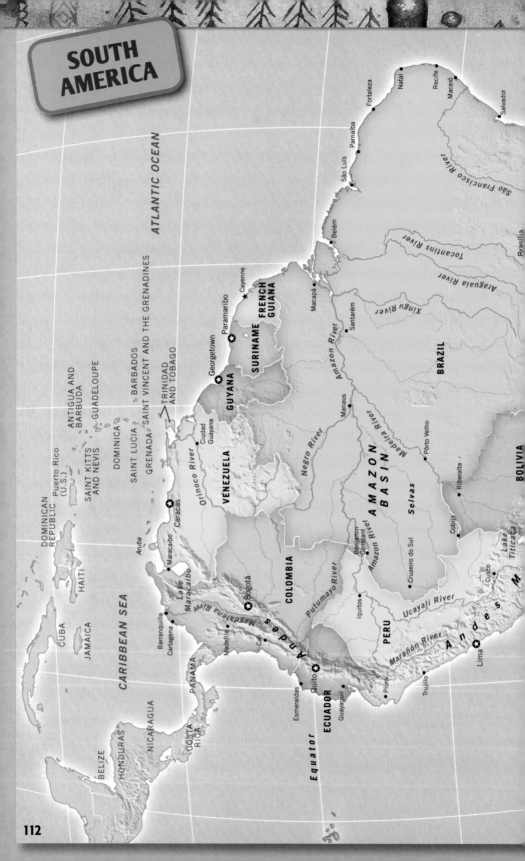

SOUTH AMERICA

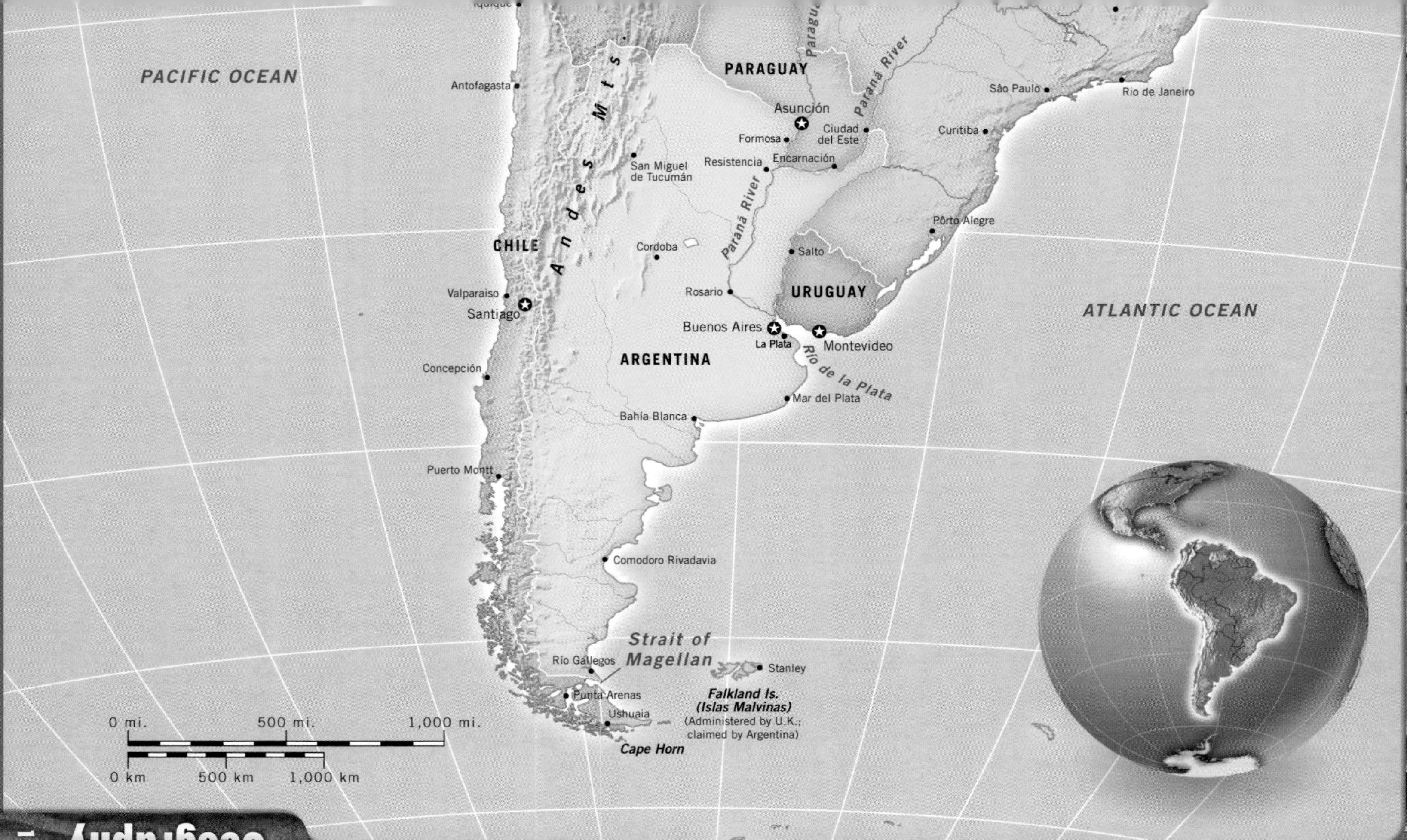

ATLANTIC OCEAN

Rio de Janeiro

São Paulo

Curitiba

Pôrto Alegre

Paraná River

Ciudad del Este

URUGUAY

Montevideo

Río de la Plata

Salto

Mar del Plata

PARAGUAY

Asunción

Formosa

Encarnación

Resistencia

Paraná River

La Plata

Buenos Aires

Rosario

ARGENTINA

Córdoba

San Miguel de Tucumán

Bahía Blanca

Stanley

Falkland Is.
(Islas Malvinas)
(Administered by U.K.;
claimed by Argentina)

Comodoro Rivadavia

Strait of Magellan

Antofagasta

Andes Mts

CHILE

Valparaíso

Santiago

Concepción

Río Gallegos

Punta Arenas

Ushuaia

Cape Horn

Puerto Montt

PACIFIC OCEAN

1,000 mi.

500 mi.

0 mi.

1,000 km

500 km

0 km

Geography

113

Government
SYMBOLS OF THE UNITED STATES

THE CONSTITUTION

The most important document in the formation of the United States government is the U.S. Constitution. Ratified on March 4, 1789, the Constitution lays out the organization of the federal government and explains the relationship between the federal and state governments and the citizens of the United States.

> The Constitution begins with a passage called the preamble, which states the document's purpose.

Many people with different opinions contributed to the Constitution. Federalists wanted to have a strong central government, while Anti-Federalists wanted the strongest powers to remain with the states. There were many angry debates and arguments, but the Constitution was approved unanimously by the members of the Constitutional Convention held in Philadelphia, Pennsylvania, in 1787. Those members then took the document back to their home states. By July 1788, it was ratified by three-quarters of the states. On March 4, 1789, the Constitution took its place as the supreme law of the land.

We the People of the United States, in order to form a more perfect union, establish justice, insure domestic tranquility, provide for the common defense, promote the general welfare, and secure the blessings of liberty to ourselves and our posterity, do ordain and establish this Constitution for the United States of America.

THE U.S. FLAG

The very first U.S. flag became official in 1777 and included 13 stripes (seven red, six white) and 13 white stars to represent the 13 colonies. The 13 stripes have remained in place, but the number of stars increased with every added state. Since 1959, when Hawaii became a state, the official flag has had 50 stars.

U.S. Marine Corps Memorial

guess what? There are a few places around the country where a law or presidential proclamation insists that a flag be flown 24 hours a day, including the Washington Monument, in Washington, D.C.; the Fort McHenry National Monument, in Baltimore, Maryland; the U.S. Marine Corps Memorial, in Arlington, Virginia; and customs ports of entry.

114

THE GREAT SEAL

Benjamin Franklin, Thomas Jefferson, and John Adams began designing the Great Seal in 1776. Congress adopted the seal as a national symbol on June 20, 1782. The current seal features a bald eagle holding a banner in its beak. Written across the banner is the national motto, "*E pluribus unum*." Translated from Latin, the motto means "Out of many, one" and refers to the many colonies that united to form one nation. The eagle clutches an olive branch in one foot, symbolizing a commitment to peace. In the other foot, the bird holds 13 arrows, to show that the nation is strong and will go to war to protect its citizens. The star at the top center of the seal is made of 13 smaller stars—one for each of the original colonies.

The Secretary of State uses the Great Seal on important documents relating to foreign affairs, such as treaties and international agreements, and on the official appointment papers given to ambassadors and other U.S. government representatives abroad. The Great Seal also appears on the $1 bill.

New York City schoolchildren recite the Pledge of Allegiance in 1958.

THE PLEDGE

Originally written in 1892, the Pledge of Allegiance is a patriotic oath that refers to the flag as the symbol of the country. In 1942, Congress recognized the words as the official national pledge. The words have changed slightly since 1892. For example, President Dwight Eisenhower added "under God" to the oath in 1954. Here is the current wording:

"I pledge allegiance to the flag of the United States of America and to the Republic for which it stands, one nation under God, indivisible, with liberty and justice for all."

At first, schoolchildren were expected to stand, salute, and recite the pledge every morning in class. But in 1943, the Supreme Court ruled that kids in public schools could not be forced to recite the Pledge of Allegiance.

Government

115

SEPARATION OF POWERS

The Constitution divides the basic structure of the U.S. government into three branches.

The purpose of this structure is to provide a separation of powers among three equally important branches—one that makes laws, another that carries out those laws, and a third that determines whether those laws are constitutional.

EXECUTIVE BRANCH
Made up of the President, the Vice President, and the Cabinet

LEGISLATIVE BRANCH
Includes the Senate and the House of Representatives

JUDICIAL BRANCH
Includes the Supreme Court, and is in charge of the country's courts of law

CHECKS AND BALANCES

The three branches of government have different responsibilities. But they also work together to keep any one branch from becoming too powerful. For example, the legislative branch creates laws, but the judicial branch can strike down a law if it conflicts with the spirit of the Constitution. This system of checks and balances has been a model of democracy for other nations in the world.

To keep Congress in check, the President has the power to veto, or refuse to approve, bills that have been written and okayed by both houses of Congress. In return, if two-thirds of the lawmakers in the house that wrote the original bill can agree, Congress can overturn a presidential veto.

In 1917, President Woodrow Wilson asked Congress to declare war on Germany. The President cannot make that decision alone.

In 1982, lawmakers in Chicago passed a law banning handguns. The law was challenged in lower courts. In 2010, the Supreme Court decided that it violated the Second Amendment, which gives Americans the right to bear arms, and struck down the law. This is one way that the judiciary branch checks the power of the legislature.

THE LEGISLATIVE BRANCH

The U.S. legislature has a bicameral structure, which means that it has two chambers: the House of Representatives (often referred to as "the House") and the Senate. Before a statute becomes a law, it is called a "bill." In order to become a law, a bill must be approved by both the House and the Senate. Both chambers of Congress have the power to hold hearings to gather information on the bills they are considering.

The House of Representatives

This chamber includes 435 representatives chosen based on the population of each state, with a minimum of one representative for each state. The larger a state's population, the more representatives it has. For example, California has 53 representatives and Montana has one. Representatives are elected to two-year terms. Each representative must be at least 25 years old, a U.S. citizen for at least seven years, and must live in the state he or she represents.

The House of Representatives has the following special powers and responsibilities:

• Create bills that allow the government to collect taxes

• Create bills that empower the government to spend money

• Elect the President in the event that no candidate receives a majority of electoral votes

• Vote to impeach the President, Vice President, or other elected official, which means to formally charge a public official with wrongdoing

The leader of the House of Representatives is known as the Speaker of the House. The current Speaker of the House is John Boehner of Ohio. He calls sessions to order, runs debates, and gives the oath of office to new representatives, among other things.

The Senate

This chamber includes 100 senators, two from each state. Senators are elected to six-year terms, with one-third of the Senate being elected every even-numbered year. A senator must be at least 30 years old, a U.S. citizen for at least nine years, and live in the state he or she represents. The Senate has the following special powers and responsibilities:

• Ratify, or approve, treaties made by the President. This requires a two-thirds vote of all senators.

• Accept or reject (by majority vote of all senators) the President's appointments of Supreme Court Justices and federal judges, ambassadors, Cabinet secretaries, and other high-level executive-branch officials

• Hold trials of officials impeached by the House of Representatives and convict or acquit them. A two-thirds vote of all senators is needed for conviction.

The Vice President is also the President of the Senate. He presides over the sessions, but only votes in the event of a tie. When the Vice President is not available, the president pro tempore is in charge. Daniel Inouye of Hawaii has been the president pro tempore since June 2010.

Government

117

THE EXECUTIVE BRANCH

When George Washington became President of the United States on April 30, 1789, it was the beginning of the executive branch of the U.S. government as outlined in Article II of the Constitution. The President, Vice President, and Cabinet make up this branch.

The President

The President serves a term of four years, with a maximum of two terms. A President must be a native-born U.S. citizen, at least 35 years old, and must have lived in the United States for at least 14 years. The President has the following powers and responsibilities:

- Carry out the laws of the land
- Appoint U.S. ambassadors, Supreme Court Justices, federal judges, and Cabinet secretaries (who then must be approved by the Senate)
- Give the annual State of the Union address to Congress
- Receive foreign ambassadors, thus recognizing their governments
- Propose treaties with other nations
- Serve as Commander in Chief of the armed forces; send troops overseas (he needs congressional approval to declare war)
- Call both houses of Congress to meet in a special session
- Approve or veto bills passed by Congress
- Grant pardons for federal crimes

President Barack Obama

The Vice President

Under Article I of the Constitution, the Vice President presides over the Senate, but casts a vote only in the event of a tie. Article XXV allows the Vice President to assume the office of President if the President dies, resigns, or is removed from office. The Vice President must also be a native-born U.S. citizen and meet the same age and residential qualifications as the President.

Vice President Biden joins the President in discussing the economy.

Vice President Joe Biden

The Cabinet

The Cabinet is made up of 15 department heads who advise the President. Cabinet secretaries are nominated by the President, then each nominee is questioned by the Senate. These interviews are known as confirmation hearings. Each nominee must be confirmed, or approved, by a majority of 51 or more senators.

Here are the 15 members of the Cabinet, along with a brief description of what each department handles.

President Obama and Vice President Biden pose with members of the Cabinet and other trusted advisors.

1. Secretary Robert Gates
The **Department of Defense** is in charge of the U.S. armed forces.

2. Secretary Timothy Geithner
The **Department of the Treasury** creates U.S. money and handles the collection of taxes.

3. Secretary Hillary Clinton
The **Department of State** helps to develop foreign policy and works with other countries.

4. Attorney General Eric Holder
The **Department of Justice** enforces laws and makes sure all Americans are treated fairly under the law.

5. Secretary Tom Vilsack
The **Department of Agriculture** supports farmers and develops agriculture and food policies.

6. Secretary Steven Chu
The **Department of Energy** develops energy policies and researches cleaner energy sources.

7. Secretary Janet Napolitano
The **Department of Homeland Security** works to keep the country secure and to prevent terrorist attacks.

8. Secretary Kathleen Sebelius
The **Department of Health and Human Services** works to ensure public health and food safety, and to provide assistance to low-income families.

9. Secretary Eric Shinseki
The **Department of Veterans Affairs** provides help and services to former members of the armed forces and their families.

10. Secretary Arne Duncan
The **Department of Education** develops educational policies and helps with financial aid for schooling.

11. Secretary Ray LaHood
The **Department of Transportation** manages airplane travel and the country's highways, shipping ports, and railroads.

12. Secretary Gary Locke
The **Department of Commerce** promotes business and trade within the country and with other nations.

13. Secretary Hilda Solis
The **Department of Labor** looks after the safety and rights of workers.

14. Secretary Ken Salazar
The **Department of the Interior** protects and preserves natural resources and wildlife and oversees national parks.

15. Secretary Shaun Donovan
The **Department of Housing and Urban Development** supports affordable housing and community development.

Secretary Napolitano meets with President Obama.

Government

119

Sonia Sotomayor
Stephen Breyer
Samuel Alito Jr.
Elena Kagan
Antonin Scalia
Anthony Kennedy
Clarence Thomas
Chief Justice John Roberts
Ruth Bader Ginsburg

THE JUDICIAL BRANCH

On February 1, 1790, the U.S. Supreme Court held its first session. As part of the checks and balances and the separation of powers built into the nation's governmental structure, the main task of the judicial branch, and of the Supreme Court in particular, is to make sure that the Constitution and the laws formed under its provisions are preserved and followed. The U.S. Supreme Court and federal courts interpret the way an established law must be carried out. The Supreme Court also has the power to declare a law unconstitutional.

Supreme Court Justices and federal judges are appointed by the President and confirmed by the Senate. They serve for life or until they decide to resign or retire. The Supreme Court consists of eight Associate Justices and a Chief Justice. All decisions are made by a majority vote of the Justices.

America's Newest Top Judge

By Suzanne Zimbler

The Supreme Court is our nation's top court. Its decisions on legal issues and laws are final and cannot be appealed. Elena Kagan is the newest Associate Justice on the Court.

In 2010, after John Paul Stephens announced that he would soon retire from his job as a Supreme Court Justice, President Barack Obama nominated Kagan, calling her "one of the nation's foremost legal minds."

Kagan grew up in New York City. She graduated from Princeton University in 1981 and received her law degree from Harvard in 1986.

As a lawyer, Kagan has held many high-level jobs. She worked for Supreme Court Justice Thurgood Marshall, and was an advisor in the White House while Bill Clinton was President. In 2003, she returned to Harvard to serve as the law school's first female leader.

In March 2009, Kagan became Solicitor General—the U.S. government's top lawyer. While in that job, she represented the United States in cases brought before the Supreme Court. Before becoming the 112th Supreme Court Justice, she had never served as a judge.

Kagan is the third woman on the current Court and the fourth in the history of the Supreme Court. "The Court is an extraordinary institution in the work it does and the work it can do for the American people," she said.

FROM TIME FOR KIDS MAGAZINE

120

Famous Supreme Court Cases

An integrated classroom in Washington, D.C., in 1954

In 1954, the Supreme Court issued its ruling in the case *Brown v. Board of Education*, and declared that racial segregation in public schools is unconstitutional. This judicial decision changed U.S. history and was a victory for civil rights in the United States. Since its first session in 1790, the U.S. Supreme Court has made many important legal rulings. Here are a few.

Dred Scott

Marbury v. Madison (1803)
Established the Constitution's precedence over any other law and the Supreme Court's power to decide what a law is

Dred Scott v. Sandford (1857)
Said that a slave was not a U.S. citizen. Established that all residents (including slaveholders) in a U.S. territory must be treated equally and that Congress could not outlaw slavery in the U.S. territories

Plessy v. Ferguson (1896)
Upheld a Louisiana court decision that racial segregation was legal. This decision was overturned by the Supreme Court's ruling on *Brown v. Board of Education* in 1954.

Miranda v. Arizona (1966)
Determined that suspected criminals must be read their constitutional rights before being questioned by law enforcement officers

A person suspected of criminal activity has rights, such as the right to remain silent and to have an attorney present during questioning.

President George W. Bush

Bush v. Gore (2000)
Overturned a Florida Supreme Court decision to manually recount the state's votes in the presidential election, which originally gave a slight lead to George W. Bush over Al Gore. The decision was based on the fact that the process of counting votes varies from state to state and the Supreme Court didn't have jurisdiction in the way the process was regulated. As a result, George Bush won the election.

Kelo v. City of New London (2005)
Said the government can take private land from owners without their consent to be used for private development if the new developments are deemed to have a positive impact on the area. The owners must receive fair compensation for their land.

Massachusetts et al. v. Environmental Protection Agency et al. (2007)
Declared that greenhouse gases are pollutants and that the EPA has the power to regulate them

guess what? In 1789, the Chief Justice of the U.S. Supreme Court made $3,500 a year. By 2011, the salary had risen to $223,500.

121

Time Line of Women's History in the United States

Meet some amazing women who helped shape our country's history.

1869 **Elizabeth Cady Stanton** (seated) and **Susan B. Anthony** organize the National Woman Suffrage Association to fight for women's rights, especially the right to vote. More than a century later, Anthony is honored when the U.S. Mint creates a coin featuring her image.

Women work during World War II.

1942 About 350,000 women serve in the armed forces during World War II. Many more provide support services. About 100,000 of those women serve in the U.S. Navy as WAVES (Women Accepted for Volunteer Emergency Service).

1920 After 72 years of struggle, women win the right to vote with the 19th Amendment to the U.S. Constitution. Shortly afterwards, the League of Women Voters is formed to push for more reforms.

Help us to win the vote

1851

Sojourner Truth delivers her famous "Ain't I a Woman" speech at a women's rights convention in Akron, Ohio. The former slave spends 40 years of her life preaching a message of equality for all people.

Shirley Chisholm becomes **1968** the first African-American woman elected to Congress. Four years later, the New Yorker becomes the first black person to run for President in the Democratic primaries.

A woman marches for her right to vote in 1914.

Sandra Day O'Connor becomes the first woman appointed to the U.S. Supreme Court. At the time, just 6% of all federal judges are women.

1981

1983 **Sally Ride** becomes America's first female astronaut when she spends six days in space. Today, about 25% of NASA's astronauts are women.

2002–2005 Young women make their mark in the music industry. Singer, songwriter, and piano whiz **Alicia Keys** takes home five Grammy Awards in 2002, and four more in 2005. Piano-playing singer and songwriter Norah Jones and her album *Come Away with Me* snag eight Grammys in 2003. Jones wins three more of music's biggest awards in 2005.

MARCH Congress passes the Equal Rights Amendment (ERA), 49 years after it was first introduced. The ERA calls for equal rights for men and women. However, a constitutional amendment requires the approval of both Congress and the states, and the measure later fails when too few states approve it.

2000 **Hillary Clinton** becomes the first First Lady to be elected to public office. She joins Congress as a U.S. Senator for New York.

JUNE A federal law known as Title IX ensures equal funding for male and female sports in schools. As a result, women and girls have more opportunities to participate in sports. In fact, many female Olympic athletes say Title IX gave them the opportunity to attend college, participate in sports, and receive athletic scholarships.

1972

First Lady Rosalynn Carter speaks to supporters of the ERA in 1977.

Hillary Clinton becomes Secretary of State on January 21, 2009. As the President's top advisor on foreign policy, Clinton is the most powerful woman in President Obama's Cabinet. She is also one of the most powerful women in the world. Clinton is the third woman to hold this important position.

2009

History

RAmerica

TIME LINES OF HISTORY

Ancient History

5000–3500 B.C. Sumer, located in what is now Iraq, becomes the earliest known civilization. Among other innovations, Sumerians develop a written alphabet.

3500–2600 B.C. People settle in the Indus River Valley, in what is now India and Pakistan.

2600 B.C. Minoan civilization begins on the island of Crete, in the Mediterranean Sea.

circa 2560 B.C. The Egyptian king Khufu finishes building the Great Pyramid at Giza. The Great Sphinx is completed soon after by his son Khaefre.

2000 B.C. Babylonians develop a system of mathematics.
• The kingdom of Kush, in Africa, becomes a major center of trade and learning.

1792 B.C. Hammurabi becomes the ruler of Babylonia. He creates the first set of laws, now known as Hammurabi's Code.

circa 1600–1050 B.C. The Shang Dynasty is the first Chinese dynasty to leave written records.

1200 B.C. The Trojan War is fought between the Greeks and the Trojans.

814 B.C. The city of Carthage, located in what is now Tunisia, is founded by the Phoenicians.

753 B.C. According to legend, Rome is founded by Romulus.

563 B.C. Siddhartha Gautama, who becomes the Buddha, or Enlightened One, is born. He will become the founder of the Buddhist religion.

551 B.C. Chinese philosopher Confucius is born. His teachings on honesty, humanity, and how people should treat one another are the foundations of Confucianism.

510 B.C. Democracy is established in Athens, Greece.

431 B.C. The Peloponnesian War breaks out between Sparta and Athens. In 404 B.C., Sparta finally wins the war and takes over Athens.

334 B.C. Alexander the Great invades Persia. He eventually conquers lands from Greece to India. He even crosses into North Africa.

100 B.C. The great city of Teotihuacán flourishes in Mexico.

58 B.C. Julius Caesar leaves Rome for Gaul (France) and spends nine years conquering much of Central Europe. He is murdered in 44 B.C.

27 B.C. Octavian becomes the first Roman emperor, ushering in a long period of peace. He is also known by the title Augustus.

Ruins of the city of Carthage, Tunisia

Confucius

Peloponnesian War

124

World History

circa 1 A.D Jesus Christ is born. He is crucified by the Romans around 30 A.D.

66 Jews rebel against Roman rule. The revolution is put down by the Romans, who destroy Jerusalem, Israel, in 70 A.D. and force many Jews into slavery.

79 Mount Vesuvius erupts, destroying the city of Pompeii (in present-day Italy).

122 Construction on Hadrian's Wall begins. It spans northern England and offers protection from the tribes to the north.

circa 250 The classic period of Mayan civilization begins. It lasts until about 900. The Maya erect impressive stone buildings and temples in areas that are now part of Mexico and Central America.

330 Constantine the Great chooses Byzantium as the capital of the Roman Empire, and the city becomes known as Constantinople.

476 The Roman Empire collapses.

622 Muhammad, the founder of Islam, flees from Mecca to Medina in what is now Saudi Arabia. This journey is called the Hegira. After the death of Muhammad in 632, Muslims conquer much of North Africa and the Middle East. In 711, Muslims also conquer Spain.

800 Charlemagne is crowned the first Holy Roman Emperor by Pope Leo III.

960 The Song Dynasty begins in China. This dynasty is known for its advances in art, poetry, and philosophy.

circa 1000–1300 During the classic period of their culture, Anasazi people build homes and other structures in the sides of cliffs in what is now the southwestern United States.

1066 At the Battle of Hastings, the Norman king William the Conqueror invades England and defeats English king Harold II.

1095 Pope Urban II delivers a speech urging Christians to capture the Holy Land from the Muslims. The fighting between 1096 and 1291 is known as the Crusades.

circa 1200 The Inca Empire begins, and elaborate stone structures are eventually built in Cuzco and Machu Picchu, Peru. The Incas flourish until Francisco Pizarro, a Spaniard, conquers them in 1533.

1206 A Mongolian warrior named Temujin is proclaimed Genghis Khan. He expands his empire so that it includes most of Asia.

1215 A group of barons in England force King John to sign the Magna Carta, a document limiting the power of the king.

1271–95 Marco Polo, a Venetian merchant, travels throughout Asia. His book, *Il Milione* (*The Million*), is a major European source of information about Asia.

1273 The Habsburg Dynasty begins in Eastern Europe. It will remain a powerful force in the region until World War I.

1325 Aztecs begin building Tenochtitlán on the site of modern Mexico City.

Hadrian's Wall today

Charlemagne

Battle of Hastings

History

125

World History, continued

1337 The Hundred Years' War starts between the English and French. France finally wins in 1453.

1347 The Black Death, or bubonic plague, breaks out in Europe. It spreads quickly, killing more than one-third of Europe's population.

1368 The Ming Dynasty is founded in China by Buddhist monk Zhu Yuanzhang (or Chu Yuan-Chang).

1433 Portuguese explorer Gil Eannes sails past Cape Bojador, in western Africa, which was thought to be the end of the world.

1453 Constantinople falls to the Ottoman Turks, ending the Byzantine Empire.

1455 Johannes Gutenberg invents the printing press. The Gutenberg Bible is the first book printed on the press.

1478 The Spanish Inquisition begins.

1487–88 Bartholomeu Dias of Portugal leads the first European expedition around the Cape of Good Hope, at the southern tip of Africa, opening up a sea route to Asia.

1492 Christopher Columbus leaves Spain, hoping to sail to the West Indies. Instead, he and his crew land in the Bahamas and visit Cuba, Hispaniola (which is now Haiti and the Dominican Republic), and other small islands.

1497–99 Portuguese explorer Vasco da Gama leads the first European expedition to India by sea via the Cape of Good Hope.

1517 Martin Luther protests the abuses of the Catholic Church, which leads to a religious split and the rise of the Protestant faith.

1519 While exploring Mexico, Spanish adventurer Hernán Cortés conquers the Aztec Empire.

1519–22 Portuguese explorer Ferdinand Magellan's expedition circumnavigates, or sails around, the globe.

1532–33 Spanish explorer Francisco Pizarro conquers the Inca Empire in South America.

1543 Polish astronomer Copernicus releases his theory that the sun, not the Earth, is the center of the universe.

1547 Ivan the Terrible becomes the first czar, or ruler, of Russia.

1588 The English defeat the Spanish Armada, or fleet of warships, when Spain attempts to invade England.

1618 The Thirty Years' War breaks out between Protestants and Catholics in Europe.

1620 English pilgrims aboard the *Mayflower* land at Plymouth Rock.

1632 Italian astronomer Galileo, the first person to use a telescope to look into space, confirms Copernicus's theory that Earth revolves around the sun.

1642 The English Civil War, sometimes called the Puritan Revolution, begins in Britain.

1688 The Glorious Revolution, or Bloodless Revolution, takes place in England. James II is removed from the throne, and William and Mary become the heads of the country.

1721 Peter the Great becomes czar of Russia.

Victims of the bubonic plague

Hernán Cortés

English Civil War

126

1789 An angry mob storms the Bastille, a prison in Paris, setting off the French Revolution.

1819 Simón Bolívar crosses the Andes to launch a surprise attack against the Spanish, liberating New Granada (now Colombia, Venezuela, Panama, and Ecuador) from Spain.

1824 Mexico becomes independent from Spain.

1845 A blight ruins the potato crop in Ireland. More than 1 million Irish starve to death, and another million leave for America to escape the Irish Potato Famine.

1848 This is known as the year of revolutions in Europe, as there is upheaval in France, Italy, Germany, Hungary, and elsewhere.

1859 Charles Darwin publishes *On the Origin of Species.*

1871 A group of independent states unifies, creating the German Empire.

1876 Alexander Graham Bell invents the telephone.

1884 Representatives of 14 European countries meet at the Berlin West Africa Conference and divide Africa into areas of control.

1892 The diesel engine is invented by Parisian Rudolf Diesel.

1893 New Zealand becomes the first country to extend to women the right to vote. • The Columbian Exposition, also known as the Chicago World's Fair, is held.

1894 The Sino-Japanese War breaks out between China and Japan, who are fighting

for control of Korea. An 1895 treaty declares Korea independent.

1898 The Spanish-American War begins.

1899 During the Boxer Rebellion, the Chinese fight against Christian and foreign influences in their country. American, Japanese, and European forces help stop the fighting by 1901.

1904 Japan declares war on Russia, beginning the Russo-Japanese War. The countries clash over influence in Manchuria and Korea. Japan wins the conflict and becomes a world power.

1909 Robert Peary is credited as the first to reach the North Pole, although recent evidence suggests he might have been as far as 30 to 60 miles (48 to 97 km) away.

1911 Roald Amundsen, the first man to travel the Northwest Passage, reaches the South Pole.

1914 Austro-Hungarian archduke Franz Ferdinand is assassinated, setting off the chain of events that starts World War I.

1917 The United States enters World War I. • The Russian Revolution begins. The czarist government is overthrown and, in 1922, the Soviet Union is formed.

1918 A flu epidemic spreads quickly around the world, killing more than 20 million people.

1919 The Treaty of Versailles ends World War I.

1927 Philo Farnsworth invents the television.

Alexander Graham Bell

Spanish-American War

Boxer Rebellion

History

127

World History, continued

1928 Alexander Fleming discovers penicillin accidentally after leaving a dish of *staphylococcus* bacteria uncovered and finding mold.

1929 The U.S. stock market collapses, beginning the Great Depression.

1933 Adolf Hitler becomes chancellor of Germany.
• Frequency modulation, or FM, radio is developed by Edwin Armstrong.

1936 The Spanish Civil War breaks out.

1939 World War II begins when Germany invades Poland. Britain responds by declaring war on Germany. The United States declares neutrality.

1941 The Japanese launch a surprise attack on the United States, bombing U.S. ships docked in Hawaii's Pearl Harbor. In response, the U.S. declares war on Japan, and both Germany and Italy declare war on the U.S.

1945 Germany surrenders on May 7, ending the war in Europe. In August, the United States drops two atomic bombs on the Japanese cities Hiroshima and Nagasaki. Japan surrenders, ending World War II.

1947 India and Pakistan become free of British colonial rule.

1948 Israel becomes a nation.

1949 Following China's civil war, Mao Zedong sets up the Communist People's Republic of China.
• South Africa enacts apartheid laws, which make discrimination against nonwhite people part of public policy.

1950 North Korean communist forces invade South Korea, beginning the Korean War. American forces support South Korea. China backs North Korea. The war ends three years later.
• Frank McNamara develops the first credit card, the Diners' Club. It is not made out of plastic but paper stock.

1952 The hydrogen bomb is developed by Edward Teller and a team at a laboratory in Los Alamos, New Mexico.

1953 Edmund Hillary and Tenzing Norgay climb to the top of Mount Everest.

1955 Jonas Salk's polio vaccine is introduced.

1961 A group of Cuban exiles, supported by the United States, invades Cuba at the Bay of Pigs. The invasion fails, and U.S.-Cuban relations worsen.

1962 The Cuban Missile Crisis, a conflict between the United States, the Soviet Union, and Cuba, brings the world to the brink of nuclear war.

1963 U.S. President John F. Kennedy is assassinated. Vice President Lyndon B. Johnson is inaugurated.

1965 The United States begins officially sending troops to Vietnam to aid South Vietnam in its civil war with North Vietnam.

1967 The Six-Day War breaks out between Israel and neighboring Arab nations Egypt, Syria, and Jordan. Israel seizes the Golan Heights, the Gaza Strip, the Sinai Peninsula, and part of the west bank of the Jordan River.

After the bombing of Pearl Harbor **Sir Edmund Hillary** **Marchers protesting the Vietnam War in 1967**

128

1973 The Paris Peace Accords end the Vietnam War. North Vietnam later violates the terms of the treaty and, in 1975, takes control of Saigon, the capital of South Vietnam.
• Egypt and Syria launch a surprise attack on Israel, beginning the Yom Kippur War.

1978 U.S. President Jimmy Carter, Israeli President Menachem Begin, and Egyptian President Anwar Sadat sign the Camp David Accords in an attempt to achieve peace in the Middle East.

1979 Religious leader Ayatollah Khomeini declares Iran to be an Islamic republic.

1989 The Chinese army crushes a demonstration in Tiananmen Square in Beijing, killing hundreds or thousands of students and protestors.
• The Berlin Wall is torn down and the city of Berlin, Germany, is reunified.

1990 Apartheid ends in South Africa. Four years later, Nelson Mandela is elected president in the country's first free, multiracial elections.
• The Persian Gulf War begins when Iraq invades Kuwait.

1991 The Soviet Union dissolves.
• Croatia, Slovenia, and Macedonia declare independence from Yugoslavia. The next year, Bosnia and Herzegovina also declares independence, but war breaks out and does not end until 1995.
• Tim Berners-Lee develops the World Wide Web.

1994 Tensions between the Hutu majority and the Tutsi minority in the African nation of Rwanda lead to genocide, which is the systematic killing of a racial or ethnic group.

1999 Honda releases the two-door Insight, the first hybrid car mass-marketed in the United States. A year later, the Toyota Prius, the first hybrid four-door sedan, is released.

2001 After the September 11 terrorist attacks in New York City and Washington, D.C., the United States declares an international War on Terror, attacking the Taliban government in Afghanistan and searching for Osama bin Laden and al-Qaeda.

2003 With the aid of Britain and other allies, the United States invades Iraq. Though the government falls quickly, resistance and fighting continue. In 2006, Saddam Hussein is executed for crimes against humanity.
• War in the Darfur region of Sudan begins, leading to a humanitarian crisis.

2004 A powerful tsunami kills nearly 300,000 people in Indonesia, Sri Lanka, India, Thailand, and other Asian countries.

2008 A global economic crisis leads to loss of jobs and homes, and to a downturn in trade.

2010 A devastating earthquake hits Haiti.
• An oil rig in the Gulf of Mexico explodes, causing one of the largest oil spills in history.

2011 Protests erupt throughout the Middle East and North Africa, toppling leaders in Tunisia and Egypt, and causing instability throughout the region.
• A massive earthquake strikes Japan, triggering a powerful tsunami.
• Protesters in Libya are attacked by forces loyal to President Muammar Gaddafi. Several countries, including the United States, Canada, France, and Qatar, launch air strikes in Libya to protect Libyan citizens.

1978 Camp David meeting

A 2011 demonstration in Egypt

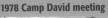

MYSTERY PERSON

I was born in Castile in 1451. My husband, King Ferdinand II, and I ruled Spain. In 1492, I sponsored Christopher Columbus's historic voyage to the New World.

WHO AM I?_____

History

Answer on page 242.

129

U.S. History

Hernando de Soto

1524 Italian explorer Giovanni da Verrazano is the first European to reach New York Harbor.

1540 In search of gold, Spanish explorer Francisco Vásquez de Coronado travels north from Mexico. One of his lieutenants is the first European to spot the Grand Canyon.

1541 Spaniard Hernando de Soto crosses the Mississippi River.

1579 Sir Francis Drake of England explores California's coastline.

1607 English settlers found Jamestown in Virginia. The colony's leader, John Smith, is captured by Native Americans. According to legend, he is saved by Pocahontas.

1609–11 Henry Hudson visits the Chesapeake, Delaware, and New York bays and becomes the first European to sail up the Hudson River.

1620 Pilgrims land at Plymouth, Massachusetts.

1626 Dutchman Peter Minuit buys the island of Manhattan from the Canarsie tribe.

1692 Accusations of witchcraft lead to the Salem witch trials and the executions of 20 people.

1770 Tensions between British soldiers and colonists erupt in the Boston Massacre, when British troops kill five men.

1773 Colonists protest a tax on tea by dressing up as Native Americans, boarding ships, and dumping tea into Boston Harbor.

Known as the Boston Tea Party, the protest angers the British, who pass other harsh taxes.

1775 Paul Revere warns the colonists that the British are coming. The Battle of Lexington and Concord is the first fight of the American Revolution. The British surrender at Yorktown, Virginia, in 1781.

1776 Drafted by Thomas Jefferson, the Declaration of Independence is signed, and the United States is formed.

1787 The U.S. Constitution is written and submitted to the states for ratification. By the end of the year, Delaware, Pennsylvania, and New Jersey have accepted it.

1789 George Washington becomes the first President of the United States.

1791 The Bill of Rights, written mostly by James Madison, becomes part of the Constitution.

1803 Thomas Jefferson buys the Louisiana Territory from France.

1804–06 Meriwether Lewis and William Clark explore the Louisiana Territory. They travel from St. Louis up the Missouri River, then over the Rockies on horseback, reaching the Pacific Ocean in November 1805.

1812 The War of 1812 breaks out between the United States and Britain because of trade and border disputes, as well as disagreements about freedom of the seas. The Treaty of Ghent ends the war in 1814.

1823 President James Monroe issues the Monroe Doctrine, warning that the Americas are not open for colonization.

Pilgrims landing in Massachusetts

Paul Revere's ride

Thomas Jefferson

130

1836 Texas declares independence from Mexico. In response, the Mexican army attacks and kills the 189 Texans defending the Alamo.

1838 In what is known as the Trail of Tears, the U.S. government forces 16,000 Cherokees to leave their land in Georgia and relocate to a reservation in Oklahoma. Roughly a quarter of the Cherokees die.

1846 The Mexican-American War begins. At the end of the fighting, in 1848, Mexico gives California and New Mexico (which also includes present-day Arizona, Utah, and Nevada) to the United States. In return, the U.S. agrees to pay Mexico $15 million.

1848 John Sutter strikes gold in California, kicking off the California gold rush.

1860 Tensions between the North and the South over slavery, taxes, and representation reach a boiling point, and South Carolina secedes from the United States.

1861 Mississippi, Florida, Alabama, Georgia, Louisiana, and Texas secede from the Union, and the Confederate government is formed. The first shots of the American Civil War are fired by Confederate soldiers at Fort Sumter, in Charleston Harbor in South Carolina. Virginia, Arkansas, Tennessee, and North Carolina also secede from the Union.

1862 The Homestead Act promises 160 acres of land to anyone who remains on the land for five years. This law encourages settlers to move west.

1863 President Abraham Lincoln issues the Emancipation Proclamation, which frees all slaves in the Confederate states. The Battle of Gettysburg is fought. It is the bloodiest battle of the Civil War.

1865 General Robert E. Lee of the Confederacy surrenders to Union general Ulysses S. Grant at Appomattox Court House, in Virginia, ending the Civil War.
• President Lincoln is assassinated at Ford's Theater by John Wilkes Booth, and Andrew Johnson becomes President.
• The 13th Amendment, which puts an end to slavery, is ratified.

1867 The United States buys Alaska from Russia for $7.2 million.

1869 The transcontinental railroad is completed when the Central Pacific and Union Pacific railroads are joined at Promontory, Utah.

1890 The Battle of Wounded Knee is the last major defeat for Native American tribes.

1898 The Spanish-American War is fought. At the end of the war, Cuba is independent, and Puerto Rico, Guam, and the Philippines become territories of the United States.

1903 Wilbur and Orville Wright complete their first airplane flight at Kitty Hawk, North Carolina.

1908 Henry Ford, founder of the Ford Motor Company, builds the Model T and sells it for $825, making automobiles much more affordable than ever before.

1917 The United States enters World War I.

1920 With the passage of the 19th Amendment, women get the right to vote.

1929 The U.S. stock market crashes, and the Great Depression begins.

Battle of Gettysburg

Model T

Opponents of the 19th Amendment

History

131

U.S. History, continued

1941 In a surprise attack, Japan bombs the U.S. fleet at Pearl Harbor, in Hawaii. The United States declares war on Japan. Germany and Italy declare war on the United States.

1945 Germany surrenders on May 7, ending the war in Europe. In August, the United States drops two atomic bombs on the Japanese cities Hiroshima and Nagasaki. Japan surrenders, ending World War II.

1946 The first bank-issued credit card is developed by John Biggins for the Flatbush National Bank of Brooklyn, in New York City.

1950 North Korean communist forces invade South Korea. American forces enter the Korean War to defend South Korea. Despite three years of bitter fighting, little land changes hands.

1954 In *Brown v. Board of Education of Topeka, Kansas,* the U.S. Supreme Court declares that segregated schools are unconstitutional.

1955 Rosa Parks is arrested for refusing to give up her bus seat to a white person, leading to a boycott of the entire bus system in Montgomery, Alabama.

1962 The United States discovers that the Soviet Union has installed missiles capable of reaching the United States on the island of Cuba. Known as the Cuban Missile Crisis, this event brings the U.S. and the U.S.S.R. to the brink of nuclear war. After two weeks of extremely tense negotiations, the crisis comes peacefully to an end.

1963 Martin Luther King Jr. delivers his famous "I Have a Dream" speech to a crowd of more than 250,000 people in Washington, D.C.
• President John F. Kennedy is assassinated.

1965 Civil-rights advocate and black militant leader Malcolm X is killed.
• A race riot in the Watts section of Los Angeles, California, is one of the worst in history.
• President Lyndon B. Johnson authorizes air raids over North Vietnam.

1968 James Earl Ray shoots and kills Martin Luther King Jr. in Memphis, Tennessee. Riots break out across the country.

1973 The Vietnam War ends when peace accords are signed. Two years later, North Vietnam takes over Saigon (or Ho Chi Minh City), the capital of South Vietnam.

1974 Due to his involvement in the Watergate scandal, President Richard Nixon resigns. Gerald Ford becomes President.

1979 Islamic militants storm the U.S. embassy in Tehran, Iran, and 52 Americans are held hostage for 444 days.

1986 The *Challenger* space shuttle explodes, killing seven crew members, including teacher Christa McAuliffe.

1991 After Iraq invades Kuwait, the United States begins bombing raids. The first Persian Gulf War ends quickly as Iraqi forces are driven from Kuwait.

1999 President Bill Clinton is acquitted of impeachment charges.

Korean War

Martin Luther King Jr.

Vietnam War

132

2000 In the extremely close election between Democrat Al Gore and Republican George W. Bush, allegations of voter fraud lead to an election recount. The U.S. Supreme Court determines the outcome, and Bush is declared the winner.

2001 On September 11, two passenger planes are hijacked and flown into the World Trade Center, in New York City, causing the buildings to collapse. Another plane is flown into the Pentagon, near Washington, D.C. A fourth hijacked plane is crashed into a field in Pennsylvania by the passengers onboard before it can reach its target. The United States and Britain respond by attacking the Taliban government in Afghanistan for harboring Osama bin Laden, the alleged mastermind of the attacks. The U.S. government declares the War on Terror.

2003 The space shuttle *Columbia* breaks apart during reentry into Earth's atmosphere, killing all seven crew members.
• Along with its allies—Britain and other countries—the United States goes to war in Iraq. Saddam Hussein's government falls quickly, but resistance and fighting continue.

2005 Hurricane Katrina hits the Gulf Coast, destroying parts of Mississippi and Louisiana, and areas along the coast of the southeastern United States. About 80% of New Orleans, Louisiana, is flooded.

2009 Barack Obama is inaugurated on January 20, becoming America's first African-American President. He quickly signs a $787 billion economic stimulus bill to combat the severe economic downturn that began in 2008.

2010 A controversial federal law is enacted to overhaul the U.S. health care system and extend health insurance to the 32 million Americans who did not have it before.
• An oil rig in the Gulf of Mexico explodes, causing one of the largest oil spills in history.

Workers rescue a pelican from the Gulf of Mexico in 2010 to clean oil from its feathers.

MYSTERY PERSON

I was born in South Adams, Massachusetts, on February 15, 1820. In 1872, I was arrested for voting. Women were not yet allowed to vote. I appear on a U.S. dollar coin.

WHO AM I? _____

Answer on page 242.

September 11, 2001

U.S. soldier in Afghanistan

Flooding from Hurricane Katrina

Inventions

Budding Inventors

By Andrea Delbanco

"When you win first place at a science fair, nobody's rushing the field or dumping Gatorade over your head," said President Barack Obama, speaking to a room full of young science scholars. But he believes that achievement in science should be celebrated more. "In many ways, our future depends on what happens in those contests," he said. That's why he invited the middle and high school winners of science, technology, engineering, and math contests to show their work at the White House Science Fair in October 2010.

Award-winning projects at the fair included a robot that plays soccer and a device designed to discourage texting while driving. There was a special wheelchair created to help a classmate, and a "smart toilet" that cuts back on water use. The President was intrigued by a test of whether foam is the best material to pad safety helmets. Obama asked seventh graders Jonathan Berman, Benjamin Kotzubei, and Austin Veseliza, from Los Angeles, California, to explain their

Students from Wissahickon High School, in Ambler, Pennsylvania, invented a soccer-playing robot.

investigation. They revealed their findings: Foam isn't the best material. A gel liner is better, but more expensive.

The President viewed the 11 projects that were on display in the State Dining Room. He had questions, and congratulations, for the presenters. "It's hard to describe just how impressive these young people are," he said.

SERIOUS ABOUT SCIENCE

Obama says the United States is being outpaced by the achievements of other countries in science and math. He challenged American students to move from the middle to the top in these important subjects. The White House Science Fair began a full week of events aimed at getting people excited about science.

"We can think of Einstein, Edison, Franklin, Tesla, and the founders of Google and Apple and Microsoft," Obama said. "But now we've got some other people to think about, like Mikayla Nelson, who's here today. . . . She and her classmates built a solar-powered car that won the design award in the National Science Bowl. . . . There's no doubt we can expect great things from her."

Mikayla Nelson, of Billings, Montana, explains her model of a solar vehicle.

134

THE COOLEST INVENTIONS OF 2010

Beef-powered trains! English-teaching robots! A suit that gives its wearer superhero powers! A car that runs on air! Do you think this sounds like life in the future? Think again. These incredible inventions are here right now. Inventors are always looking for ways to make our lives easier, greener, and a whole lot more fun. Take a look at 2010's biggest and coolest breakthroughs in science and technology. What in the world will inventors dream up next?

A TOUCH TABLET

Apple, creator of the iPhone and iPod, had another hit invention in 2010 with the iPad. The iPad is a touch-screen tablet computer. The gadget gives users video, websites, books, and games, right at their fingertips. Apple sold 3 million iPads in the first 80 days of its release.

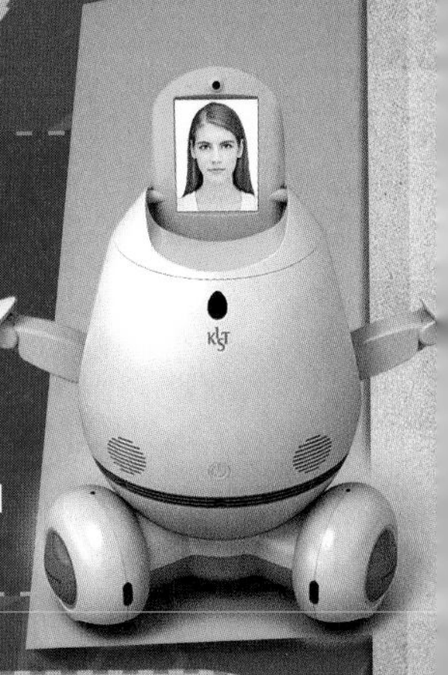

ROBO-TEACHERS

Some students in South Korea have a new language instructor: an English-teaching robot. The bots help students practice speaking English. South Korea employs 30,000 foreigners to teach English. The robot teachers are helping to solve a shortage of English teachers. Could robots replace human teachers one day?

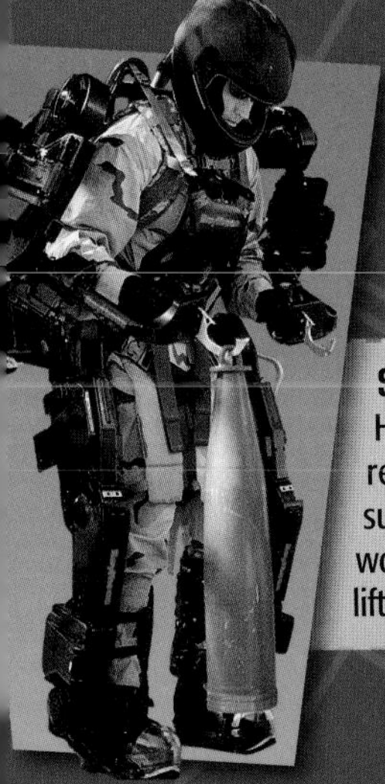

SUPERHERO SUIT

Have you ever dreamed of becoming a superhero? Dream no more. There's a real Iron Man suit, XOS 2, that instantly transforms the person wearing it. The suit provides the power to lift 200 pounds (91 kg) with ease and break slabs of wood in a single karate chop. It was designed to help the military with heavy lifting. One person in the suit can do the work of three soldiers.

ROBO-GUARD

EMILY is not your typical lifeguard. She's a robotic, 4-foot-long (1.2 m) buoy. She can swim through riptides at up to 24 miles (39 km) per hour. Her inventor, Tony Mulligan, says that's 15 times faster than human lifeguards! EMILY, or the Emergency Integrated Lifesaving Lanyard, is powered by a tiny electric pump, and operated remotely.

Inventions

135

ONE STEP AT A TIME

The makers of eLEGS hope to help people with paralyzed legs to stand and walk on their own. The device consists of robotic legs and crutches. It uses artificial intelligence to understand the wearer's arm movements through the crutches. It may be available for home use by 2013.

UP, UP, AND AWAY!

It took him 30 years to develop it, and now Glenn Martin's invention is ready to take off. The Martin Jetpack allows its operator to fly 8,000 feet (2,438 m) into the air. "I've made a Jet Ski for the sky," Martin says. Unfortunately, you can't soar through the skies too long. The jetpack holds only about 30 minutes' worth of fuel. The aircraft will sell for $100,000.

HARDWORKING ROBOT

The EMIEW2 robot is the perfect office helper. Need a document delivered? No problem! It can also guide visitors to their destinations. The 3-foot-tall (1 m) bot can identify different human voices and respond to commands. One day, it may serve as a receptionist or a security guard.

SUPER-MOLDABLE GLUE

Sugru looks like Play-Doh but acts like Super Glue. It's a brightly colored silicone rubber that is soft enough to mold, yet strong enough to fix everyday objects so they work better. Sugru sticks to everything from metal to fabric.

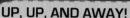

136

ON THE ROAD

No traffic jam here! Space-saving, eco-friendly vehicles keep traffic moving. The partly solar-powered straddling bus spans two lanes of road. It can carry 1,200 people, and its carriage is raised so cars can pass underneath. The Antro Solo is a lightweight electric car that holds up to three people. Two Solos can combine to form a bigger car, the Duo.

GREEN MACHINE

Say goodbye to gasoline! The AirPod car runs on—you guessed it—air power. That means this car won't pollute. A high-pressure air tank can fill the car in minutes. The three-wheeler can travel about 130 miles (209 km) between fill-ups.

BEEF POWER

All aboard the beef train! Amtrak's Heartland Flyer runs partly on fuel that is made from cow fat. The goal is to reduce carbon emissions by 10%. The train travels between Oklahoma City, Oklahoma, and Fort Worth, Texas.

UNDERWATER KITE

The Deep Green kite is no toy. As it dives in the ocean currents, a turbine engine attached to the kite collects energy. Just one hour of the kite's work could supply about two weeks of power for the average home. The device can generate 800 times more power than if it were in the sky.

MYSTERY PERSON

I was an inventor and a scientist born in 1706. I invented the first stove that gave off more heat than a fireplace. I was also a Founding Father of the United States. In 1776, I suggested to Congress that the turkey be the national symbol, rather than the bald eagle.

WHO AM I?

Answer on page 242.

Inventions

137

Language

Learning Chinese

By Jaime Joyce

A growing number of American students are learning Chinese. As China becomes a more powerful country, Chinese speakers may have greater opportunities.

Jingjing Wu greets her American students as they enter the room. "*Ni hao (nee how)*," she says. In Mandarin Chinese, *ni hao* means "hello." For the next hour, Chinese is all the children will hear. They are learning the language through songs, games, and talking. "They pick it up really fast," Wu says. "Kids remember so much."

你好

Here is how you write "hello" in Chinese.

The students go to Lomond Elementary School, in Shaker Heights, Ohio. Each week, all students in grades 1 through 5 in this school district have a one-hour Chinese class. "We're trying to generate great interest in the language," school official James J. Paces told TFK.

Other U.S. schools are too. Ten years ago, about 300 schools had Chinese programs. Today, about 1,600 schools teach Chinese. "China is becoming a real powerhouse nation," says Nancy C. Rhodes, a language expert. "It makes sense that we have young people who not only know the language, but understand the culture."

One-fifth of the world's people live in China. Its products, including clothes, toys, and electronics, are sold around the world. More people speak Chinese than any other language.

STARTING YOUNG

Yinghua (yeeng hwa) Academy is a K–8 Chinese immersion school in Minneapolis, Minnesota. Instead of studying only the language itself, students learn all of their subjects in Chinese. They don't start to use English in class until they are in the second grade.

"When you're younger, it's easier to learn a different language," says fifth grader Zoë Lindberg. She has been studying Chinese since kindergarten. Experts say it's best to start language instruction early.

OPENING DOORS

"If you know how to speak Mandarin Chinese, you open a huge door for yourself," says Yinghua's academic director, Luyi Lien. In Shaker Heights, Paces agrees. "It's really important that all children receive this instruction," he says. "We'd like to do even more."

guess what? The Chinese language is made up of more than 50,000 symbols. Each one represents a syllable or a concept instead of a sound. To be considered literate, a person must know at least 3,000 of these symbols.

TOP 10

Languages Spoken in the United States

About 80% of Americans over age 5 speak only English at home. That's about 225,500,000 people. Here are some of the other languages that 55,400,000 Americans are speaking at home.

LANGUAGE	APPROXIMATE NUMBER OF SPEAKERS
1. Spanish or Spanish Creole	34,547,077
2. Chinese	2,464,572
3. French	1,355,805
4. Tagalog	1,480,429
5. Vietnamese	1,207,004
6. German	1,104,354
7. Korean	1,062,337
8. Russian	851,174
9. Italian	798,801
10. Arabic	767,319

Tagalog is the most common language spoken in the Philippines.

SPEAKING WITHOUT SOUND

American Sign Language is a system of hand signals that hearing-impaired people use to communicate. The chart below illustrates the hand sign for each letter of the alphabet.

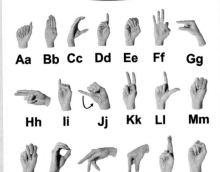

Aa Bb Cc Dd Ee Ff Gg

Hh Ii Jj Kk Ll Mm

Nn Oo Pp Qq Rr Ss

Tt Uu Vv Ww Xx Yy Zz

TOP 10

Languages Spoken Worldwide

LANGUAGE	APPROXIMATE NUMBER OF SPEAKERS
1. Chinese (Mandarin)	1,213,000,000
2. Spanish	329,000,000
3. English	328,000,000
4. Arabic	221,000,000
5. Hindi	182,000,000
6. Bengali	181,000,000
7. Portuguese	178,000,000
8. Russian	144,000,000
9. Japanese	122,000,000
10. German	90,000,000

Language

2010 SCRIPPS NATIONAL SPELLING BEE

On June 4, 2010, 14-year-old Anamika Veeramani, from Cleveland, Ohio, won the 83rd annual Scripps National Spelling Bee. She beat out 273 other students who participated in the big event. She correctly spelled words such as *nahcolite*, *epiphysis*, and *juvia* before winning with the medical term, *stromuhr*. A stromuhr is a tool used to measure the speed of blood as it moves through an artery. Here are 10 winning words from spelling bees that have come before.

2008
guerdon
a reward or payment

1999
logorrhea
extreme talkativeness; using lots and lots of words (and often not making much sense)

1998
chiaroscurist
an artist who uses light and shade (instead of using color) to create depth in a work of art

1995
xanthosis
a yellow discoloration of the skin

1992
lyceum
a hall for public lectures

1976
narcolepsy
a sleep disorder; people with narcolepsy fall deeply asleep suddenly and uncontrollably ▼

1961
smaragdine
emerald green

1955
crustaceology
branch of study that deals with crustaceans, a group of mostly water-dwelling animals that includes lobsters, shrimp, crabs, and barnacles

1934
deteriorating
falling apart

1930
fracas
a noisy fight

guess what? Recent research suggests that writing by hand exercises your brain in a way that typing on a computer does not. It may help you learn and remember new information better.

140

UPDATE YOUR DICTIONARY

Each new edition of the dictionary includes new words and terms. This time around, some of the words came from a growing interest in the environment. Others relate to computer activities and social networking. Even some texting abbreviations, such as BFF (best friend forever) and TTYL (talk to you later), have been included. Here are some of the other new additions to *The New Oxford American Dictionary*.

defriend: to remove someone from a list of friends on a social networking site like Facebook. *Unfriend*, which means the same thing, was added in 2009.

gal pal: an informal term for a female friend

green audit: an assessment of a business in terms of its impact on the environment

green-collar: an adjective used to describe jobs designed to improve the environment

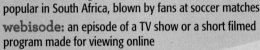
Installing solar panels is a green-collar job.

vuvuzela: a long horn, popular in South Africa, blown by fans at soccer matches

webisode: an episode of a TV show or a short filmed program made for viewing online

Many people were introduced to the vuvuzela during the 2010 World Cup soccer tournament, held in South Africa.

EASILY CONFUSED WORDS

WORDS	MEANING/USAGE	EXAMPLE
affect	to have an influence on	*Your grades can affect your future.*
effect	the result of a cause	*Studying has a good effect on grades.*
beside	next to	*Please sit beside me.*
besides	also	*Besides, I like you.*
capital	the city in which the government works	*Washington, D.C., is the capital of the United States.*
Capitol	the building in which members of government meet	*The Senate meets in the Capitol.*
farther	more distant	*We traveled farther than you did.*
further	to a greater extent	*We need to study further in order to understand this problem.*
few	used with countable items	*There are fewer kids in the third grade this year.*
less	used with uncountable amounts	*The school is less crowded.*
laid	past tense of *lay*	*I laid the blanket on the lawn.*
lay	past tense of *lie*	*I lay down and took a nap.*
lightening	to make brighter or to reduce in weight	*She was lightening the load by removing heavy items from her purse.*
lightning	an electrical charge in the sky	*The lightning lit up the night sky.*
passed	past tense of *pass*	*He passed the library on his way home.*
past	an earlier time	*He liked reading about the past.*
stationary	not moving	*You can exercise on a stationary bike.*
stationery	letter paper	*The letter was written on pretty stationery.*

Language

141

POEMS

You use your language skills all the time: when you order a pizza, type a text message, write an essay in English class, or tell jokes with your friends. Another way to exercise your language skills is to write poetry. Many poems are written in free verse, which means that they do not have a rhyme scheme, the length of the lines vary, and there is not a predictable rhythm to the poem. There are many other kinds of poems that have a particular form. Here are two types of poems you might try to write.

SONNETS

A sonnet is a 14-line rhyming lyric poem. The most famous sonnet writer is probably William Shakespeare (1564–1616). He divided his sonnets into four stanzas, or sections. The first three stanzas are four lines each. The last stanza is a pair of rhyming lines called a couplet.

Shall I compare thee to a Summer's day?
Thou art more lovely and more temperate.
Rough winds do shake the darling buds of May,
And Summer's lease hath all too short a date.

Sometime too hot the eye of heaven shines,
And often is his gold complexion dimm'd;
And every fair from fair sometime declines,
By chance or nature's changing course untrimm'd:

But thy eternal Summer shall not fade,
Nor lose possession of that fair thou owest,
Nor shall Death brag thou wanderest in his shade,
When in eternal lines to time thou growest.

So long as men can breathe, or eyes can see,
So long lives this, and this gives life to thee.

HAIKU

A traditional haiku (hy-*koo*) is a three-line poem that consists of 17 syllables. The first line has five syllables, the second line has seven syllables, and the last line has five. Here are two examples from the Japanese haiku master Matsuo Basho (1644–1694).

Clouds appear and bring
to men a chance to rest from
looking at the moon.

Pond there, still and old.
A frog has jumped from the shore.
A splash can be heard.

guess what? Research shows that young children who enjoy rhyming, making up words, and playing with words are better readers than those who don't.

142

WORD WORDS

There are countless ways to use language to explain a situation, make a point, or make a story spooky, funny, or sweet. Here are just a few of the techniques and figures of speech that can be used when writing.

simile: a figure of speech comparing two things, using the words *like or as*
- *After lunch, she fell asleep and slept like a baby.*
- *Be as quiet as a mouse and you won't disturb anyone.*

metaphor: a figure of speech comparing two things without using the words *like or as*
- *I hate exams—tests stink!*
- *He can eat anything—his stomach is a bottomless pit.*

alliteration: more than two words in a row that begin with the same consonant
- *Several snakes slithered slowly toward unsuspecting Sally.*
- *Tim taped a tiny sign on Tina's T-shirt: "Tickle me."*

hyperbole: an exaggeration
- *I almost died laughing.*
- *I have a mountain of homework to do!*

antonym: a word that has the opposite meaning of another word
enormous/tiny   always/never
hot/cold   strong/weak

synonym: a word with a similar, or the same, meaning as another
beautiful/gorgeous   hop/jump
fast/quick   cry/weep

USING LANGUAGE TO WIN WARS

During World War II, thousands of Native Americans served in the United States armed forces. Some fought with words instead of weapons.

U.S. troops needed a way to send secret messages. Very few people speak the Navajo language, and it is incredibly hard to learn. So Navajo soldiers used their language to make a code. This kept the enemy fighters from learning U.S. plans. Known as "code talkers," these Navajo soldiers helped the United States win many battles.

The code talkers chose Navajo words to stand for English letters. The word *ma-e* means *fox.* They used *ma-e* for *f,* because *fox* starts with *f.* Even other Navajos could not understand the coded messages. Use the chart below to decode our message. Write the correct letter under each Navajo word.

Navajo code talkers

Navajo	English
LHA-CHA-EH	DOG
AH-JAH	EAR
MA-E	FOX
BE-TAS-TNI	MIRROR
A-CHIN	NOSE
TLO-CHIN	ONION
GAH	RABBIT
KLESH	SNAKE

KLESH   AH-JAH   A-CHIN   LHA-CHA-EH
  S   ___   ___   ___

BE-TAS-TNI   TLO-CHIN   GAH   AH-JAH
   ___   ___   ___   ___

MA-E   TLO-CHIN   TLO-CHIN   LHA-CHA-EH
 ___   ___   ___   ___

Answer on page 242.   143

Language

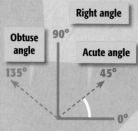

GEOMETRIC TERMS

An *ANGLE* is formed every time two lines meet, or intersect.
A *RIGHT ANGLE* is an angle that measures 90°.
An *ACUTE ANGLE* measures less than 90°.
An *OBTUSE ANGLE* measures more than 90°.

PARALLEL LINES are lines that will never meet, or intersect.
PERPENDICULAR LINES form a right angle where they meet.

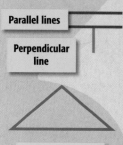

A *TRIANGLE* has three sides.
In an *EQUILATERAL TRIANGLE,* all sides are the same length.
An *ISOSCELES TRIANGLE* has at least two sides of the same length.
In a *SCALENE TRIANGLE,* each side is a different length.
A *RIGHT TRIANGLE* is a triangle with a right angle.
On a right triangle, the side opposite the right angle is called
the *HYPOTENUSE.*

A *QUADRILATERAL* is a geometric figure with four sides.
A *RECTANGLE* is a quadrilateral with four right angles. A *SQUARE* is a
rectangle with four equal sides. A *TRAPEZOID* is a quadrilateral with one set
of parallel sides. A *PARALLELOGRAM* is a four-sided figure with two pairs of
parallel sides. A *RHOMBUS* is a parallelogram with sides of equal length.

GEOMETRIC PUZZLES

You are never too old to have fun with simple
shapes. Try your hand at making tangrams! A
tangram is a Chinese puzzle that is made up of
seven pieces that fit together into a square. These
pieces include five triangles, one square, and one
rhomboid. The pieces of a tangram can be put
together in different ways to form all sorts of
shapes, such as animals or people. The object of
the game is to make a certain shape by using all of
the puzzle pieces—no more and no less.

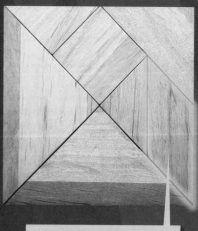

A rhomboid is a special kind of
parallelogram. It has four sides,
but is not a square, a rectangle, or
a rhombus. Think of it as a slanted
rectangle.

COMMON FORMULAS

TO FIND THE AREA OF A TRIANGLE:
Multiply the base of the triangle by the height of the triangle. Divide by 2.

area = (base x height) ÷ 2

EXAMPLE: **area = (6 x 8) ÷ 2, or 24 square units**

TO FIND THE AREA OF A RECTANGLE:
Multiply the base of the rectangle by its height.

area = base x height

EXAMPLE: **area = 6 x 3, or 18 square units**

TO FIND THE AREA OF A SQUARE:
Multiply the length of one side of the square by itself.

area = side x side

EXAMPLE: **area = 4 x 4, or 16 square units**

The **radius** of a circle is the length between the center of the circle and any point on the perimeter of the circle.

TO FIND THE AREA OF A CIRCLE:
Multiply the radius by itself. Then multiply the product by 3.14 (which is also known as π, or **pi**).

area = radius x radius x 3.14
(or area = πr^2)

EXAMPLE: **area = 5 x 5 x 3.14, or 78.5 square units**

The **diameter** of a circle is the length of a straight line beginning on the perimeter of the circle, passing through the center and ending on the perimeter of the circle. The diameter is twice as long as the radius. The **circumference** of a circle is the distance around the entire circle.

TO FIND THE CIRCUMFERENCE OF A CIRCLE:
Multiply the diameter by 3.14.

circumference = diameter x 3.14
(or circumference = diameter x π)

EXAMPLE: **circumference = 10 x 3.14, or 31.4**

EASY AS PI?

The number 3.14, used in some common mathematical formulas (above), is π rounded to two decimal places. Pronounced like *pie*, π is a Greek letter. The actual value of π continues for trillions of digits. Here are the first 50 digits after the decimal point.

3.14159265358979323846264338327950288419716939937510

WHAT IS AN INTEGER?

An integer is a whole number. It can be a positive number or a negative number. The number 0 is also an integer. Decimals, fractions, and percentages are not integers.

Positives and Negatives

When you add, subtract, multiply, and divide whole numbers, certain rules always apply.

- If you multiply two positive numbers, the result will be positive.

- If you divide two positive numbers, the result will be positive.

- If you multiply or divide a positive number and a negative number, the result will be negative.

- If you multiply or divide two negative numbers, the result will be positive.

REMEMBER:
Two negatives cancel each other out.

Evens and Odds

Based on whether numbers are even or odd, you can predict whether their sums and remainders will be even or odd.

Even numbers end in 0, 2, 4, 6, or 8. Odd numbers end in 1, 3, 5, 7, or 9.

When you add and subtract even and odd numbers, other rules apply.

ADDITION	SUBTRACTION
even + even = even	even − even = even
odd + odd = even	odd − odd = even
even + odd = odd	even − odd = odd
	odd − even = odd

MAKING SENSE OF FRACTIONS

Fractions are not integers. They are used to express portions of a whole. In a fraction, the number below the bar is called the denominator. The denominator is the total number of parts that a whole has been divided into.

The number above the bar is called the numerator. The top number is the amount of these parts.

Numerator

1/4

Denominator

EXAMPLE: This circle has been divided into 6 equal parts. One of these parts is red. The other five are blue. This can be expressed in fractions:

$\frac{1}{6}$ of the circle is **red**

$\frac{5}{6}$ of the circle is **blue**

When the numerator is smaller than the denominator, it's a proper fraction.

If the denominator is larger than the numerator, it is an improper fraction. This means the value of the fraction is greater than 1. For example, when 7 parts are green, it could be expressed as: $\frac{7}{6}$ or $1\frac{1}{6}$

Unless the numerator and the denominator are the same, dividing the numerator by the denominator will turn a fraction into a decimal.

EVERYDAY MATH

Ever wonder why you have to memorize multiplication tables or work out those tough long-division problems? Here are just a few times when your mathematical knowledge can come in handy.

- When you need to make a double-size batch of brownies

- After a meal, when it is time to calculate a tip at a restaurant

- Before you buy something, when you must make sure you have enough money for the item you want plus the sales tax

- In order to find the best shopping bargain based on price and quantity

- When you need to know what time it is in a different time zone

- During sporting events, to determine and predict athletes' statistics

- After the pizza delivery person has arrived, and you need to know how much to contribute for each slice you plan to eat

There are also countless jobs that make regular use of arithmetic, algebra, geometry, calculus, statistics, and more. Here are just a few: farmer, architect, accountant, carpenter, geologist, bridge engineer, construction manager, computer programmer, doctor, handyman, meteorologist, and, of course, math teacher.

TIME FOR KIDS GAME

APPLE PICKING TIME!

You will often need to use math in the grocery store and in the kitchen. Show off your skills by answering these delicious questions.

3 medium apples = 1 pound (.5 kg)
1 bushel = 42 pounds (19 kg)

1. About three apples make one pound. How many apples make two pounds?

2. It takes two pounds of apples to make one apple pie. How many pies can you make with six pounds of apples?

3. One bushel of apples weighs 42 pounds (19 kg). How many pounds would five bushels weigh?

BONUS: Apples are measured in bushels. How many apples are in five bushels?

Answers on page 242.

Math and Money

147

HANDLING MONEY

Do you get an allowance? Make money babysitting? Receive checks from your grandparents on your birthday? No matter how much money you have, it is important to budget. When you create a budget, you estimate how much money you will be earning and list how much money you can spend and save. Without a budget, you might go broke!

A bank account helps you keep track of your money while storing it safely. You can add money to your account by making a deposit and take money out with a withdrawal.

With a savings account, you can collect interest. Interest is a small percentage of money that the bank pays you in exchange for letting it hold on to your money. If you put $100 in the bank, after a year you might have $103! It doesn't sound like much, but it can add up over time.

You may also decide to put money in a checking account, which allows you to write checks or use a debit card to pay for purchases or bills instead of using cash.

Using a credit card allows you to buy things now and pay later. But be careful—you will be charged interest for using credit, so you may end up paying a lot more than you bargained for!

THE VALUE OF MONEY

You probably have a clear idea of what you can buy for $1 or $10 or $20. But if you were to travel to a different country, the value of the currency might be totally different. Here are some things you can buy for a dollar around the world.

CANADA:
½ of a tube of toothpaste

BRAZIL:
1/10 of a pizza

BANGLADESH:
⅓ of a sari, which is a dress worn traditionally by Hindu women

KENYA:
8 cups (1.89 L) of milk

PHILIPPINES:
1 pound (.5 kg) of apples, or half of a Big Mac

JAPAN:
10 days of electricity

SOUTH KOREA:
1 bar of soap

RUSSIA:
2.2 pounds (1 kg) of spaghetti

PERU:
1 haircut, plus tip

PAPER TRAIL

Benjamin Franklin just got a makeover. In 2010, the U.S. Bureau of Engraving and Printing unveiled the new $100 bill. It is the highest-denomination note in circulation. The bill can withstand seven years of use.

Here is the new $100 bill. A blue 3-D security ribbon appears on the front, along with a color-changing bell in an inkwell.

The $100,000 gold certificate was printed from 1934 to 1935 but was not released. It features President Woodrow Wilson.

Martha Washington was the only woman to appear on a U.S. currency note. The $1 silver certificate circulated in the late 1800s.

This is one of a series of bills made up of 3¢, 5¢, 10¢, 15¢, 25¢, and 50¢ notes. They were first issued in 1862.

guess what? Paper money in the United States is made of 75% cotton and 25% linen.

going green

In an effort to reduce the amount of shredded money rotting away in landfills, some Federal Reserve banks are recycling old bills. Retired banknotes can be shredded, treated, and used as material in pencils, pens, stationery, roofing tiles, jewelry, and more.

INCOMES AROUND THE WORLD

The average annual income of residents of different countries varies greatly. The average annual income of a person in the United States is $47,240. How does that compare to other countries?

Armenia	$3,100
Australia	$43,770
Bangladesh	$590
Botswana	$6,240
Burundi	$150
Chile	$9,420
China	$3,590
France	$42,680
Indonesia	$2,230
Iran	$4,530
Mexico	$8,920
Niger	$340
South Africa	$5,770
Sweden	$48,930
United Kingdom	$41,520
Vietnam	$1,010

Math and Money

149

Looking Back on Harry Potter

By Vickie An

Daniel Radcliffe spoke to TFK about playing Harry Potter for the past decade.

TFK: How does it feel now that you're done filming?

DANIEL RADCLIFFE: Obviously, toward the end, it was very emotional. We all cried a lot. The first month away was very strange. But I've always said this about Harry Potter: Once you're in, you're never really out. There is some sadness in leaving it, but I'm excited about the future.

TFK: Can you talk about the emotional journey Harry goes through in *Deathly Hallows*?

RADCLIFFE: One of the major themes of *Deathly Hallows*, particularly *Part 1*, is the theme of faith. Harry's faith in Dumbledore is being tested. Dumbledore has died, and he leaves Harry with this mission and almost no information on which to work. As far as his relationship with Ron and Hermione, they gradually realize that Harry has no plan; he's just winging it. As they lose faith in him, he becomes more isolated and desperate.

TFK: Did you take any souvenirs from the set?

RADCLIFFE: I only wanted Harry's glasses. I didn't want the wand. I definitely didn't want the broom. I ended up getting two pairs of the glasses. I have one pair that is lensless. Often the glasses I wear on set are lensless, because there are camera reflections. Those are from the seventh film, and I also got a pair with lenses from the very first film.

TFK: What's your best Harry Potter memory from the past 10 years?

RADCLIFFE: It's not necessarily my favorite memory, but it was one of the moments where I took a step back and thought, "No matter how long I act, I will never get another moment like this again." It was the scene in the sixth film where I burst out of the water in the cave, surrounded by a ring of fire. For the past few years, I've taken for granted that I get to play an action hero. It's rare that actors get to do that. It's a lot of fun, and I'll miss that, certainly.

TFK: What was your favorite experience at the the Wizarding World of Harry Potter theme park in Orlando?

RADCLIFFE: The Dragon Challenge ride is the best part. I rode it five times. It was awesome! I went on the front of the ride; I went on the back; we rode it at night. The Phelps twins [who play Fred and George Weasley in the films] were on the other dragon. We saw our faces steaming towards each other at 60 miles an hour, almost colliding, and then veering away sharply at the last minute. It was great!

TFK: After 10 years, what do you walk away with as an actor and as a person?

RADCLIFFE: I will never be able to watch one scene in any of these films without immediately connecting it to the memory of that day on set or to the memory of what was happening in my life at the time. I walk away with a wealth of experience that many actors would kill for in terms of the people I've worked with and learned from. And I walk away, most importantly, with a love of film, and the most amazing group of friends anyone could wish for. These are people I will know forever, and I feel very lucky.

Emma Watson, Daniel Radcliffe, and Rupert Grint in 2000

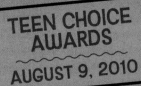

TEEN CHOICE
AWARDS
AUGUST 9, 2010

FILM

SCI-FI: *Avatar*
ACTOR, SCI-FI: Sam Worthington, *Avatar*
ACTRESS, SCI-FI: Zoë Saldana, *Avatar*
ACTION/ADVENTURE: *Sherlock Holmes*
FANTASY: *The Twilight Saga: New Moon*
DRAMA: *The Blind Side*
ACTOR, DRAMA: Robert Pattinson, *Remember Me*
ACTRESS, DRAMA: Sandra Bullock, *The Blind Side*
COMEDY: *Date Night*
ACTOR, COMEDY: Ashton Kutcher, *Killers*
ACTRESS, COMEDY: Tina Fey, *Date Night*
ANIMATED: *Toy Story 3*
ACTOR, ACTION/ADVENTURE: Channing Tatum, *G.I. Joe: The Rise of Cobra*
ACTRESS, ACTION/ADVENTURE: Rachel McAdams, *Sherlock Holmes*
ACTOR, FANTASY: Taylor Lautner, *The Twilight Saga: New Moon*
ACTRESS, FANTASY: Kristen Stewart, *The Twilight Saga: New Moon*
ROMANTIC COMEDY: *Valentine's Day*
ACTOR, ROMANTIC COMEDY: Ashton Kutcher, *Valentine's Day*
ACTRESS, ROMANTIC COMEDY: Sandra Bullock, *The Proposal*
VILLAIN: Rachelle Lefevre, *The Twilight Saga: New Moon*
FIGHT: Mia Wasikowska vs. the Jabberwocky, *Alice in Wonderland*
HISSY FIT: Miley Cyrus, *The Last Song*
DANCE: Sandra Bullock and Betty White, *The Proposal*
CHEMISTRY: Kristen Stewart and Robert Pattinson,
The Twilight Saga: New Moon

Sandra Bullock

Taylor Lautner

TELEVISION

COMEDY: *Glee*
ACTOR, COMEDY: Jonas Brothers, *JONAS*
ACTRESS, COMEDY: Selena Gomez, *Wizards of Waverly Place*
DRAMA: *Gossip Girl*
ACTOR, DRAMA: Chace Crawford, *Gossip Girl*
ACTRESS, DRAMA: Leighton Meester,
Gossip Girl
ACTION: *NCIS: Los Angeles*
ACTOR, ACTION: Zachary Levi, *Chuck*
ACTRESS, ACTION:
Yvonne Strahovski, *Chuck*
REALITY SHOW COMPETITION:
American Idol
PERSONALITY: Ryan Seacrest
PARENTAL UNIT:
Mike O'Malley, *Glee*

Selena Gomez

Zachary Levi and
Yvonne Strahovski

Movies and TV

151

Colin Firth

The King's Speech, starring Colin Firth, Geoffrey Rush, and Helena Bonham Carter, was the big winner of the 83rd Annual Academy Awards. The event, held in the Kodak Theatre in Los Angeles, California, was hosted by actors James Franco and Anne Hathaway.

The King's Speech tells the story of King George VI (played by Firth) who suffers from a speech impediment. The king goes to a speech therapist (played by Rush) in order to overcome his stutter, and the two form an incredible bond. This inspiring tale took home the awards for Best Picture, Best Direction, and Best Original Screenplay. Colin Firth won the Oscar for Best Actor.

Two kids' movies were also honored at the Oscars.

BEST ANIMATED FEATURE FILM	*Toy Story 3*
BEST ORIGINAL SONG	*Toy Story 3*
BEST ART DIRECTION	*Alice in Wonderland*
BEST COSTUME DESIGN	*Alice in Wonderland*

Alice in Wonderland

NICKELODEON KIDS' CHOICE AWARDS
APRIL 2, 2011

TV
FAVORITE TV SHOW: *iCarly*
FAVORITE REALITY SHOW: *American Idol*
FAVORITE CARTOON: *SpongeBob SquarePants*
FAVORITE TV ACTOR: Dylan Sprouse
FAVORITE TV ACTRESS: Selena Gomez
FAVORITE TV SIDEKICK: Jennette McCurdy

Jennette McCurdy

MOVIES
FAVORITE MOVIE: *The Karate Kid*
FAVORITE MOVIE ACTOR: Johnny Depp
FAVORITE MOVIE ACTRESS: Miley Cyrus
FAVORITE ANIMATED MOVIE: *Despicable Me*

Miley Cyrus

PEOPLE'S CHOICE AWARDS
JANUARY 5, 2011

Conan O'Brien

FAVORITE MOVIE: *The Twilight Saga: Eclipse*
FAVORITE MOVIE ACTOR: Johnny Depp
FAVORITE MOVIE ACTRESS: Kristen Stewart
FAVORITE ACTION MOVIE: *Iron Man 2*
FAVORITE ACTION STAR: Jackie Chan
FAVORITE DRAMA MOVIE: *The Twilight Saga: Eclipse*
FAVORITE FAMILY MOVIE: *Toy Story 3*
FAVORITE COMEDIC STAR: Adam Sandler
FAVORITE ONSCREEN TEAM: Robert Pattinson, Kristen Stewart, Taylor Lautner, *The Twilight Saga: Eclipse*
FAVORITE MOVIE STAR UNDER 25: Zac Efron
FAVORITE TV DRAMA: *House*
FAVORITE TV DRAMA ACTOR: Hugh Laurie
FAVORITE TV DRAMA ACTRESS: Lisa Edelstein
FAVORITE TV COMEDY: *Glee*
FAVORITE TV COMEDY ACTOR: Neil Patrick Harris
FAVORITE TV COMEDY ACTRESS: Jane Lynch
FAVORITE TALK SHOW HOST: Conan O'Brien
FAVORITE FAMILY TV MOVIE: *Camp Rock 2: The Final Jam*
FAVORITE NEW TV DRAMA: *Hawaii Five-O*

Robert Pattinson, Kristen Stewart, and Taylor Lautner

Zac Efron

Glee cast members Cory Monteith, Jane Lynch, and Chris Colfer

guess what?
The bestselling DVD on Amazon.com for 2010 was *The Blind Side*, starring Sandra Bullock.

TOP 10 Highest-Grossing Movies in the U.S.

RANK	MOVIE TITLE	YEAR RELEASED	U.S. BOX OFFICE TOTAL
1.	*Avatar*	2009	$760,505,847
2.	*Titanic*	1997	$600,779,824
3.	*The Dark Knight*	2008	$533,316,061
4.	*Star Wars: Episode IV—A New Hope*	1977	$460,935,665
5.	*Shrek 2*	2004	$436,471,036
6.	*E.T.: The Extra-Terrestrial*	1982	$434,949,459
7.	*Star Wars: Episode I—The Phantom Menace*	1999	$431,065,444
8.	*Pirates of the Caribbean: Dead Man's Chest*	2006	$423,032,628
9.	*Toy Story 3*	2010	$414,984,497
10.	*Spider-Man*	2002	$403,706,375

Movies and TV

153

FROM TIME FOR KIDS MAGAZINE

Bieber Fever

By Claire Suddath

Justin Bieber has a warm smile and overgrown hair that he brushes forward into his face. His oversized high-tops are always untied. The singer seems at first like nothing more than the latest in a line of teen idols, such as Britney Spears, Miley Cyrus, and the Jonases. But Bieber is something else entirely: the first real teen idol of the digital age, a star who became famous thanks to the Internet.

THE PATH TO FAME

Bieber didn't arrive through the normal channels. He wasn't a child model; he was never on *Star Search* or the Disney Channel; his parents didn't audition him for commercials. In 2007, he was 12 years old and living in Stratford, Ontario, in Canada, with his mother, Pattie Mallette.

Mallette began posting videos of her son's musical performances on YouTube so that relatives could see him in action: Bieber participating in a local talent show, or singing and playing guitar at home. He covered pop and R&B songs: Matchbox Twenty, Stevie Wonder, Alicia Keys. And he was good. Really good. So good that strangers started watching his videos. Within months, his Internet following numbered in the thousands. Not bad for a middle school student.

Late one night in 2007, Scooter Braun, an Atlanta-based promoter and music manager, was surfing the Internet when he stumbled upon a grainy home video of Bieber belting out "Respect."

"It was such raw talent," Braun said. Two weeks later, he flew Bieber and his mother to Atlanta and became the young singer's manager.

BUILDING A FAN BASE

Braun and Bieber spent the next six months building a fan base. Bieber would post new songs on YouTube, respond to messages from fans, and interact with them. Even now, with more than 5 million Twitter followers, he frequently responds to fans' questions and retweets their greetings. "I also try to read all of my fan mail," he said.

Among other artists, word of Bieber's talent quickly spread. Justin Timberlake wanted to work with him. So did Usher. "He sang and played the guitar for me, and I was like, wow, this kid has even more talent than I did at that age," said Usher. The R&B star struck a business deal with Braun; a record contract soon followed.

By the time Bieber released his first, seven-song album, *My World*, in November 2009, he had 50 million YouTube subscribers and was one of the most discussed topics on Twitter. Bieber is simply grateful for what's already happened. "I feel like I just won the lotto," he said.

THE AMERICAN MUSIC AWARDS

FAVORITE SOUL/R&B ALBUM: Usher, *Raymond v. Raymond*

FAVORITE POP ROCK BAND/DUO/GROUP: The Black Eyed Peas

FAVORITE COUNTRY FEMALE ARTIST: Taylor Swift

FAVORITE LATIN MUSIC ARTIST: Shakira

FAVORITE SOUL/R&B FEMALE ARTIST: Rihanna

FAVORITE COUNTRY MALE ARTIST: Brad Paisley

FAVORITE BREAKTHROUGH ARTIST: Justin Bieber

The Black Eyed Peas

FAVORITE POP/ROCK MALE ARTIST: Justin Bieber

FAVORITE COUNTRY BAND/DUO/GROUP: Lady Antebellum

FAVORITE ALTERNATIVE ROCK MUSIC ARTIST: Muse

FAVORITE ADULT CONTEMPORARY MUSIC ARTIST: Michael Bublé

FAVORITE SOUL/R&B MALE ARTIST: Usher

Michael Bublé

FAVORITE ARTIST OF THE YEAR: Justin Bieber

FAVORITE COUNTRY ALBUM: Carrie Underwood, *Play On*

FAVORITE RAP/HIP-HOP MALE ARTIST: Eminem

FAVORITE POP/ROCK ALBUM: Justin Bieber, *My World 2.0*

FAVORITE POP/ROCK FEMALE ARTIST: Lady Gaga

FAVORITE CONTEMPORARY INSPIRATIONAL ARTIST: MercyMe

FAVORITE RAP/HIP-HOP ALBUM: Eminem, *Recovery*

FAVORITE SOUNDTRACK ALBUM: *Glee: The Music, Volume 3 Showstoppers*

Rihanna

Guess what? Eminem began rapping in Detroit clubs when he was only 14 years old.

NICKELODEON KIDS' CHOICE AWARDS

FAVORITE MUSIC GROUP: The Black Eyed Peas

FAVORITE FEMALE SINGER: Katy Perry

FAVORITE MALE SINGER: Justin Bieber

FAVORITE SONG: "Baby," Justin Bieber featuring Ludacris

Music

TEEN CHOICE AWARDS

FEMALE ARTIST: Lady Gaga

MALE ARTIST: Justin Bieber

GROUP: Selena Gomez & The Scene

ALBUM, COUNTRY: *Fearless,* Taylor Swift

ALBUM, RAP: *Relapse,* Eminem

ALBUM, ROCK: *Brand New Eyes,* Paramore

ALBUM, POP: *My World 2.0,* Justin Bieber

ALBUM, R&B: *Jason Derülo,* Jason Derülo

ROCK TRACK: "Ignorance," Paramore

Jason Derülo

R&B TRACK: "OMG," Usher

Usher

RAP/HIP-HOP TRACK: "Love The Way You Lie," Eminem featuring Rihanna

LOVE SONG: "When I Look At You," Miley Cyrus

Katy Perry

HOOK UP: "Airplanes," B.o.B featuring Hayley Williams

Justin Bieber

SINGLE: "California Gurls," Katy Perry

ROCK GROUP: Paramore

BREAKOUT ARTIST, MALE: Justin Bieber

BREAKOUT ARTIST, FEMALE: Selena Gomez & The Scene

RAP ARTIST: Eminem

R&B ARTIST: Beyoncé

COUNTRY GROUP: Lady Antebellum

MALE COUNTRY ARTIST: Keith Urban

FEMALE COUNTRY ARTIST: Taylor Swift

COUNTRY SONG: "Fifteen," Taylor Swift

Taylor Swift

guess what? Taylor Swift's grandmother was a professional opera singer.

156

MTV VIDEO MUSIC AWARDS

Florence + The Machine

VIDEO OF THE YEAR: "Bad Romance," Lady Gaga

BEST NEW ARTIST: Justin Bieber

BEST HIP HOP: "Not Afraid," Eminem

BEST POP: "Bad Romance," Lady Gaga

BEST MALE VIDEO: "Not Afraid," Eminem

BEST ROCK: "Kings and Queens," 30 Seconds to Mars

BEST FEMALE VIDEO: "Bad Romance," Lady Gaga

BEST DANCE MUSIC VIDEO: "Bad Romance," Lady Gaga

BEST COLLABORATION: "Video Phone (Extended Remix)," Lady Gaga featuring Beyoncé

BEST CINEMATOGRAPHY: "Empire State of Mind," Jay-Z and Alicia Keys

BEST ART DIRECTION: "Dog Days Are Over," Florence + The Machine

BEST CHOREOGRAPHY: "Bad Romance," Lady Gaga

Lady Gaga

BEST DIRECTION: "Bad Romance," Lady Gaga

BEST EDITING: "Bad Romance," Lady Gaga

Broadway Royalty

By Sarah Horbacewicz

Ever wonder what it's like to be in a Broadway show? For many actors, performing in a top show in New York City is a career highlight. It's hard to make it on Broadway. It's even more difficult if you're a kid.

Alphonso Jones II was 10, in 2009, when he landed the part of young Simba in *The Lion King.* Alphonso tried out for Simba when he was 8. He didn't get the part until two years later. At the auditions,

Alphonso sang "I Just Can't Wait to Be King." "I was a bit nervous when I first started," he admits. "But it got easier."

Now, he performs in four shows each week. Another actor shares his role. It is a great opportunity, but it's also a great deal of work. Alphonso sings, dances, and acts. But he still has to do homework. Before arriving at the theater for the weekday evening shows, Alphonso attends a full day of school.

He has to be at the theater before 6:00 p.m. The play doesn't start until 7:00 or 8:00 p.m., but it takes time to get ready. After hair and makeup, it's showtime!

Alphonso Jones II

Music

FROM TIME FOR KIDS MAGAZINE

157

GRAMMY AWARDS FEBRUARY 13, 2011

RECORD OF THE YEAR: *Need You Now,* Lady Antebellum

ALBUM OF THE YEAR: *The Suburbs,* Arcade Fire

SONG OF THE YEAR: "Need You Now," Lady Antebellum

BEST NEW ARTIST: Esperanza Spalding

BEST FEMALE POP VOCAL PERFORMANCE: "Bad Romance," Lady Gaga

Esperanza Spalding

BEST MALE POP VOCAL PERFORMANCE: "Just the Way You Are," Bruno Mars

BEST POP PERFORMANCE BY A DUO OR GROUP: "Hey, Soul Sister" (Live), Train

BEST POP VOCAL ALBUM: *The Fame Monster,* Lady Gaga

BEST TRADITIONAL POP VOCAL ALBUM: *Crazy Love,* Michael Bublé

BEST SOLO ROCK VOCAL PERFORMANCE: "Helter Skelter," Paul McCartney

BEST ROCK SONG: "Angry World," Neil Young

BEST ROCK ALBUM: *The Resistance,* Muse

BEST R&B SONG: "Shine," John Legend & The Roots

BEST CONTEMPORARY R&B ALBUM: *Raymond v. Raymond,* Usher

Bruno Mars

BEST RAP SONG: "Empire State of Mind," Jay-Z and Alicia Keys

BEST FEMALE COUNTRY VOCAL PERFORMANCE: "The House That Built Me," Miranda Lambert

BEST MALE COUNTRY VOCAL PERFORMANCE: "'Til Summer Comes Around," Keith Urban

BEST COUNTRY SONG: "Need You Now," Lady Antebellum

BEST COUNTRY ALBUM: *Need You Now,* Lady Antebellum

BEST MUSICAL SHOW ALBUM: *American Idiot* (Featuring Green Day)

Guess what?
Lady Gaga's real name is Stefani Joanne Angelina Germanotta.

Lady Antebellum

158

TOP 5 MUSICAL INSTRUMENTS

Strike up the band! Americans buy more musical instruments than anyone else in the world. Here are the top sellers.

1. FRETTED INSTRUMENTS (GUITARS, BANJOS, ETC.) $1.4 billion per year
Fretted instruments have strings stretched across a neck, which are plucked to play notes and chords. The strings cross over raised parts (frets) on the neck, which act as a guide to help musicians to play in tune.

2. PIANOS (INCLUDING ELECTRONIC KEYBOARDS) $1.1 billion per year
A traditional piano has 88 keys. When keys are pushed down, they cause soft hammers to strike specific strings in the back, which produces the sound.

3. PERCUSSION (DRUMS, ETC.) $572.6 million per year
Hit it, shake it, scrape it, bang it, clang it. These are some of the many ways in which musicians use percussion instruments to keep rhythm, make unique sounds, or add effects to a musical piece.

4. WIND INSTRUMENTS (HORNS, FLUTES, OBOES, ETC.) $470.3 million per year
With wind instruments, you use your breath to make a sound. They are made from either wood or metals. Wood instruments need a thin piece of wood, or reed, to play a note.

5. STRINGED INSTRUMENTS (VIOLINS, CELLOS, ETC.) $68.4 million per year
Most stringed instruments have the same basic shape, but the differences in their size create the differences in their sound. For most of these instruments, a horsehair bow is drawn across the strings to create sound. For a harp, strings are plucked.

MYSTERY PERSON?

guess what? A harmonica is made from reeds. There are two rows of holes, each containing two reeds. A sound is produced when the player blows out or sucks in air through the holes.

I was born in 1756, in Salzburg, Austria, to a musical family. By age 5, I was composing my own pieces. At 7, I was performing across Europe. In my short lifetime, I wrote more than 600 works, including symphonies and operas. Among my best-known operas are *The Magic Flute* and *The Marriage of Figaro*.

WHO AM I? _____

Answer on page 242.

Music

159

JFK's Life of Service

By Nellie Gonzalez Cutler

Crowds lined the streets of Dallas, Texas, hoping to catch a glimpse of the youthful President and his popular young wife. The couple smiled and waved from the backseat of an open convertible. Suddenly, shots rang out. The President slumped over. His car raced to Parkland Memorial Hospital, where, at 1:00 p.m. on November 22, 1963, he was pronounced dead.

John Fitzgerald Kennedy (JFK) was 46 years old. He served as President for only 1,037 days. In that short time, he changed the way Americans viewed themselves and the world.

President Kennedy's children, John Jr. and Caroline, visit the Oval Office.

THE WAR HERO

JFK was born into a wealthy Irish-American family. His father, Joseph P. Kennedy, expected his children to excel at school and sports. "You can go a long way," he once wrote to his son.

After graduating from college, JFK joined the Navy. During World War II, he commanded a small patrol boat in the South Pacific. His job was to search for enemy ships. One night, a Japanese warship rammed his boat. Despite serious injuries, Kennedy swam through dangerous waters to lead his men to safety. He was awarded the Navy and Marine Corps Medal for his bravery.

A CHALLENGE TO AMERICANS

Kennedy often said he wanted to be remembered for keeping the peace during difficult times. He pushed for equality for all Americans, asking Congress to pass a civil-rights bill. "This nation, for all its boasts, will not be fully free until all its citizens are free," he said in a televised speech. He promoted understanding around the world, establishing the Peace Corps. Since its founding, more than 200,000 volunteers have served in 139 countries. President Kennedy also encouraged space exploration.

"Ask not what your country can do for you; ask what you can do for your country," JFK said on the day he took office. His words still inspire people to serve others. His daughter, Caroline Kennedy, wrote that the commitment to public service is one of her father's greatest legacies.

Kennedy delivering the famous 1961 speech in which he vowed to put an American on the moon before the end of the decade.

PRESIDENTIAL SHAKE-UPS

If a U.S. President dies while in office, becomes too ill to continue serving, or is removed from office for any other reason, the Vice President is next in line to lead the country. In the history of the United States, this has happened nine times.

Who's Next in Line?

This list shows the order of people who would take over if a sitting President died, resigned, or was removed from office.

1. Vice President
2. Speaker of the House
3. President Pro Tempore of the Senate
4. Secretary of State
5. Secretary of the Treasury
6. Secretary of Defense
7. Attorney General
8. Secretary of the Interior
9. Secretary of Agriculture
10. Secretary of Commerce
11. Secretary of Labor
12. Secretary of Health and Human Services
13. Secretary of Housing and Urban Development
14. Secretary of Transportation
15. Secretary of Energy
16. Secretary of Education
17. Secretary of Veterans Affairs
18. Secretary of Homeland Security

DEATH OF A PRESIDENT

Four U.S. Presidents have died of natural causes while in office.

• In 1841, **William Henry Harrison** died after only 32 days in office. John Tyler took over.

• Zachary Taylor passed away in 1850, so Millard Fillmore became President.

• After Warren Harding had a heart attack in 1923, Calvin Coolidge took the top job.

• While serving his fourth term in office, Franklin Roosevelt suffered a stroke and died. Harry Truman became President in 1945.

IMPEACHMENT

If the members of the House of Representatives vote to **impeach** a President, or formally charge him of wrongdoing, then the President must stand trial before the Senate. Two-thirds of all senators must agree in order to convict an official. Only one President has left office after being impeached.

• In 1974, Richard Nixon was impeached for the role he played in covering up a break-in known as the Watergate burglary. He resigned and left office. **Gerald Ford** became President and later pardoned Nixon in an effort to get the country to move on.

ASSASSINATION

Four U.S. Presidents have been assassinated, or killed, while in office.

• In 1865, John Wilkes Booth shot and killed Abraham Lincoln. Andrew Johnson was later sworn in.

• Charles Guiteau shot James Garfield in 1881. Vice President Chester Arthur became President.

• Theodore Roosevelt became President after **William McKinley** was shot by Leon Czolgosz during the Buffalo Pan-American Exposition in 1901.

• Lyndon Johnson was sworn in as President aboard Air Force One after John F. Kennedy's death. Kennedy was assassinated by Lee Harvey Oswald while riding in a motorcade in Dallas, Texas, in 1963.

Presidents

161

U.S. PRESIDENTS IN ORDER

GEORGE WASHINGTON 1

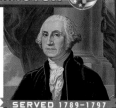

Born: February 22, 1732, in Virginia **Died:** December 14, 1799
Political Party: None (first term), Federalist (second term)
Vice President: John Adams   **First Lady:** Martha Dandridge Custis

guess what? *At the time of his presidency, George Washington had only one tooth. He wore dentures, which were made from such things as gold, ivory, lead, animal teeth, and even human teeth, but never from wood.*

SERVED 1789–1797

2 JOHN ADAMS

Born: October 30, 1735, in Massachusetts **Died:** July 4, 1826
Political Party: Federalist
Vice President: Thomas Jefferson   **First Lady:** Abigail Smith

guess what? *The United States capital was moved from Philadelphia to Washington, D.C., during John Adams's presidency.*

SERVED 1797–1801

THOMAS JEFFERSON 3

Born: April 13, 1743, in Virginia **Died:** July 4, 1826
Political Party: Democratic-Republican
Vice Presidents: Aaron Burr, George Clinton
First Lady: Martha Wayles Skelton

guess what? *Thomas Jefferson was a keen inventor. Some of his inventions include a macaroni-making machine and a spherical sundial, a round object that uses shadows to tell time during the day.*

SERVED 1801–1809

4 JAMES MADISON

Born: March 16, 1751, in Virginia **Died:** June 28, 1836
Political Party: Democratic-Republican
Vice Presidents: George Clinton, Elbridge Gerry
First Lady: Dorothy "Dolley" Payne Todd

guess what? *At 5 feet 4 inches (163 cm) tall, James Madison was the shortest President. He weighed less than 100 pounds (45 kg).*

SERVED 1809–1817

JAMES MONROE 5

Born: April 28, 1758, in Virginia **Died:** July 4, 1831
Political Party: Democratic-Republican
Vice President: Daniel D. Tompkins   **First Lady:** Elizabeth "Eliza" Kortright

guess what? *In 1817, James Monroe became the first President to ride on a steamboat.*

SERVED 1817–1825

6 JOHN QUINCY ADAMS

Born: July 11, 1767, in Massachusetts **Died:** February 23, 1848
Political Party: Democratic-Republican
Vice President: John C. Calhoun   **First Lady:** Louisa Catherine Johnson

guess what? *John Quincy Adams had a pet alligator, which he kept in the East Room of the White House.*

SERVED 1825–1829

162

ANDREW JACKSON 7

Born: March 15, 1767, in South Carolina **Died:** June 8, 1845
Political Party: Democratic
Vice Presidents: John C. Calhoun, Martin Van Buren
First Lady: Rachel Donelson Robards

guess what? *The U.S. government paid off the country's debts during the presidency of Andrew Jackson. He is the only President to serve in a debt-free United States.*

SERVED 1829–1837

8 MARTIN VAN BUREN

SERVED 1837–1841

Born: December 5, 1782, in New York **Died:** July 24, 1862
Political Party: Democratic
Vice President: Richard M. Johnson **First Lady:** Hannah Hoes

guess what? *Martin Van Buren was the first U.S. President to be born a citizen of the United States. The others were former British subjects.*

WILLIAM HENRY HARRISON 9

Born: February 9, 1773, in Virginia **Died:** April 4, 1841
Political Party: Whig
Vice President: John Tyler **First Lady:** Anna Tuthill Symmes

guess what? *William Henry Harrison is the only President who studied to become a doctor.*

SERVED 1841

10 JOHN TYLER

SERVED 1841–1845

Born: March 29, 1790, in Virginia **Died:** January 18, 1862
Political Party: Whig
Vice President: None **First Ladies:** Letitia Christian (d. 1842), Julia Gardiner

guess what? *John Tyler had more children than any other President. He had seven girls and eight boys for a total of 15 kids!*

JAMES K. POLK 11

Born: November 2, 1795, in North Carolina **Died:** June 15, 1849
Political Party: Democratic
Vice President: George M. Dallas **First Lady:** Sarah Childress

guess what? *James Polk admired Andrew Jackson. Polk was known as "Young Hickory," which was similar to Jackson's nickname, "Old Hickory."*

SERVED 1845–1849

12 ZACHARY TAYLOR

SERVED 1849–1850

Born: November 24, 1784, in Virginia **Died:** July 9, 1850
Political Party: Whig
Vice President: Millard Fillmore **First Lady:** Margaret Mackall Smith

guess what? *Zachary Taylor did not vote until he was 62 years old.*

MILLARD FILLMORE 13

Born: January 7, 1800, in New York Died: March 8, 1874
Political Party: Whig
Vice President: None First Lady: Abigail Powers (d. 1853)

guess what? *Although Millard Fillmore served as Zachary Taylor's Vice President, the pair did not meet until after they were elected.*

SERVED 1850–1853

14 FRANKLIN PIERCE

SERVED 1853–1857

Born: November 23, 1804, in New Hampshire Died: October 8, 1869
Political Party: Democratic
Vice President: William R. King First Lady: Jane Means Appleton

guess what? *Franklin Pierce gave his inaugural address completely from memory—all 3,329 words of it!*

JAMES BUCHANAN 15

Born: April 23, 1791, in Pennsylvania Died: June 1, 1868
Political Party: Democratic
Vice President: John C. Breckinridge First Lady: None

guess what? *James Buchanan often angled his head to one side because one of his eyes was near-sighted and the other was far-sighted.*

SERVED 1857–1861

16 ABRAHAM LINCOLN

Born: February 12, 1809, in Kentucky Died: April 15, 1865
Political Party: Republican
Vice Presidents: Hannibal Hamlin, Andrew Johnson First Lady: Mary Todd

guess what? *Abraham Lincoln was watching a play called* Our American Cousin *at Ford's Theater when he was assassinated in 1865.*

SERVED 1861–1865

ANDREW JOHNSON 17

Born: December 29, 1808, in North Carolina Died: July 31, 1875
Political Parties: Union, Democratic
Vice President: None First Lady: Eliza McCardle

guess what? *Before entering politics, Andrew Johnson was a tailor. As President, he only wore suits that he custom-tailored.*

SERVED 1865–1869

18 ULYSSES S. GRANT

Born: April 27, 1822, in Ohio Died: July 23, 1885
Political Party: Republican
Vice Presidents: Schuyler Colfax, Henry Wilson First Lady: Julia Boggs Dent

guess what? *Ulysses S. Grant's Inauguration Day in 1873 was the coldest March 4th on record. The inaugural ball ended early after the food froze and the guests, who kept their hats and overcoats on in the unheated celebration building, went home to warm up.*

SERVED 1869–1877

164

RUTHERFORD B. HAYES 19

Born: October 4, 1822, in Ohio **Died:** January 17, 1893
Political Party: Republican
Vice President: William A. Wheeler **First Lady:** Lucy Ware Webb

guess what? *In Rutherford B. Hayes's campaign, he promised not to run for reelection—and he didn't.*

SERVED 1877–1881

20 JAMES A. GARFIELD

Born: November 19, 1831, in Ohio **Died:** September 19, 1881
Political Party: Republican
Vice President: Chester A. Arthur **First Lady:** Lucretia Rudolph

guess what? *James A. Garfield could write with both hands. Occasionally, he would entertain people by writing in Latin with one hand and in Greek with the other—at the same time!*

SERVED 1881

CHESTER A. ARTHUR 21

Born: October 5, 1829, in Vermont **Died:** November 18, 1886
Political Party: Republican
Vice President: None **First Lady:** Ellen Lewis Herndon

guess what? *Chester Arthur liked to change his pants several times a day. It is said that he owned about 80 pairs.*

SERVED 1881–1885

22 GROVER CLEVELAND

Born: March 18, 1837, in New Jersey **Died:** June 24, 1908
Political Party: Democratic
Vice President: Thomas A. Hendricks **First Lady:** Frances Folsom

guess what? *Before becoming the mayor of Buffalo, New York, Grover Cleveland was sheriff of Erie County, New York. He also served as the public executioner.*

SERVED 1885–1889

BENJAMIN HARRISON 23

Born: August 20, 1833, in Ohio **Died:** March 13, 1901
Political Party: Republican
Vice President: Levi P. Morton **First Lady:** Caroline Lavina Scott (d. 1892)

guess what? *Benjamin Harrison had the White House wired for electricity, but he wouldn't touch the light switches because he was afraid of being shocked.*

SERVED 1889–1893

24 GROVER CLEVELAND

Born: March 18, 1837, in New Jersey **Died:** June 24, 1908
Political Party: Democratic
Vice President: Adlai E. Stevenson **First Lady:** Frances Folsom

guess what? *Grover Cleveland's parents named him Stephen Grover Cleveland. As a child, he decided he preferred to be called by his middle name.*

SERVED 1893–1897

Presidents

165

WILLIAM McKINLEY 25

Born: January 29, 1843, in Ohio Died: September 14, 1901
Political Party: Republican
Vice Presidents: Garret A. Hobart, Theodore Roosevelt
First Lady: Ida Saxton

guess what? *William McKinley's picture was on the $500 bill.*

SERVED 1897–1901

26 THEODORE ROOSEVELT

Born: October 27, 1858, in New York Died: January 6, 1919
Political Party: Republican
Vice President: Charles W. Fairbanks First Lady: Edith Kermit Carow

guess what? *Theodore Roosevelt was awarded a Nobel Peace Prize in 1906 for his work on the Treaty of Portsmouth, which ended the Russo-Japanese War.*

SERVED 1901–1909

WILLIAM H. TAFT 27

Born: September 15, 1857, in Ohio Died: March 8, 1930
Political Party: Republican
Vice President: James S. Sherman First Lady: Helen Herron

guess what? *According to popular legend, the tradition of the seventh-inning stretch began when William Taft stood up during a baseball game. As a sign of respect, the rest of the crowd rose. When Taft sat back down, everyone else returned to their seats, too.*

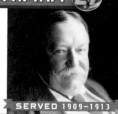

SERVED 1909–1913

28 WOODROW WILSON

Born: December 28, 1856, in Virginia Died: February 3, 1924
Political Party: Democratic
Vice President: Thomas R. Marshall
First Ladies: Ellen Louise Axson (d. 1914), Edith Bolling Galt

guess what? *Woodrow Wilson is the only President to be buried in Washington, D.C. Visitors can pay their respects at the Washington National Cathedral.*

SERVED 1913–1921

WARREN G. HARDING 29

Born: November 2, 1865, in Ohio Died: August 2, 1923
Political Party: Republican
Vice President: Calvin Coolidge First Lady: Florence Kling

guess what? *Warren G. Harding was the first President to give a speech on the radio.*

SERVED 1921–1923

30 CALVIN COOLIDGE

Born: July 4, 1872, in Vermont Died: January 5, 1933
Political Party: Republican
Vice President: Charles G. Dawes First Lady: Grace Anna Goodhue

guess what? *Calvin Coolidge was vacationing in Vermont when President Harding died. Coolidge was sworn into office by his father, a notary public, before returning to Washington.*

SERVED 1923–1929

166

HERBERT C. HOOVER 31

Born: August 10, 1874, in Iowa **Died:** October 20, 1964
Political Party: Republican
Vice President: Charles Curtis   **First Lady:** Lou Henry

guess what? *Herbert Hoover was one of two Presidents who donated his salary to charity. (The other was John F. Kennedy.)*

SERVED 1929–1933

32 FRANKLIN D. ROOSEVELT

Born: January 30, 1882, in New York **Died:** April 12, 1945
Political Party: Democratic
Vice Presidents: John Garner, Henry Wallace, Harry S Truman
First Lady: Anna Eleanor Roosevelt

guess what? *Franklin Roosevelt was the first President to appear on television.*

SERVED 1933–1945

HARRY S TRUMAN 33

Born: May 8, 1884, in Missouri **Died:** December 26, 1972
Political Party: Democratic
Vice President: Alben W. Barkley
First Lady: Elizabeth "Bess" Virginia Wallace

guess what? *Many newspapers wrongly declared Harry Truman's opponent, Thomas Dewey, the winner of the 1948 election.*

SERVED 1945–1953

34 DWIGHT D. EISENHOWER

Born: October 14, 1890, in Texas **Died:** March 28, 1969
Political Party: Republican
Vice President: Richard M. Nixon   **First Lady:** Mamie Geneva Doud

guess what? *Dwight Eisenhower was a skilled cook. He was well known for his vegetable soup, steaks, and cornmeal pancakes.*

SERVED 1953–1961

JOHN F. KENNEDY 35

Born: May 29, 1917, in Massachusetts **Died:** November 22, 1963
Political Party: Democratic
Vice President: Lyndon B. Johnson   **First Lady:** Jacqueline Lee Bouvier

guess what? *John F. Kennedy is one of two Presidents buried in Arlington National Cemetery. The other is William Taft.*

SERVED 1961–1963

36 LYNDON B. JOHNSON

Born: August 27, 1908, in Texas **Died:** January 22, 1973
Political Party: Democratic
Vice President: Hubert H. Humphrey
First Lady: Claudia Alta "Lady Bird" Taylor

guess what? *Lyndon B. Johnson was sworn in aboard Air Force One, the President's official plane, after the assassination of President Kennedy.*

SERVED 1963–1969

Presidents

RICHARD M. NIXON 37

Born: January 9, 1913, in California **Died:** April 22, 1994
Political Party: Republican
Vice Presidents: Spiro T. Agnew, Gerald R. Ford
First Lady: Thelma Catherine "Pat" Ryan

guess what? *Richard Nixon was impeached and left the presidency in disgrace. Later, he wrote several books, including* The Real War, Seize the Moment: America's Challenge in a One-Superpower World, *and* Beyond Peace.

SERVED 1969–1974

38 GERALD R. FORD

Born: July 14, 1913, in Nebraska **Died:** December 26, 2006
Political Party: Republican
Vice President: Nelson A. Rockefeller
First Lady: Elizabeth "Betty" Anne Bloomer Warren

guess what? *Both Gerald Ford and his wife, Betty, were models before they were married.*

SERVED 1974–1977

JIMMY CARTER 39

Born: October 1, 1924, in Georgia
Political Party: Democratic
Vice President: Walter F. Mondale **First Lady:** Rosalynn Smith

guess what? *Jimmy Carter was once a peanut farmer.*

SERVED 1977–1981

40 RONALD REAGAN

Born: February 6, 1911, in Illinois **Died:** June 5, 2004
Political Party: Republican
Vice President: George H.W. Bush **First Lady:** Nancy Davis

guess what? *Ronald Reagan loved jellybeans, particularly Jelly Belly® candies. The blueberry-flavored Jelly Belly was developed specifically for him so that he could serve red, white, and blue sweets at his Inauguration parties.*

SERVED 1981–1989

GEORGE H.W. BUSH 41

Born: June 12, 1924, in Massachusetts
Political Party: Republican
Vice President: J. Danforth Quayle **First Lady:** Barbara Pierce

guess what? *In 1943, days before he turned 19, George H. W. Bush became a Navy pilot. At the time, he was the youngest pilot in the U.S. Navy.*

SERVED 1989–1993

42 BILL CLINTON

Born: August 19, 1946, in Arkansas
Political Party: Democratic
Vice President: Albert Gore Jr. **First Lady:** Hillary Rodham

guess what? *Bill Clinton was nicknamed Bubba as a child.*

SERVED 1993–2001

168

GEORGE W. BUSH 43

Born: July 6, 1946, in Connecticut
Political Party: Republican
Vice President: Richard B. "Dick" Cheney **First Lady:** Laura Welch

guess what? *George W. Bush was part-owner of the Texas Rangers baseball team.*

SERVED 2001–2009

44 BARACK OBAMA

Born: August 4, 1961, in Hawaii
Political Party: Democratic
Vice President: Joe Biden
First Lady: Michelle Robinson

guess what? *Barack Obama collects Spider-Man and Conan the Barbarian comic books.*

To find out what the President does each day, check out *TIME FOR KIDS President Obama: A Day in the Life of America's Leader.*

SERVED 2009–

MYSTERY PERSON

I was born in 1890 in Denison, Texas. I was in the U.S. military for 41 years and earned the high rank of five-star general. I became the 34th President of the United States in 1953 and served two terms. In 1954, I signed a bill that made November 11 Veterans Day, a national salute to former members of the military.

WHO AM I? _____

Answer on page 242.

THE STATE OF THE UNION ADDRESS

Once a year, the President is expected to deliver an important speech before both houses of Congress. In non-election years, this is known as the State of the Union address. Traditionally delivered in January, the speech will include the President's thoughts on how the country is doing and goals for the future. In addition to members of Congress, most members of the Cabinet and the Supreme Court attend, as well as newsworthy guests.

guess what?

The first—and shortest—presidential message to Congress lasted six minutes. Now, they are about one hour long. Bill Clinton gave the longest State of the Union address. His 2000 speech lasted for 1 hour, 28 minutes, 49 seconds.

Presidents

169

Science

Branches of Science

Science is the field of knowledge that systematically studies and organizes information, and draws conclusions based on measurable results. Traditionally, scientists have classified their fields into three branches: physical sciences, Earth sciences, and life sciences. Social sciences, technology, and mathematics may also be included. Each branch has many smaller branches of study; some are described here.

Botanist

LIFE SCIENCES

These sciences explore the nature of living things. **Biology** covers how living things evolve, reproduce, thrive, and relate to one another. It is further divided into many branches, including **botany**, which focuses on plants; **zoology**, which deals with animals; and **microbiology**, which zeroes in on microscopic organisms.

guess what? Entomologists (en-ta-*mal*-oh-jists) are zoologists who study insects. Some entomologists dicovered that you can estimate the temperature outside based on cricket chirps. Here's one way to approximate degrees Fahrenheit: count the number of cricket chirps in a 14-second period and add 40.

PHYSICAL SCIENCES

These sciences study the properties of energy and matter, as well as their relationship to one another. **Physics** seeks to explain how the universe behaves through the workings of matter, energy, force, and time. **Chemistry** is the study of chemical elements and how they interact on an atomic level. **Astronomy** is the study of space, its galaxies, and all objects beyond Earth's atmosphere.

Astronomer

EARTH SCIENCES

These sciences focus on the Earth and its composition and structure. **Geology** is the study of Earth's rock formations. **Geography** concerns the study and mapping of Earth's terrain. **Oceanography** focuses on Earth's oceans, and their currents and habitats. **Meteorology** is the study of weather. **Paleontology** focuses on the remains of ancient plants and animals.

guess what? A dendrochronologist (den-dro-kra-*nal*-oh-jist) is a type of paleontologist who studies tree rings. He or she can look at the rings visible on a cross-section of a tree's trunk and determine the age of the tree. Each ring represents one year of the tree's life. Wide rings indicate mostly wet weather, and narrow rings indicate dry seasons.

Geologist

SOCIAL SCIENCES

These sciences investigate how humans behave and live together. **Psychology** explores individual human behavior, and **sociology** analyzes group behavior. **Anthropology** is the study of human physical traits, as well as cultures and languages. **Archaeology** is a branch of anthropology in which scientists learn about the past by looking at the objects people left behind. **Economics** is the study of how money, goods, and businesses affect society. **Law** focuses on the rules of society, and **political science** examines governmental processes and institutions.

Archaeologists

guess what? Some anthropologists study hieroglyphics, a form of writing used by ancient Egyptians. Instead of letters, hieroglyphics are made up of pictures or symbols.

Computer scientist

TECHNOLOGY

This branch is about the practical application of scientific knowledge. **Engineering** is concerned with the design and construction of objects, machines, and systems. **Biotechnology** is the application of biological processes to create medicines and vaccines, and to alter food and crops. **Computer science** focuses on meeting industrial and research needs by creating computers and developing new software.

MATHEMATICS

This science differs from other branches because it deals with concepts rather than physical evidence. Its focus is on measuring numeric relationships, analyzing data, and predicting outcomes. **Arithmetic** uses only numbers to solve problems, while **algebra** uses both numbers and unknown variables in the form of letters. **Geometry** is the study of two- and three-dimensional shapes. **Calculus** involves the computation of problems that contain constantly changing measurements. Nearly all scientists use mathematics in their research.

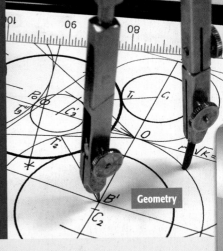
Geometry

Science

171

What Is Ecology?

Ecology is the scientific study of plants and animals in their natural environments. Our environment is constantly changing, and ecologists examine the effects of growing populations, rising temperatures, forest fires, construction projects, and other factors on the plants and animals in a particular habitat. These scientists also study the impact of human activities on nature and identify the lasting effects we have on the environment. Because ecology deals with so many areas of science, ecologists need to know a great deal about biology. They often also need to know about weather patterns and bodies of water, types of soil, different rocks and minerals, and other topics in life and Earth science.

Rocks and Minerals

Minerals are naturally occurring substances found on Earth. They can be found in dirt or water. They are solid chemicals that often form into crystals. Some minerals are made from a single element, like gold, copper, or nickel, but most are a combination of elements. Gemstones like diamonds, rubies, and sapphires are minerals that are cut and polished to be used in fancy jewelry.

Rocks are made up of combinations of minerals, and belong to one of three categories: sedimentary, igneous, or metamorphic.

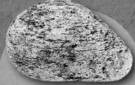

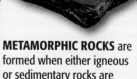

SEDIMENTARY ROCKS are made from bits of larger rocks, other pieces of earth, and even seashells, that get washed into rivers, lakes, and oceans. These particles settle under the water, and more and more pieces of earth are piled on top of them. Over extremely long periods of time, these fragments harden into rock. Limestone and sandstone are examples of sedimentary rocks.

IGNEOUS ROCKS are made from molten magma. This burning-hot substance, found deep inside Earth, cools and hardens once it reaches the air. Granite and basalt are common igneous rocks.

METAMORPHIC ROCKS are formed when either igneous or sedimentary rocks are subject to so much heat or pressure underground that they change form. Marble and slate are both well-known metamorphic rocks.

Molten rock gushing from a volcano

172

Botany and Trees

Botany is the study of plants, from moss and ferns to flowers and giant redwood trees. The Greek philosopher Aristotle developed a system for categorizing plants more than 2,000 years ago, and we now know of more than 400,000 different species of plants on Earth. Plants and trees can offer animals shade from the hot sun, provide nutrition for humans and animals, supply people with sturdy building materials, or simply be colorful and beautiful (and fun to climb). They also play an important role in our environment.

Many human activities—including breathing, driving cars, and creating electricity—add carbon dioxide (CO_2) to the atmosphere. Too much CO_2 in the atmosphere causes global warming, which can have disastrous effects on the environment (see page 85). Plants help to purify our air and keep the planet healthy by using up this harmful CO_2.

Through a process called photosynthesis (foh-toh-*sin*-thah-sis), plants help to replenish our oxygen supply. Here is how photosynthesis works.

Plants absorb carbon dioxide from the air, and water and minerals from the soil.	**Plants use energy from sunlight to convert these materials into food for themselves while releasing oxygen into the atmosphere.**	**Animals and people use the oxygen to breathe.**

In addition to cleaning up the air we breathe, plants give us energy. When humans and animals eat plants, they convert the raw materials in the plants into energy.

Parts of a Flowering Plant

Many people find flowers beautiful and fill their gardens with colorful blossoms, or give bouquets as presents. But flowers are more than just pretty decorations. They create the seeds that help a plant to reproduce. The plants that produce blossoms are known as flowering plants.

Each part of a plant helps it to grow and survive. Here are the parts of a daffodil.

guess what? Not all plants have flowers. Mosses, liverworts, and ferns reproduce using tiny particles called spores. The seeds of conifer trees, like pines, spruces, and cedar trees, are in their cones.

The flower makes the plant's seeds. Its bright color may attract helpful insects.

The stem supports the leaves and flowers. It carries water and minerals throughout the plant.

The leaves trap sunlight to make food for the plant.

Some plants grow from bulbs. The bulb stores food for the plant during the winter.

going green Raising animals for food produces lots of carbon dioxide, which is bad for the environment. So by eating more fruits and vegetables and less meat, not only will you improve your health, but you'll also improve the health of the planet!

A plant's roots are underground. They hold the plant in place and absorb water and minerals from the soil.

Science

How Science Helped Solve the Mystery of KING TUT

The funerary mask of King Tut

In 1922, a British archaeologist named Howard Carter stumbled onto an incredible discovery that would puzzle and delight scientists for nearly 80 years. Inside a small tomb in the Valley of the Kings, in Egypt, he found a mummy. Many tombs in the area had been broken into before, and the objects inside had been stolen or disturbed. This tomb, however, remained untouched, and the mummy was incredibly well preserved.

The mummy was the young pharaoh Tutankhaton. Most of us know him as King Tut. Some facts were already known about him from his tomb. He lived in Amarna, near the Nile Valley in northern Egypt. He was only 9 or 10 years old when he became king in 1333 B.C. He changed his name to Tutankhamen, and, by the age of 13, married a girl named Ankhesenamen. X-rays of the mummy's teeth taken in 1968 led scientists to conclude King Tut was only 19 years old when he died. Yet the question remained: How did he die?

Doctors today often use special equipment to perform CT scans to help diagnose different illnesses or injuries. This test helps doctors to see internal organs, bones, blood vessels, and more. In 2005, scientists did a CT scan and discovered that King Tut had been 5 feet 6 inches (1.7 m) tall, and that he had an overbite similar to other kings from his family. The scan also showed that he had a small cleft palate, which is a birth defect that affects the upper lip and the roof of one's mouth. Today, doctors and plastic surgeons can often fix cleft palates, but that was not an option in ancient Egypt.

Howard Carter

A Missing Stone

For decades, there were many theories about Tut's ancestry. One theory suggested he was either the son of Smenkhkare, a minor king, or Amenhotep III, the father of Akhenaten, one of Egypt's greatest pharaohs. Another theory supposed he was the son of Akhenaten himself. The truth of his ancestry was proved using a mixture of old-fashioned detective work and up-to-date scientific tests.

In 2008, Zahi Hawass, chief of Egypt's Supreme Council of Antiquities, discovered a piece of a limestone block that helped to fill in the blanks about Tut's family. When pieced together, the block showed the young Tutankhamen and his wife, Ankhesenamen, seated together. The inscriptions on the ancient piece of stone indicated that King Tut and his wife had the same father—Akhenaten.

DNA Tests

Over the next two years, scientists conducted DNA tests. DNA is found inside every living cell. It acts like a set of instructions that tell a cell what kind of organism it is part of and what to do. Every person's DNA is different, but the DNA of people who are related to one another is very similar. Tests showed that King Tut's DNA was a lot like the DNA of Amenhotep III and Akhenaten, proving that Amenhotep III was Tut's grandfather and Akhenaten was Tut's father.

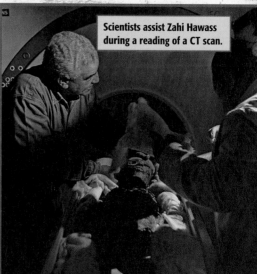

Scientists assist Zahi Hawass during a reading of a CT scan.

174

Disproving Old Theories

X-rays of the mummy done in 1968 showed pieces of bone loose in his skull. That led some scientists to believe King Tut may have been murdered, probably by a blow to the head. But the 2005 CT scans revealed that the skull had been broken after death, not while the boy was alive. Another early theory was that King Tut had fallen from a chariot and died from his injuries. The CT scan ruled out this explanation, too.

So, How Did He Die?

Scans done in 2010 showed that King Tut had a clubfoot, which meant that one of his feet turned inward at the ankle. He was also missing the middle bone from one of his toes, making one foot shorter than the other. Other tests proved that he had a bone disorder in his foot known as Köhler disease II, which would have made walking difficult. Artifacts found in the tomb supported the scientists' finding. In fact, about 130 canes were found in his burial chamber.

A CT scan of Tut's head

According to the recent scans, King Tut fractured his thigh bone, most likely in a fall. That injury did not properly heal, and may have become infected. Scientists also found a malaria parasite present in his mummy. Malaria is a disease that still exists. Often carried by mosquitoes in tropical areas, malaria causes fever, chills, and other flulike symptoms, and can be deadly.

Scientists from Egypt, Italy, and Germany analyzed all of the data, or information, that they uncovered in CT scans, DNA tests, and other observations of the mummy, and they concluded that Köhler disease II and the complications from his leg injury weakened King Tut's immune system. Since he was already unwell, he was unable to fight the malaria. The famous boy king most likely died from the combination of his bone disorder, the leg infection, and malaria.

TIME FOR KIDS GAME

PIONEERS IN SCIENCE

Match the face with the find.

LOUIS PASTEUR · JANE GOODALL · JONAS SALK

MARIE CURIE · ISAAC NEWTON · RACHEL CARSON

1. I made many discoveries, the most important being the law of universal gravitation, or gravity.

2. I was the first scientist to discover that illnesses are caused by germs, and that these microorganisms could be killed by heat and disinfectant. There is a process of ridding milk of harmful bacteria that is named after me.

3. I spent decades working with African chimpanzees. I discovered that chimps eat meat as well as plants, and that they have tool-making and communication skills.

4. I wrote many scientific pamphlets, articles, and books, including *Silent Spring*, which exposed the dangers of pesticides to the environment and led to the banning of DDT, a chemical used to kill insects and battle malaria.

5. I created a vaccine against the polio virus, which causes paralysis. My vaccine saved the lives of hundreds of thousands of people and prevented the disability of many more.

6. After discovering the properties of two new chemical elements, radium and polonium, I won a Nobel Prize in Physics. Eight years later, I won a Nobel Prize in Chemistry for my work showing the practical uses of radioactivity.

Science

Answers on page 242.

Space

FROM TIME FOR KIDS MAGAZINE

Found: An Earthlike Planet, at Last

By Michael D. Lemonick for TIME

The star known as Gliese 581 is a red dwarf, the most common type of star in our galaxy, the Milky Way. At 20 light-years away, it is relatively nearby. A light-year is about 5.88 trillion miles (9.46 trillion km). (And yes, a trillion is a million millions!) There are 116 stars closer to us than Gliese 581. You can't even see Gliese 581 without a telescope.

On September 29, 2010, a team of astronomers announced that they had found two more planets circling the star, bringing the total to six. And one of the planets, which was given the name Gliese 581g, may be of truly historic significance.

WHAT'S SO SPECIAL ABOUT GLIESE 581G?

Gliese 581g is in the "Goldilocks" zone. It is far enough away from its home star that temperatures are not too hot, but it's close enough that they're not too cold either, and thus just right for the possibility of life. In that way, Gliese 581g is a lot like Earth. Gliese 581g probably has a solid surface just like Earth. It orbits at just the right distance from the star to let water remain liquid rather than freezing solid or boiling away. As far as we know, that's a minimum requirement for the presence of life.

For thousands of years, scientists have wondered whether other Earthlike planets existed out in the universe. Now they have succeeded in identifying one. "We're pretty excited about it," admits Steve Vogt, of the University of California at Santa Cruz, and a member of the team that found the planet. But at this point, there's no way to determine whether there is life on the new planet.

A REMARKABLE ACHIEVEMENT

Detecting a planet this small is incredibly hard. It would have been impossible when Vogt and codiscoverer Paul Butler, of the Carnegie Institution of Washington, first got into the planet-hunting game in the early 1990s. The instruments simply were not sensitive enough. Since then, says Vogt, he has been working hard "to improve the instruments." And, he says, Butler has been working just as hard to do the observations.

At this point, there is no proof that there is water on Gliese 581g. "Those are things we just have to speculate about," says Vogt. But he goes on to point out where there is water. "There's water on Earth," he says, "and on the moon, and Mars, and on Jupiter's moon, Europa, and Saturn's moon, Enceladus, and in interstellar space." It's not hard to imagine, in other words, that Gliese 581g might have plenty of water as well. "It could have quite a good ocean," Vogt says. Maybe there's no life in that ocean. But unlike any planet found until now, there's nothing to rule out the idea that it could be full of life.

An artist created this image of Gliese 581g (right). It is orbiting around the star Gliese 581 (left) just as Earth travels around the sun.

THE SOLAR SYSTEM

The sun is at the center of our solar system. It consists mostly of ionized gas and supports life on Earth. Planets orbit around the sun. While traveling around the sun, each planet is also spinning on its own axis.

Early astronomers were able to see the six planets closest to the sun, but Uranus, Neptune, and Pluto (which is now considered a dwarf planet) were all discovered by telescope. Some planets are made of liquid and gas, such as Saturn. Others, like Mars, are rocky. A planet, such as Venus, can be broiling hot. Or, like Neptune, it can be freezing cold. The planets differ in size, too. The largest planet, Jupiter, has a diameter at its equator of 88,736 miles (142,800 km). Earth's diameter is 7,926 miles (12,756 km) at its equator. Mercury is the smallest planet, measuring just 3,032 miles (4,880 km) across.

These are called the terrestrial planets because they have solid, rocky bodies.

The outer four planets are made up of gases and do not have surfaces at all. You could not stand on Jupiter like you stand on Earth.

MERCURY
EARTH
VENUS
MARS
JUPITER
SATURN
URANUS
NEPTUNE

GALAXIES

The universe consists of trillions of billions of stars. Some of these stars have planets orbiting them. Scientists aren't sure if every star has other bodies orbiting it, because many stars are simply too far away to observe with today's tools. A group of millions of stars (along with dust, gas, and debris) bound together by gravity is known as a galaxy. (Think of galaxies as the various enormous neighborhoods that make up the universe.)

Our sun and its planets exist in a part of the universe called the Milky Way galaxy. The Milky Way is huge. If it were possible to travel at the speed of light (186,282 miles per second/299,792 km per second!), it would still take 100,000 years to go from one end of the Milky Way to the other.

NASA's Hubble Space Telescope captured this photo of a distant spiral galaxy known as NGC 4603.

guess what?

The sun is huge! It's so big that 1.3 million planets the size of Earth could fit inside it.

TWINKLE, TWINKLE

Stars and planets look almost exactly alike in the night sky, but there are a couple of ways to tell them apart. Because stars are so much farther away from us than planets, they twinkle. A planet's light remains steady.

Space

177

SPACE WASTE

In addition to the sun and its eight large planets, there are a few dwarf planets (including Pluto), and about 160 moons in our solar system. There is also a lot of space junk, such as hunks of rock and ice, old satellites, pieces broken off man-made spacecraft, and objects dropped or left behind by astronauts. Space waste can be dangerous for astronauts in space. Even tiny particles can damage sensitive equipment. And, in March 2009, astronauts aboard the International Space Station actually prepared to evacuate because a piece of fast-moving space junk was headed straight for the station. Objects orbiting Earth can get moving at nearly 5 miles (7.7 km) per second. That's fast!

MILESTONES AT ZERO GRAVITY

Here are some of the many milestones in space exploration that have occurred since humans first figured out how to put objects in space.

1957: Russian scientists launch Sputnik, the first man-made satellite, into space.

1958: NASA (National Aeronautics and Space Administration) is founded. It launches *Explorer 1*, the first U.S. satellite, into the atmosphere.

1961: Cosmonaut (the Russian equivalent of an astronaut) Yuri Gagarin becomes the first person to see Earth from space. Later that year, aboard the *Freedom 7*, Alan Shepard is the first American in space.

1962: John Glenn is the first American to orbit Earth in a spaceship.

1969: Neil Armstrong walks on the surface of the moon.

1971: The Russians launch Salyut I, the first space station.

1976: NASA's Viking 1 lands on Mars.

1978: NASA's Pioneer 1 and Pioneer 2 reach Venus's atmosphere.

1979–81: NASA's Voyager craft passes Saturn and Jupiter, taking the first close-up pictures of these planets.

1981: The first space shuttle, *Columbia*, is launched by NASA.

1990: The Hubble Space Telescope is launched.

1998: Construction begins on the International Space Station (ISS).

2002: NASA's Mars Odyssey space probe maps the surface of Mars.

2004: *SpaceShipOne*, the first privately launched spacecraft, lifts off from Mojave, California.

SPACE TIME

All planets in our solar system orbit the sun. The time it takes to make a complete trip around the sun is that planet's year. Each planet also spins on its axis, turning toward and away from the sun. The time it takes to finish a full rotation is the length of that planet's day. How long is a day? How long is a year? It depends which planet you're on.

Planet	Length of Day	Length of Year
Mercury	59 Earth days	88 Earth days
Venus	243 Earth days	222 Earth days
Earth	24 hours	365¼ days
Mars	24 hours and 40 minutes	687 Earth days
Jupiter	10 hours	12 Earth years
Saturn	10 hours	29 Earth years
Uranus	17 hours	84 Earth years
Neptune	16 hours	165 Earth years

TIME FOR KIDS GAME

ASTRO-NUTS

Can you imagine looking behind you and seeing Earth in the distance? Astronauts aboard the International Space Station (ISS) sure can! In this NASA photo, astronaut Clay Anderson waves to the camera from outside the ISS.

These two amazing space photos look a lot alike. But look closely, and you'll see that 10 things have changed. Can you spot all of the differences?

Answers on page 243.

guess what?

In order to stay healthy in space, astronauts on the International Space Station spend at least two hours a day working out.

Space

179

Sports

Star on Ice

By TFK Kid Reporter Gabe Roy

Imagine trying to prepare mentally for a 40-second race that could change your life. Apolo Anton Ohno deals with this all the time. Ohno is a world-famous speed skater. With eight medals, he holds the record for a U.S. Winter Olympian. Recently, Apolo competed in the 2010 Winter Olympics in Vancouver, Canada, where he won a silver and two bronze medals in short track speed skating. Ohno participated in the 2002 and 2006 Olympics, where he took home gold, silver, and bronze medals. He is also a three-time World Cup overall champion.

Being a speed skater means you have to practice a lot—eight to 12 hours a day, Ohno says. But Ohno took some time from his demanding training schedule to talk to TFK about his autobiography, *Zero Regrets: Be Greater than Yesterday.*

TFK: How did you first become interested in speed skating?

APOLO ANTON OHNO: I saw speed skating when I was 12 years old on the Olympic Games with my father, and I thought it was the coolest thing I had ever seen in my life. I didn't think it was real. I thought it was little superheroes racing on a track on blades. That's when I first got hooked.

TFK: As a kid, did you speed skate? If not, what activities did you enjoy?

OHNO: I didn't speed skate. I played sports. I was a swimmer. I did inline skating, but I jamskated [a mix of dancing, skating, and gymnastics]. I don't know if that counts.

TFK: Before a race, how do you overcome being nervous, or are you not nervous at all?

OHNO: I don't know if I get nervous anymore. I think it is more that I get anxious. But it happens every time and I try to use it to my advantage. You know, I tell myself it's a natural function and it just means I'm getting ready for the race.

TFK: What would you like to tell the young athletes of America?

OHNO: I would say to follow your dreams, and to realize whatever path you want to do. Whether you want to be an athlete, you want to focus full time on school, and to really dedicate 100% of yourself to that. I know it's hard, you're so young, but try and realize you guys have an opportunity to be the best you can be every single day. Believe in yourself and don't listen to anybody who says you can't do it.

TFK: If you could make any wish come true, what would it be?

OHNO: Oh, I'm living a dream, man! I'm living my own personal dream. I wouldn't change anything for myself right now. Everything has happened for a reason. Win, lose, or draw, it's all part of the process. So I try to enjoy every single step of the way.

180

WINTER SPORTS

SNOWBOARDING

The 2011 International Ski Federation Snowboard World Championship took place in La Molina, Spain, January 14–23, 2011.

SNOWBOARDCROSS
MEN: Alex Pullin
WOMEN: Lindsey Jacobellis

PARALLEL GIANT SLALOM
MEN: Benjamin Karl
WOMEN: Alena Zavarzina

Alex Pullin

PARALLEL SLALOM
MEN: Benjamin Karl
WOMEN: Hilde-Katrine Engeli

HALF-PIPE
MEN: Nathan Johnstone
WOMEN: Holly Crawford

BIG AIR
MEN: Petja Piiroinen

ALPINE SKIING

The 2011 International Ski Federation Alpine World Ski Championships took place in Garmisch-Partenkirchen, Germany, from February 8–20, 2011. Here are the big winners.

DOWNHILL
MEN: Erik Guay
WOMEN: Elisabeth Goergl

SUPER-G
MEN: Christof Innerhofer
WOMEN: Elisabeth Goergl

Christof Innerhofer

SUPER COMBINED
MEN: Aksel Lund Svindal
WOMEN: Anna Fenninger

GIANT SLALOM
MEN: Ted Ligety
WOMEN: Tina Maze

SLALOM
MEN: Jean-Baptiste Grange
WOMEN: Marlies Schild

CROSS-COUNTRY SKIING

The 2011 U.S. Cross Country Championships took place in Rumford, Maine, from January 1 to 8, 2011. Nineteen-year-old Jessica Diggins won the women's freestyle sprint event. Torin Koos took home the men's freestyle sprint title.

FIGURE SKATING

The 2011 United States Figure Skating Championships were held in Greensboro, North Carolina, from January 22–30, 2011.

MEN
1. Ryan Bradley
2. Richard Dornbush
3. Ross Miner

WOMEN
1. Alissa Czisny
2. Rachael Flatt
3. Mirai Nagasu

Alissa Czisny

Elisabeth Goergl

Sports

181

SUPER BOWL XLV

On February 6, 2011, the NFC champions, the Green Bay Packers, and the AFC winners, the Pittsburgh Steelers, played against each other in Super Bowl XLV in Dallas, Texas. The Steelers had won two Super Bowls in the past six seasons. The Packers, on the other hand, had not played in football's biggest game since 1998 (when they lost to the Broncos).

The big game featured two of the NFL's best quarterbacks: Green Bay's Aaron Rodgers and Pittsburgh's Ben Roethlisberger. Rodgers led his youthful team to their first Super Bowl win since the 1996 season. This was the first Super Bowl loss for Roethlisberger, who already has two Super Bowl rings. He played well, but threw two costly interceptions in the first half that allowed Green Bay to take an early 21–3 lead. The Steelers made a comeback, and with two minutes left in the game, trailed by only six points. In the end, the Steelers could not make up for their rough first half, and they lost 31–25.

Aaron Rodgers, who has only played six seasons of pro football, was named Super Bowl MVP. During the game, he threw for 304 yards and three touchdown passes.

guess what? Only one player on the Green Bay Packers 2011 championship team had ever played in a Super Bowl before. It was Aaron Rodgers.

RECORD BREAKER Super Bowl XLV aired on Fox and averaged 111 million viewers, making it the most-watched television program in U.S. history.

2010-2011 NFL AWARD WINNERS

MOST VALUABLE PLAYER
Tom Brady, quarterback, New England Patriots

OFFENSIVE PLAYER OF THE YEAR
Tom Brady, quarterback, New England Patriots

DEFENSIVE PLAYER OF THE YEAR
Troy Polamalu, safety, Pittsburgh Steelers

OFFENSIVE ROOKIE OF THE YEAR
Sam Bradford, quarterback, St. Louis Rams

DEFENSIVE ROOKIE OF THE YEAR
Ndamukong Suh, defensive tackle, Detroit Lions

COACH OF THE YEAR
Bill Belichick, New England Patriots

COMEBACK PLAYER OF THE YEAR
Michael Vick, quarterback, Philadelphia Eagles

Tom Brady

Ndamukong Suh tackles Jay Cutler.

RECORD BREAKER The Seattle Seahawks became the first team to win their division with a losing record. During the 2010–2011 regular season, they won seven games and lost nine. But they still ranked higher than the St. Louis Rams, San Francisco 49ers, and Arizona Cardinals to win the NFC West, a division of the NFL's National Football Conference. This automatically earned them a spot in the playoffs. They made the most of the opportunity and beat the defending champions, the New Orleans Saints, in the first round of the playoffs.

2010 BCS BOWL GAMES AND SCORES

Glendale, Arizona | January 10, 2010
Final score: Auburn 22, Oregon 19
The final game of the BCS (Bowl Championship Series) featured a pair of undefeated teams: the Auburn Tigers and the Oregon Ducks. It was both teams' first appearance in the championship game.

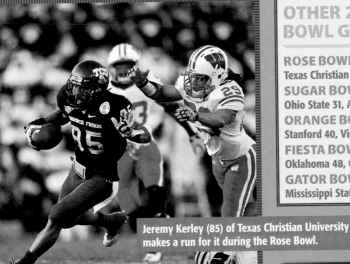

Jeremy Kerley (85) of Texas Christian University makes a run for it during the Rose Bowl.

OTHER 2010 BCS BOWL GAMES

ROSE BOWL (PASADENA, CA)
Texas Christian University 21, Wisconsin 19
SUGAR BOWL (NEW ORLEANS, LA)
Ohio State 31, Arkansas 26
ORANGE BOWL (MIAMI, FL)
Stanford 40, Virginia Tech 12
FIESTA BOWL (GLENDALE, AZ)
Oklahoma 48, Connecticut 20
GATOR BOWL (JACKSONVILLE, FL)
Mississippi State 52, Michigan 14

HEISMAN TROPHY

Every year, the Heisman award, named after legendary coach John Heisman, is given to the most outstanding player in college football, "whose performance best exhibits the pursuit of excellence with integrity." The winner of this important award is chosen by a panel of sportswriters from around the country.

Quarterback Cam Newton won the 2010 Heisman Trophy for leading the Auburn Tigers to an undefeated season and their first national championship since 1957. He threw for 2,589 yards passing and 28 touchdown passes.

RECORD BREAKER In his 45th season as head coach of Penn State, Joe Paterno won his 400th game, becoming the first major college coach to reach that milestone. Paterno also holds the record for most bowl wins (24).

Cam Newton

Sports

183

BASEBALL

2010 WORLD SERIES

Tim Lincecum

The Texas Rangers met the San Francisco Giants in the 2010 World Series. To get to baseball's biggest game, the Rangers beat the 2009 champion New York Yankees in the American League Championship Series. It was the Rangers' first World Series appearance. But it was the Giants, led by their outstanding young pitcher Tim Lincecum, who would eventually be crowned champions, beating the Rangers four games to one. This was the first championship win for the Giants since moving to San Francisco in 1957. (They won the World Series as the New York Giants in 1954.) The Giants won both games that Lincecum pitched, including Game 5, the series clincher. Giants shortstop Edgar Renteria was named MVP of the series.

Edgar Renteria

guess what? *Prior to the World Series every year, teams from the American League mostly play other teams in the American League. And teams in the National League mostly play other teams from the National League. But on June 12th, 1997, the Rangers hosted the Giants in the first-ever regular season game between two teams from different leagues. The Giants won that one, too, with a score of 4 to 3.*

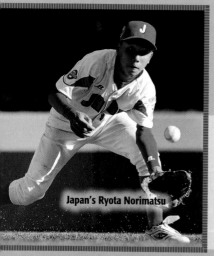

Japan's Ryota Norimatsu

guess what?

In 1994, the World Series was canceled because of a players' strike that lasted 232 days.

2010 LITTLE LEAGUE WORLD SERIES

In the 64th Little League World Series, the Edogawa Minami Little League team from Tokyo, Japan, beat the Waipio Little League team from Waipahu, Hawaii. The boys from Tokyo won 4 to 1 in the championship game. It was the seventh time a team from Japan has captured the Little League World Series. The last time was in 2003.

going green

Baseball has gotten into the green game. In 2005, the Oakland Athletics began using biodegradable cups at the McAfee Coliseum. Since 2007, there has been a composting program at the Seattle Mariners' Safeco Field. And, in 2008, the San Francisco Giants became the first team to install a solar energy system in its stadium.

184

2010 MLB LEAGUE LEADERS

BATTING

HOME RUNS
AMERICAN LEAGUE: Jose Bautista, right fielder, Toronto Blue Jays, 54
NATIONAL LEAGUE: Albert Pujols, first baseman, St. Louis Cardinals, 42

BATTING AVERAGE
AMERICAN LEAGUE: Josh Hamilton, left fielder, Texas Rangers, .359
NATIONAL LEAGUE: Carlos Gonzalez, center fielder, Colorado Rockies, .336

PITCHING

EARNED RUN AVERAGE
AMERICAN LEAGUE: Felix Hernandez, Seattle Mariners, 2.27
NATIONAL LEAGUE: Josh Johnson, Florida Marlins, 2.30

STRIKEOUTS
AMERICAN LEAGUE: Jered Weaver, Los Angeles Angels, 233
NATIONAL LEAGUE: Tim Lincecum, San Francisco Giants, 231

Felix Hernandez

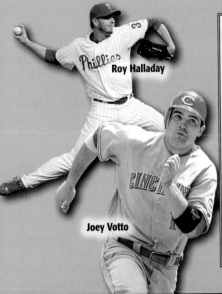

Roy Halladay

Joey Votto

2010 MLB AWARD WINNERS

MOST VALUABLE PLAYERS
AMERICAN LEAGUE: Josh Hamilton, Texas Rangers
NATIONAL LEAGUE: Joey Votto, Cincinnati Reds

CY YOUNG AWARD (BEST PITCHER)
AMERICAN LEAGUE: Felix Hernandez, Seattle Mariners
NATIONAL LEAGUE: Roy Halladay, Philadelphia Phillies

ROOKIE OF THE YEAR
AMERICAN LEAGUE: Neftali Feliz, Texas Rangers
NATIONAL LEAGUE: Buster Posey, San Francisco Giants

MANAGER OF THE YEAR
AMERICAN LEAGUE: Ron Gardenhire, Minnesota Twins
NATIONAL LEAGUE: Bud Black, San Diego Padres

Alex Rodriguez

RECORD BREAKER In the first inning of a game against the Toronto Blue Jays, 35-year-old Alex Rodriguez—third baseman for the New York Yankees--hit a two-run homer off of pitcher Shaun Marcum. This made A-Rod the youngest player ever to reach 600 career home runs. Only six others have reached that baseball milestone: Barry Bonds (762 homers), Hank Aaron (755), Babe Ruth (714), Willie Mays (660), Ken Griffey Jr. (630), and Sammy Sosa (609).

Sports

2009–2010 NBA LEADERS

SCORING

	Name	Team	Games Played	Points per Game
1.	Kevin Durant	Oklahoma City Thunder	82	30.1
2.	LeBron James	Cleveland Cavaliers	76	29.7
3.	Carmelo Anthony	Denver Nuggets	69	28.2

ASSISTS

	Name	Team	Games Played	Assists per Game
1.	Steve Nash	Phoenix Suns	81	11.0
2.	Chris Paul	New Orleans Hornets	45	10.7
3.	Deron Williams	Utah Jazz	76	10.5

REBOUNDS

	Name	Team	Games Played	Rebounds per Game
1.	Dwight Howard	Orlando Magic	82	13.2
2.	Marcus Camby	Los Angeles Clippers/ Portland Trail Blazers	74	11.8
3.	Zach Randolph	Memphis Grizzlies	81	11.7

Kevin Durant

Steve Nash

2010 NBA FINALS

The 2010 NBA finals pitted the Boston Celtics against the Los Angeles Lakers. Neither team was new to the finals. In fact, the Celtics have won the most championships and the Lakers the second most. The two teams last met in the finals in 2008, which the Celtics won. A year later, the Lakers beat the Magic for the NBA's top spot.

With the two most successful franchises in NBA history facing off, the series was billed as one of the best NBA finals ever. After the first five games of the series, the Celtics led three games to two. The Lakers won Game 6, tying up the series. In a hard-fought game, the Lakers were victorious, winning Game 7, 83–79, to defend their title. The final game was the second-most-watched game in NBA history, with 28.2 million viewers tuning in. Lakers star Kobe Bryant won his second NBA Finals MVP award in a row.

Kobe Bryant

guess what? *The 2009–2010 NBA season was truly an international affair. Eighty-three foreign-born players (from 36 different countries and territories) started the season on NBA rosters, tying the record for most ever. Omri Casspi of Israel, Jonas Jerebko of Sweden, and Hasheem Thabeet of Tanzania were the first players from their countries to play in the NBA.*

going green

During the NBA's second annual Green Week, in April 2010, players wore shooting shirts made from 50% recycled material. They autographed basketballs made from recycled materials and sold them to raise funds for the Natural Resources Defense Council. Individual teams also hosted events to encourage their fans to participate in recycling drives, nature cleanups, tree plantings, and other eco-friendly initiatives.

Sue Bird

WNBA REGULAR SEASON

2010 WNBA SEASON LEADERS

SCORING

	Name	Team	Games Played	Points per Game
1.	Diana Taurasi	Phoenix Mercury	31	22.6
2.	Cappie Poindexter	New York Liberty	34	21.4
3.	Angel McCoughtry	Atlanta Dream	34	21.1

ASSISTS

	Name	Team	Games Played	Assists per Game
1.	Ticha Penicheiro	Los Angeles Sparks	32	6.9
2.	Sue Bird	Seattle Storm	33	5.8
3.	Lindsay Whalen	Minnesota Lynx	33	5.6

REBOUNDS

	Name	Team	Games Played	Rebounds per Game
1.	Tina Charles	Connecticut Sun	34	11.7
2.	Rebekkah Brunson	Minnesota Lynx	30	10.3
3.	Sylvia Fowles	Chicago Sky	34	9.9

2010 WNBA Championship

The Seattle Storm beat the Atlanta Dream in Game 3. Lauren Jackson was named the Finals MVP.

Game 1: Storm 79, Dream 77

Game 2: Storm 87, Dream 84

Game 3: Storm 87, Dream 84

Tina Charles

COLLEGE BASKETBALL

2010 NCAA Men's Division 1 Championship
(April 5, 2010 | Indianapolis, Indiana)

Duke's Kyle Singler and Butler's Willie Veasley battle for the ball.

TEAM	1ST HALF POINTS	2ND HALF POINTS	FINAL SCORE
Duke Blue Devils	33	28	61
Butler Bulldogs	32	27	59

2010 NCAA Women's Division 1 Championship
(April 6, 2010 | San Antonio, Texas)

TEAM	1ST HALF POINTS	2ND HALF POINTS	FINAL SCORE
Connecticut Huskies	12	41	53
Stanford Cardinals	20	27	47

Sports

HOCKEY

2010 STANLEY CUP

In the 2010 Stanley Cup finals, the Chicago Blackhawks took on the Philadelphia Flyers, beating them four games to two. The Blackhawks won Game 6 with an exciting overtime goal by Patrick Kane. Chicago had not won the Stanley Cup since 1961— that's the longest championship drought of any team in the NHL.

guess what? *The Conn Smythe Trophy, which is awarded to the playoffs MVP, went to Blackhawks team captain Jonathan Toews.*

Ryan Miller

2010 NHL AWARD WINNERS

Like most professional sports leagues, the NHL hands out end-of-season awards to its best players and coaches. Here are some of the awards given out in 2010.

AWARD	GIVEN TO...	2010 WINNER (TEAM)
Hart Memorial Trophy	Most valuable player	Henrik Sedin (Canucks)
Vezina Trophy	Best goalie	Ryan Miller (Sabres)
James Norris Memorial Trophy	Outstanding defenseman	Duncan Keith (Blackhawks)
Calder Memorial Trophy	Outstanding rookie	Tyler Myers (Sabres)
Lady Byng Memorial Trophy	Player who displays sportsmanship and gentlemanly conduct	Martin St. Louis (Lightning)
Frank J. Selke Trophy	Outstanding defensive forward	Pavel Datsyuk (Red Wings)
Jack Adams Award	Outstanding coach	Dave Tippett (Coyotes)
Ted Lindsay Award	Most outstanding player as voted by fellow NHL members	Alex Ovechkin (Capitals)

Martin St. Louis

SOCCER

In the months leading up to the 2010 World Cup, organizations in South Africa launched tree-planting initiatives to help offset the upcoming rise in pollution. The various programs led to the planting of more than 200,000 trees across the country.

2010 WORLD CUP

South Africa hosted the 2010 FIFA World Cup from June 11 to July 11, 2010. In the final match of the international series, Spain defeated the Netherlands, 1 to 0. Germany came in third, and Uruguay finished fourth in the tournament.

Here are a few of the awards given out for outstanding work on the field.

Adidas Golden Ball: Diego Forlán (Uruguay)

Adidas Golden Boot: Thomas Mueller (Germany)

Adidas Golden Glove: Iker Casillas (Spain)

FIFA Fair Play Award: Spain

Best Young Player Award: Thomas Mueller (Germany)

Diego Forlán

AUTO RACING

2010 CHASE FOR THE SPRINT CUP RACE RESULTS

The Sprint Cup Series consists of 36 races, starting with the prestigious Daytona 500, and is considered the top racing series of the National Association for Stock Car Auto Racing (NASCAR). The first 26 races make up the regular season as drivers rack up points for their finishes. After that, the 12 drivers with the most points compete in the Chase, the final 10 races of the series. The driver with the most points after those 10 races is awarded the Sprint Cup, NASCAR's greatest prize. In 2010, the Chase ended with the Ford 400 on November 21.

RACE	TRACK	WINNER
Sylvania 300	New Hampshire Motor Speedway	Clint Bowyer
AAA 400	Dover International Speedway	Jimmie Johnson
Price Chopper 400 Presented by Kraft Foods	Kansas Speedway	Greg Biffle
Pepsi Max 400	Auto Club Speedway	Tony Stewart
Bank of America 500	Charlotte Motor Speedway	Jamie McMurray
Tums Fast Relief 500	Martinsville Speedway	Denny Hamlin
Amp Energy Juice 500	Talladega Superspeedway	Clint Bowyer
AAA Texas 500	Texas Motor Speedway	Denny Hamlin
Kobalt Tools 500	Phoenix International Raceway	Carl Edwards
Ford 400	Homestead-Miami Speedway	Carl Edwards

Jimmie Johnson

2010 CHASE FOR THE SPRINT CUP FINAL STANDINGS

1. Jimmie Johnson — 6,622 points
2. Denny Hamlin — 6,583 points
3. Kevin Harvick — 6,581 points

guess what? NASCAR's biggest event is the Daytona 500. Unlike the Super Bowl or the World Series, this race comes at the beginning of the season, not the end.

INDIANAPOLIS 500

The Indianapolis 500, or Indy 500, is one of the largest single-day sporting events in the world. Held at the Indianapolis Motor Speedway, the race covers a full 500 miles (805 km) and is viewed live by more than 250,000 people. The 94th Indy 500 took place on May 30, 2010, and was won by Dario Franchitti of Scotland. Musicians played bagpipes to celebrate his second Indy 500 win (he first won in 2007).

Dario Franchitti

Sports

189

TENNIS

In 1962, Rod Laver became the first person to win all four of the major tennis tournaments (Australian Open, French Open, Wimbledon, and U.S. Open) in a single year. In 1969, he did it again!

RECORD BREAKER

2010–2011 TENNIS CHAMPIONS

AUSTRALIAN OPEN
MEN'S SINGLES: Roger Federer
WOMEN'S SINGLES: Serena Williams
MEN'S DOUBLES: Bob Bryan, Mike Bryan
WOMEN'S DOUBLES: Venus Williams, Serena Williams

FRENCH OPEN
MEN'S SINGLES: Rafael Nadal
WOMEN'S SINGLES: Francesca Schiavone
MEN'S DOUBLES: Daniel Nestor, Nenad Zimonjic
WOMEN'S DOUBLES: Serena Williams, Venus Williams

WIMBLEDON
MEN'S SINGLES: Rafael Nadal
WOMEN'S SINGLES: Serena Williams
MEN'S DOUBLES: Jürgen Melzer, Philipp Petzschner
WOMEN'S DOUBLES: Vania King, Yaroslava Shvedova

U.S. OPEN
MEN'S SINGLES: Rafael Nadal
WOMEN'S SINGLES: Kim Clijsters
MEN'S DOUBLES: Bob Bryan, Mike Bryan
WOMEN'S DOUBLES: Vania King, Yaroslava Shvedova

Davis Cup (Men's International Team Tennis)
Serbia defeated France, three matches to two.

Fed Cup (Women's International Team Tennis)
Italy defeated the United States, three matches to one.

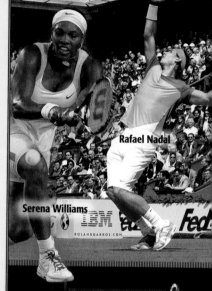

Serena Williams

Rafael Nadal

GOLF

2010 MAJOR EVENT WINNERS

MEN
MASTERS: Phil Mickelson
U.S. OPEN: Graeme McDowell
BRITISH OPEN: Louis Oosthuizen
PGA CHAMPIONSHIP: Martin Kaymer
U.S. AMATEUR CHAMPIONSHIP: Peter Uihlein

WOMEN
KRAFT NABISCO CHAMPIONSHIP: Yani Tseng
LPGA CHAMPIONSHIP: Cristie Kerr
U.S. WOMEN'S OPEN: Paula Creamer
WOMEN'S BRITISH OPEN: Yani Tseng
U.S. AMATEUR CHAMPIONSHIP: Danielle Kang

Yani Tseng

Graeme McDowell

GYMNASTICS

2010 WORLD CHAMPIONSHIPS

The World Artistic Gymnastics Championships were held in Rotterdam, Netherlands, October 16–24, 2010.

EVENT	GOLD MEDAL	COUNTRY
Men's Individual All-Around	Kohei Uchimura	Japan
Men's Floor	Eleftherios Kosmidis	Greece
Men's Pommel Horse	Krisztian Berki	Hungary
Men's Rings	Yibing Chen	China
Men's Vault	Thomas Bouhail	France
Men's Parallel Bars	Zhe Feng	China
Men's High Bar	Chenglong Zhang	China
Women's Individual All-Around	Aliya Mustafina	Russia
Women's Vault	Alicia Sacramone	USA
Women's Uneven Bars	Beth Tweddle	Great Britain
Women's Balance Beam	Ana Porgras	Romania
Women's Floor	Lauren Mitchell	Australia

Alicia Sacramone

COLLEGE GYMNASTICS

In 2010, the NCAA Women's Gymnastics Championship title went to the University of California, Los Angeles (UCLA), ending the Georgia Bulldogs' five-win streak. For the men, Michigan State took the top title.

SURFING

2010 WORLD SURFING CHAMPIONSHIPS

Four champions are recognized every year by the Association of Surfing Professionals (ASP). The titles for best male, female, and longboard surfers are awarded based on points that surfers receive in competitions on the ASP World Tour. In 2010, Australian Stephanie Gilmore took her fourth straight title for the women's championship, and U.S. surfer Kelly Slater won the men's championship. For the longboard championships, Duane DeSoto took the men's title, while Cori Schumacher took the women's. Both longboard champs are from the United States.

Kelly Slater

Sports

CYCLING

Alberto Contador

Guess what?

Henri Cornet of France was the youngest cyclist to win the Tour de France. In 1904, at the age of 19, he took home cycling's top prize.

2010 TOUR DE FRANCE TOP FINISHES

The Tour de France is an exhausting bike race that takes place every summer. The 2010 race began in Rotterdam, Netherlands, and ended in Paris, France. Here are the first five riders to complete the race.

	NAME	COUNTRY	RACE TIME
1.	Alberto Contador	Spain	91 hours, 58 minutes, 48 seconds
2.	Andy Schleck	Luxembourg	91 hours, 59 minutes, 27 seconds
3.	Denis Menchov	Russia	92 hours, 00 minutes, 49 seconds
4.	Samuel Sánchez	Spain	92 hours, 02 minutes, 28 seconds
5.	Jurgen Van Den Broeck	Belgium	92 hours, 05 minutes, 42 seconds

Kathryn Hoff

SWIMMING

2010 FINA WORLD SWIMMING CHAMPIONSHIPS

The 2010 FINA World Swimming Championships were held in Dubai, United Arab Emirates, December 15–19, 2010. Here are some results.

Matthew Mitcham

EVENT	GOLD MEDAL
Men's 4x100 Meter Medley Relay	USA
Women's 4x100 Meter Medley Relay	China
Men's 400-m Freestyle	Paul Biedermann (Germany)
Women's 400-m Freestyle	Kathryn Hoff (USA)
Women's 800-m Freestyle	Erika Villaecija García (Spain)
Men's 1500-m Freestyle	Oussama Mellouli (Tunisia)

DIVING

The 2010 FINA Diving World Cup was held in Changzhou, China, June 2–6, 2010. Australia's Matthew Mitcham won the gold medal in the men's 10-meter platform event. Yadan Hu, of China, scored highest in the women's 10-meter platform event.

HORSE RACING

2010 TRIPLE CROWN

The three biggest horse races in the United States are the Kentucky Derby, at Churchill Downs in Louisville, Kentucky; the Preakness Stakes, at Pimlico Race Course in Baltimore, Maryland; and the Belmont Stakes, at Belmont Park in Elmont, New York. These three races take place within a five-week period from early May to early June, and make up the Triple Crown of Thoroughbred Racing, or Triple Crown, for short.

Lookin at Lucky

2010 TRIPLE CROWN RACE RESULTS

Here are the horses that finished in the top three for each of the races that make up the Triple Crown.

KENTUCKY DERBY
1. Super Saver
2. Ice Box
3. Paddy O'Prado

PREAKNESS STAKES
1. Lookin at Lucky
2. First Dude
3. Jackson Bend

BELMONT STAKES
1. Drosselmeyer
2. Fly Down
3. First Dude

Super Saver

RECORD BREAKER Jockey Calvin Borel rode Super Saver to victory in the 2010 Kentucky Derby. It was Borel's third Derby victory in four years. He rode Mine That Bird in 2009 and Street Sense in 2007.

DOGSLEDDING

Alaska's Big Sled Dog Race

On March 16, 2010, Lance Mackey blazed to first place in the Iditarod Trail Sled Dog Race, in Nome, Alaska. He ran the race in 8 days, 23 hours, 59 minutes, and 9 seconds—the second-fastest finish in the event's history. Mackey is the only person with four straight Iditarod victories. He won $50,400 and a new truck.

During the 1,150-mile (1,917 km) trip, teams endure bitter temperatures. Veterinarians give the dogs checkups along the way. Some animal-rights groups say the race is cruel. But Mackey says his dogs are his family. "These are my heroes," he said.

Lance Mackey checks in with his sled dog Rev at a race checkpoint in Takotna, Alaska.

FROM TIME FOR KIDS MAGAZINE

Sports

X GAMES

The X Games, held every winter and summer, showcase the best in extreme sports. Athletes from all over the world participate, showing off their skills with a skateboard, snowboard, bike, rally car, snowmobile, or pair of skis. Some events are based on pure speed, while others reward competitors for style and tricks.

Ashley Fiolek

2010 SUMMER X GAMES JULY 29–AUGUST 1, 2010

SKATEBOARDING

Jake Brown (Big Air), **Gaby Ponce** (Women's Vert), **Pierre-Luc Gagnon** (Men's Vert), **Italo Penarrubia** (Vert Am), **Pierre-Luc Gagnon** (Best Trick), **Ryan Sheckler** (Men's Street), **Alexis Sablone** (Women's Street), **Christian Hosoi** (Park Legends), **Pedro Barros** (Park)

Pierre-Luc Gagnon

MOTO X

Josh Grant (Men's Super X), **Ashley Fiolek** (Women's Super X), **Travis Pastrana** (Freestyle), **Matt Buyten** (Step Up), **Cam Sinclair** (Best Trick), **Todd Potter** (Best Whip)

BMX

Jamie Bestwick (Vert), **Daniel Dhers** (Park), **Chad Kagy** (Big Air), **Garrett Reynolds** (Street)

RALLY CAR RACING

Tanner Foust

guess what? During a 2009 competition in Spain, motocross rider Cam Sinclair had a terrible accident. Doctors predicted it would take him two years to recover from his injuries. But the very next year, he won the gold medal for Motocross Best Trick at the 2010 Summer X Games by performing a double backflip—the same trick that nearly killed him the year before.

2011 WINTER X GAMES JANUARY 26–30, 2011

SKIING

Josh Deuck (Mono Skier X), **Alex Schlopy** (Big Air), **John Teller** (Men's Skier X), **Kelsey Serwa** (Women's Skier X), **Sammy Carlson** (Men's Slopestyle), **Kaya Turksi** (Women's Slopestyle), **Kevin Rolland** (Men's SuperPipe), **Sarah Burke** (Women's SuperPipe)

SNOWBOARDING

Torstein Horgmo (Big Air), **Nick Baumgartner** (Men's Snowboarder X), **Lindsey Jacobellis** (Women's Snowboarder X), **Sebastien Toutant** (Men's Slopestyle), **Enni Rukajärvi** (Women's SlopeStyle), **Shaun White** (Men's SuperPipe), **Kelly Clark** (Women's SuperPipe), **Nic Sauvé** (Snowboard Street)

SNOWMOBILING

Daniel Bodin (Freestyle), **Joe Parsons** (Speed & Style), **Tucker Hibbert** (SnoCross), **Mike Schultz** (SnoCross Adaptive), **Daniel Bodin** (Best Trick)

Nic Sauvé

Torstein Horgmo

Lindsey Jacobellis

194

TIME FOR KIDS GAME

GIFT MIX-UP

Answers on page 243.

What's the ballerina doing with a hockey stick? It looks like this holiday gift swap got all mixed up! Look at each person in this picture for clues to what they like to do best. Then write the correct person's letter next to the gift meant for him or her. (Look for clues in what they wear or do.)

○ skateboard   ○ ballet shoes   ○ saddle   ○ holiday songbook

○ chef's hat   ○ hockey stick   ○ dog collar   ○ football

UPCOMING OLYMPICS

The Olympics are held every two years. They alternate between featuring winter sports like ice hockey, figure skating, speed skating, luge, snowboarding, and bobsledding, and summer events like swimming, soccer, basketball, gymnastics, volleyball, archery, wrestling, and weight lifting. In 2010, the Winter Olympics were held in Vancouver, British Columbia, in Canada. The next Winter Games will be held in Sochi, Russia, in 2014. London, England, is hosting the 2012 Summer Olympics. In 2016, the summer games will be held in Rio de Janeiro, Brazil.

MYSTERY PERSON

I was born in 1956 in Chicago, Illinois. At 19, I captured America's heart when I won a gold medal in figure skating at the 1976 Winter Olympics, in Innsbruck, Austria. I have also enjoyed a successful professional skating career.

WHO AM I? _____

Answer on page 243.

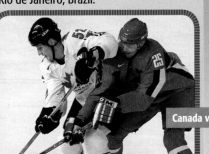

Canada vs. Russia in the 2010 Olympics

Sports

195

Will You Drive an Electric Car One Day?

By Brian Dumaine for TIME

Soon, electric cars may be whirring through your neighborhood. These quiet, clean, battery-powered vehicles can be charged in a wall outlet, like a giant power tool. And some people believe the cars cannot come soon enough.

Automakers say that the world's population is slated to jump from 6.8 billion to 9 billion by 2050. So the supply of petroleum (which is turned into gasoline) won't keep up with the number of cars on the road. "Everyone agrees we have to get off of oil," says Tony Posawatz, who works for General Motors (GM) and is in charge of the Chevy Volt project. The Volt runs on electricity, but also has a gas engine. "In 10 years," Posawatz says, "the number of cars around the globe will rise from 800 million to 1.1 billion. We know the price of oil will go up."

CHARGE IT

To help car companies develop gas-free electric vehicles, the U.S. government has given billions of dollars to makers of electric cars. But huge roadblocks remain. It can take as much as eight hours to charge a car for only 100 miles (161 km) of driving. And the distance the car can go changes depending on driving conditions. According to Nissan, its all-electric Leaf

The Chevy Volt can run for 25 to 50 miles (40 to 80 km) on electricity alone. In January 2011, the Volt was named the North American Car of the Year.

can go 100 miles (161 km) on cool, sunny days and on flat roads. On a hot day in heavy traffic, that drops to 47 miles (76 km).

Price is a problem, too. Electric models cost much more than similar gasoline-powered cars. The good news is that electric-car technology is improving, and the prices of the vehicles are dropping as it does. Where will drivers be able to charge the cars? The U.S. Department of Energy is giving grants to pay for at least 10,000 charging stations around the nation.

GEARING UP

Private businesses are also gearing up. Richard Lowenthal is the head of Coulomb Technologies, a company in California. He says that his firm will install about 4,500 charging stations, mostly at office parks and homes. The stations are rectangular boxes about the size of parking meters. Each has a plug and cord. The cost? About $3 per charge. "The typical car is parked 23 hours a day. You can charge it while you work and while you sleep," Lowenthal says.

Much of the interior of the Nissan Leaf is made from recycled materials—mostly plastic water bottles.

Alternative Fuels

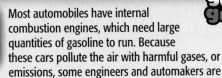

Most automobiles have internal combustion engines, which need large quantities of gasoline to run. Because these cars pollute the air with harmful gases, or emissions, some engineers and automakers are hard at work developing alternate engine systems. Others are working on identifying new types of fuel for vehicles and making them practical. For example, **biofuels** blend petroleum with plant materials. Ethanol, a type of biofuel, is made from corn, barley, wheat, or other grains and grasses. In the United States, ethanol usually comes from corn. Some critics warn that the amount of energy used to transform the corn into fuel is so high that it cancels out ethanol's environmental benefits. As more research and trials are done, ethanol makers hope to find a better, more efficient process.

Biodiesel is another alternative to gasoline. It is biodegradable and made from renewable resources like new or used vegetable oil and animal fats. Some people have found ways to power cars using the oil left over from restaurant deep fryers. But you can't just pour cooking oil into your gas tank! The liquid needs to be processed into a usable substance first. In the United States, biodiesel is often made from soybean oil.

Be on the lookout for more eco-friendly transportation news. Many companies are investing more time and money than ever into the research and development of green vehicles. In the meantime, try to walk or ride your bike when traveling short distances. Taking mass transit, like buses, trains, and subways, also helps lessen the environmental impact of transportation.

This biodiesel plant, in Washington state, creates fuel from canola oil, soybeans, and other crops.

TILT AND TRAVEL

Nearly everyone has ridden a tricycle or a bike and been a passenger in a car. But what about a Segway™ Human Transporter? Released in 2001, the Segway is a self-balancing, two-wheeled vehicle that responds to the movements of its rider. If the rider leans forward, the Segway moves forward. When the rider leans back, the Segway moves in reverse. What's so special about the Segway is that it doesn't run on gasoline. It uses electricity and relies on gyroscopes for its unique type of movement. Gyroscopes are spinning objects that resist change in certain directions. They are similar to tops that spin and spin but resist falling down. Inside the Segway are five gyroscopes, along with tilting sensors, and a computer. They help the machine respond to the rider but keep a person from falling down or knocking it over. Segways are now being used within large hotels and malls and by police forces.

guess what? Police officers use Segways for many reasons: to patrol large areas quickly, to cover more ground than they can on foot, and to elevate themselves so they can see over crowds. But there is another major reason for police to use the two-wheeled machines: Segways get people talking and interacting with one another and with their local officers.

Transportation

197

Milestones in Transportation History

In 1860, it could take half a year to travel from the East Coast to the West Coast of the United States. Now, passengers can fly across the country in six or seven hours. In 1950, putting a human on the moon was the stuff of science fiction films. But in 1969, a space vehicle made it happen for real. Here are just a few of the major inventions and events in the history of transportation.

1783 The Montgolfier brothers create the first hot air balloons.

1787 The first successful steam-powered ship is introduced in the United States. By 1807, there is regular steamboat service along the Hudson River in New York and along the Mississippi River. In 1822, the SS *Robert Fulton* completes the first steamboat trip from New York to New Orleans, Louisiana.

1803 The first steam-powered locomotive (an early type of train) is invented by Richard Trevithick.

1830 The first passenger railroad in the United States opens. Part of the Baltimore & Ohio Railroad, this 13-mile (21 km) line connects Baltimore and Ellicott City, Maryland.

1832 People begin traveling through New York City aboard horse-drawn streetcars.

1863 The world's first subway opens in London, England.

1869 The transcontinental railroad in the United States is complete. The Central Pacific and Union Pacific railroads are connected at Promontory Point, Utah. Using the transcontinental railroad, it only takes six days for a person to travel from Omaha, Nebraska, to Sacramento, California.

1871 The cable car is invented by Andrew Hallidie. A cable car system is introduced in San Francisco in 1873. Later, Hallidie's inventions are used to set up cable cars in Chicago, Los Angeles, Cincinnati, and other cities.

1885 German engineer Gottlieb Daimler invents the first car with an internal combustion engine in Germany. It is considered a forerunner of the type of gasoline-powered car that many people drive today.

1897 *Argonaut I*, a gasoline-powered vehicle, is the first successful submarine to operate in the open sea.

1903 Wilbur and Orville Wright design and build the first engine-powered airplane. Over a period of four days, they complete several successful but short flights in Kitty Hawk, North Carolina. The longest one lasts 59 seconds. The plane travels 852 feet (260 m).

SPOTLIGHT ON HENRY FORD

Henry Ford founded the Ford Motor Company in 1903. At first, Ford built only a few cars a day. But demand for Model Ts was so high, Ford developed a way to make more cars in an inexpensive, efficient way. In 1913, he rolled out a moving assembly line. Workers stood in front of a conveyor belt, and each completed one task on every car that passed by. Ford's method of mass production revolutionized car manufacturing. It also changed life in the U.S. More people could travel. Highways grew. Suburbs developed outside of cities.

1908 On October 1, 1908, the Ford Motor Company introduces the Model T. It is an instant hit. At $825, it costs about half as much as other cars on the market. By 1918, half of all the cars in the United States are Model Ts. The Ford Motor Company stops making the Model T in 1927.

1927 Charles Lindbergh is the first person to fly by himself and without stopping from New York to France. It takes him 33.5 hours to fly 3,610 miles (5,810 km). Five years later, Amelia Earhart is the first woman to make a solo flight across the Atlantic Ocean.

1947 The first supersonic jet flight with a pilot takes place in California. Captain Charles Yeager flies faster than the speed of sound.

1970 Pan Am operates the first commercial jumbo jet, the Boeing 747.

1981 NASA launches the space shuttle *Columbia*. For more info on space firsts, see page 178.

2000 Amtrak launches the Acela, a high-speed train. It can travel at speeds up to 150 miles (241 km) per hour.

2005 The "Super Jumbo" Airbus A380, makes its first flight. The world's largest passenger plane, it can seat 853 people.

2010 Trains on a railway line between Shanghai and Hangzhou, China, travel at an average of 217 miles (350 km) per hour. These high-speed trains set records for going faster than 258 miles (416 km) per hour.

TIME FOR KIDS GAME

GET MOVING!

From leaning on a Segway to flying aboard a double-decker jumbo jet, there are many ways to get around. Can you find all of the transportation words listed below in this grid? The words can go up, down, sideways, or diagonally.

Acela
electric
engine
ethanol
Ford
gyroscope

hybrid
railroad
streetcar
subway
supersonic
train

F	U	L	G	H	Y	B	R	I	D
I	R	S	Y	N	A	P	Q	W	A
E	W	T	R	A	I	N	J	U	D
T	L	R	O	Z	A	C	E	L	A
H	P	E	S	O	K	Q	N	G	O
A	K	E	C	C	J	U	G	I	R
N	B	T	O	T	E	D	I	K	L
O	H	C	P	T	R	O	N	P	I
L	U	A	E	X	R	I	E	M	A
F	O	R	D	I	G	F	C	H	R
E	S	U	B	W	A	Y	I	R	F
S	U	P	E	R	S	O	N	I	C

Transportation

Answers on page 243.

199

United States

ALABAMA

CAPITAL: Montgomery

LARGEST CITY: Birmingham

POSTAL CODE: AL

LAND AREA: 50,750 square miles (131,443 sq km)

POPULATION (2010): 4,779,736

ENTERED UNION (RANK): December 14, 1819 (22)

MOTTO: *Audemus jura nostra defendere.* (We dare maintain our rights.)

TREE: Southern longleaf pine

FLOWER: Camellia

BIRD: Yellowhammer (also known as the northern flicker or yellow-shafted flicker)

NICKNAMES: Yellowhammer State, Cotton State, Heart of Dixie

FAMOUS ALABAMIAN: Harper Lee, Pulitzer Prize–winning author of *To Kill a Mockingbird*

guess what? *A monument dedicated to the boll weevil, a destructive insect, can be found in Enterprise, Alabama.*

ALASKA

CAPITAL: Juneau

LARGEST CITY: Anchorage

POSTAL CODE: AK

LAND AREA: 570,374 square miles (1,477,267 sq km)

POPULATION (2010): 710,231

ENTERED UNION (RANK): January 3, 1959 (49)

MOTTO: North to the future

TREE: Sitka spruce

FLOWER: Forget-me-not

BIRD: Willow ptarmigan

NICKNAMES: The Last Frontier, Land of the Midnight Sun

FAMOUS ALASKAN: Scott Gomez, hockey player

guess what? *The aurora borealis, also known as the northern lights, is a phenomenon that occurs in Earth's atmosphere. It looks like glowing, colorful bands of moving light, and can be seen in the night sky of Fairbanks, Alaska.*

ARKANSAS

CAPITAL: Little Rock

LARGEST CITY: Little Rock

POSTAL CODE: AR

LAND AREA: 52,075 square miles (134,874 sq km)

POPULATION (2010): 2,915,918

ENTERED UNION (RANK): June 15, 1836 (25)

MOTTO: *Regnat populus.* (The people rule.)

TREE: Pine

FLOWER: Apple blossom

BIRD: Mockingbird

NICKNAME: Natural State

FAMOUS ARKANSAN: Johnny Cash, singer and songwriter

guess what? *The state beverage, established in 1985, is milk.*

Little Rock

ARIZONA

CAPITAL: Phoenix

LARGEST CITY: Phoenix

POSTAL CODE: AZ

LAND AREA: 113,642 square miles (296,400 sq km)

POPULATION (2010): 6,392,017

ENTERED UNION (RANK): February 14, 1912 (48)

MOTTO: *Ditat deus.* (God enriches.)

TREE: Palo verde

FLOWER: Saguaro cactus blossom

BIRD: Cactus wren

NICKNAME: Grand Canyon State

FAMOUS ARIZONAN: Joan Ganz Cooney, founder of *Sesame Street*

guess what? *Arizona is the only state to have official state neckwear. It is the bola tie, which is a cord worn around the neck and fastened with a decorative clasp.*

Phoenix

United States

Alaska

COLORADO

CAPITAL: Denver

LARGEST CITY: Denver

POSTAL CODE: CO

LAND AREA:
103,730 square miles (268,660 sq km)

POPULATION (2010): 5,029,196

ENTERED UNION (RANK):
August 1, 1876 (38)

MOTTO: *Nil sine numine* (Nothing without the deity)

TREE: Colorado blue spruce

FLOWER: Rocky Mountain columbine

BIRD: Lark bunting

NICKNAME: Centennial State

FAMOUS COLORADAN: Jack Dempsey, boxer

guess what? *In 1972, Colorado became the first and only state to reject the Olympics. The 1976 Winter Games had been scheduled for Denver, but the state government decided to pass because of the high cost of hosting the Games and worries about negative environmental impact.*

CALIFORNIA

CAPITAL: Sacramento

LARGEST CITY:
Los Angeles

POSTAL CODE: CA

LAND AREA: 155,973 square miles (403,970 sq km)

POPULATION (2010): 37,253,956

ENTERED UNION (RANK):
September 9, 1850 (31)

MOTTO: *Eureka!* (I have found it!)

TREE: California redwood

FLOWER: Golden poppy

BIRD: California valley quail

NICKNAME: Golden State

FAMOUS CALIFORNIAN: Zac Efron, actor

guess what? *The largest landlocked harbor in the world is San Francisco Bay, in California.*

DELAWARE

CAPITAL: Dover

LARGEST CITY: Wilmington

POSTAL CODE: DE

LAND AREA: 1,955 square miles (5,063 sq km)

POPULATION (2010): 897,934

ENTERED UNION (RANK): December 7, 1787 (1)

MOTTO: Liberty and independence

TREE: American holly

FLOWER: Peach blossom

BIRD: Blue hen chicken

NICKNAMES: Diamond State, First State, Small Wonder

FAMOUS DELAWAREAN: Henry Heimlich, surgeon and inventor of the Heimlich maneuver

guess what? *Peaches were introduced to the state when Delaware was still a U.S. colony, and have been important to its farming industry ever since. In 2009, the state government named peach pie Delaware's official dessert.*

Wilmington

Dover

CONNECTICUT

CAPITAL: Hartford

LARGEST CITY: Bridgeport

POSTAL CODE: CT

LAND AREA: 5,018 square miles (12,997 sq km)

POPULATION (2010): 3,574,097

ENTERED UNION (RANK): January 9, 1788 (5)

MOTTO: *Qui transtulit sustinet.* (He who transplanted sustains.)

TREE: White oak

FLOWER: Mountain laurel

BIRD: American robin

NICKNAMES: Constitution State, Nutmeg State

FAMOUS NUTMEGGER: Marcus Camby, basketball player

guess what? *The name of Connecticut comes from the Indian word Quinnehtukqut, which means "beside the long tidal river."*

Hartford

Bridgeport

United States

FLORIDA

CAPITAL: Tallahassee

LARGEST CITY: Jacksonville

POSTAL CODE: FL

LAND AREA: 53,927 square miles (139,670 sq km)

POPULATION (2010): 18,801,310

ENTERED UNION (RANK): March 3, 1845 (27)

MOTTO: In God we trust.

TREE: Sabal palm (cabbage palmetto)

FLOWER: Orange blossom

BIRD: Mockingbird

NICKNAME: Sunshine State

FAMOUS FLORIDIAN: Janet Reno, first female Attorney General

guess what? *Cape Canaveral, Florida, is home to the Kennedy Space Center. The National Aeronautics and Space Administration (NASA) launches space flights from Cape Canaveral.*

GEORGIA

CAPITAL: Atlanta

LARGEST CITY: Atlanta

POSTAL CODE: GA

LAND AREA: 57,919 square miles (150,010 sq km)

POPULATION (2010): 9,687,653

ENTERED UNION (RANK): January 2, 1788 (4)

MOTTO: Wisdom, justice, and moderation

TREE: Live oak

FLOWER: Cherokee rose

BIRD: Brown thrasher

NICKNAMES: Peach State, Empire State of the South

FAMOUS GEORGIAN: John Pemberton, inventor of Coca-Cola

guess what? *A sculpture carved into Stone Mountain, near Atlanta, depicts Stonewall Jackson, Jefferson Davis, and Robert E. Lee with his horse, Traveler. The image is 190 feet (58 m) long and 90 feet (27 m) tall. At its deepest point (Lee's elbow), the sculpture is cut 12 feet (4 m) into the face of the mountain.*

HAWAII

CAPITAL: Honolulu (on the island of Oahu)

LARGEST CITY: Honolulu

POSTAL CODE: HI

LAND AREA: 6,423 square miles (16,636 sq km)

POPULATION (2010): 1,360,301

ENTERED UNION (RANK): August 21, 1959 (50)

MOTTO: *Ua mau ke ea o ka aina i ka pono.* (The life of the land is perpetuated in righteousness.)

TREE: Kuku'i (candlenut)

FLOWER: Yellow hibiscus

BIRD: Nene (Hawaiian goose)

NICKNAME: Aloha State

FAMOUS HAWAIIAN: Bette Midler, singer and actress

guess what? *The state fish of Hawaii is the* humuhumunukunukuapua'a. *(hoo-moo-hoo-moo-noo-koo-noo-koo-ah-poo-ah-ah). It can swim backwards, and it grunts like a pig when approached or when taken out of water.*

Honolulu

PACIFIC OCEAN

IDAHO

CAPITAL: Boise

LARGEST CITY: Boise

POSTAL CODE: ID

LAND AREA: 82,751 square miles (214,325 sq km)

POPULATION (2010): 1,567,582

ENTERED UNION (RANK): July 3, 1890 (43)

MOTTO: *Esto perpetua.* (Let it be perpetual.)

TREE: Western white pine

FLOWER: Syringa

BIRD: Mountain bluebird

NICKNAME: Gem State

FAMOUS IDAHOAN: Gutzon Borglum, Mount Rushmore sculptor

guess what? *Seventy-two types of precious and semiprecious stones are mined in Idaho. The star garnet, the state stone, is found only in Idaho and India.*

Boise

United States

ILLINOIS

CAPITAL: Springfield

LARGEST CITY: Chicago

POSTAL CODE: IL

LAND AREA:
55,593 square miles (143,986 sq km)

POPULATION (2010): 12,830,632

ENTERED UNION (RANK):
December 3, 1818 (21)

MOTTO: State sovereignty, national union

TREE: White oak

FLOWER: Purple violet

BIRD: Cardinal

NICKNAMES: Prairie State, Land of Lincoln

FAMOUS ILLINOISAN:
Ronald Reagan,
40th U.S. President

guess what? *In the comics, Superman lives in the town of Metropolis—which really exists in southern Illinois. A 15-foot-tall (4.5 m) bronze statue of Superman was erected in 1993 to honor this small-town hero.*

Chicago

Springfield

INDIANA

CAPITAL: Indianapolis

LARGEST CITY:
Indianapolis

POSTAL CODE: IN

LAND AREA: 35,870 square miles (92,903 sq km)

POPULATION (2010): 6,483,802

ENTERED UNION (RANK):
December 11, 1816 (19)

MOTTO: The crossroads of America

TREE: Tulip tree, or yellow poplar

FLOWER: Peony

BIRD: Cardinal

NICKNAMES: Hoosier State, Crossroads of America

FAMOUS INDIANAN, OR HOOSIER:
Will Shortz, crossword puzzle creator and editor

guess what? *Wabash, Indiana, was the first U.S. city to be entirely lit by electricity.*

Indianapolis

206

IOWA

CAPITAL: Des Moines

LARGEST CITY: Des Moines

POSTAL CODE: IA

LAND AREA: 55,875 square miles (144,716 sq km)

POPULATION (2010): 3,046,355

ENTERED UNION (RANK): December 28, 1846 (29)

MOTTO: Our liberties we prize, and our rights we will maintain.

TREE: Oak

FLOWER: Wild prairie rose

BIRD: Eastern goldfinch (also known as the American goldfinch)

NICKNAME: Hawkeye State

FAMOUS IOWAN: William "Buffalo Bill" Cody, scout and entertainer

guess what? *The Eskimo Pie, the first chocolate-covered ice cream bar, was invented in Onawa, Iowa, in 1921.*

Des Moines

KANSAS

CAPITAL: Topeka

LARGEST CITY: Wichita

POSTAL CODE: KS

LAND AREA: 81,823 square miles (211,922 sq km)

POPULATION (2010): 2,853,118

ENTERED UNION (RANK): January 29, 1861 (34)

MOTTO: *Ad astra per aspera* (To the stars through difficulties)

TREE: Cottonwood

FLOWER: Sunflower

BIRD: Western meadowlark

NICKNAMES: Sunflower State, Jayhawk State, Wheat State

FAMOUS KANSAN: Amelia Earhart, first woman to fly solo across the Atlantic Ocean

guess what? *The first express mail line across the United States was operated by relays of mail-carrying riders on horseback. An original, unchanged station from the Pony Express stands near Hanover, Kansas. It is the Hollenberg Station.*

Topeka

Wichita

Iowa

KENTUCKY

CAPITAL: Frankfort

LARGEST CITY: Louisville

POSTAL CODE: KY

LAND AREA:
39,732 square miles (102,906 sq km)

POPULATION (2010): 4,339,367

ENTERED UNION (RANK):
June 1, 1792 (15)

MOTTO: United we stand, divided we fall.

TREE: Tulip poplar

FLOWER: Goldenrod

BIRD: Cardinal

NICKNAME: Bluegrass State

FAMOUS KENTUCKIAN: Diane Sawyer, news anchor and journalist

 Mammoth Cave is the longest cave in the world, with more than 390 miles (628 km) of cave passages explored.

Louisville
Frankfort

LOUISIANA

CAPITAL: Baton Rouge

LARGEST CITY:
New Orleans

POSTAL CODE: LA

LAND AREA: 43,566 square miles (112,836 sq km)

POPULATION (2010): 4,533,372

ENTERED UNION (RANK):
April 30, 1812 (18)

MOTTO: Union, justice, and confidence

TREE: Bald cypress

FLOWER: Magnolia

BIRD: Eastern brown pelican

NICKNAME: Pelican State

FAMOUS LOUISIANAN: Harry Connick Jr., actor and singer

 Louisiana has an official state crustacean. It is the crawfish.

New Orleans
Baton Rouge

MARYLAND

CAPITAL: Annapolis

LARGEST CITY: Baltimore

POSTAL CODE: MD

LAND AREA: 9,775 square miles (25,317 sq km)

POPULATION (2010): 5,773,552

ENTERED UNION (RANK): April 28, 1788 (7)

MOTTO: *Fatti maschii, parole femine* (Manly deeds, womanly words)

TREE: White oak

FLOWER: Black-eyed Susan

BIRD: Baltimore oriole

NICKNAMES: Free State, Old Line State

FAMOUS MARYLANDER: Harriet Tubman, abolitionist, Underground Railroad operator

guess what? *The official state cat of Maryland is the calico. Its orange, black, and white coloring is shared by Maryland's state bird, the Baltimore oriole, and the state butterfly, the Baltimore checkerspot.*

Baltimore

Annapolis

MAINE

CAPITAL: Augusta

LARGEST CITY: Portland

POSTAL CODE: ME

LAND AREA: 30,865 square miles (79,940 sq km)

POPULATION (2010): 1,328,361

ENTERED UNION (RANK): March 15, 1820 (23)

MOTTO: *Dirigo.* (I lead.)

TREE: White pine

FLOWER: White pine cone and tassel

BIRD: Black-capped chickadee

NICKNAME: Pine Tree State

FAMOUS MAINER: Olympia Snowe, U.S. Senator

guess what? *Scary story–writer and Maine native Stephen King built a baseball field in a park behind his house, which locals have dubbed Field of Screams.*

Augusta

Portland

MASSACHUSETTS

CAPITAL: Boston

LARGEST CITY: Boston

POSTAL CODE: MA

LAND AREA:
7,838 square miles (20,300 sq km)

POPULATION (2010): 6,547,629

ENTERED UNION (RANK):
February 6, 1788 (6)

MOTTO: *Ense petit placidam sub libertate quietem.* (By the sword we seek peace, but peace only under liberty.)

TREE: American elm

FLOWER: Mayflower

BIRD: Black-capped chickadee

NICKNAMES: Bay State, Old Colony State, Baked Bean State

FAMOUS BAY STATER: Alicia Sacramone, gymnast and Olympic medalist

guess what? *The first subway in the United States, the T, opened in Boston in 1897.*

Boston ✪

MICHIGAN

CAPITAL: Lansing

LARGEST CITY: Detroit

POSTAL CODE: MI

LAND AREA:
56,809 square miles (147,135 sq km)

POPULATION (2010): 9,883,640

ENTERED UNION (RANK):
January 26, 1837 (26)

MOTTO: *Si quaeris peninsulam amoenam circumspice.* (If you seek a pleasant peninsula, look about you.)

TREE: White pine

FLOWER: Apple blossom

BIRD: American robin

NICKNAMES: Wolverine State, Great Lakes State

FAMOUS MICHIGANDER OR MICHIGANIAN:
Stevie Wonder, singer

guess what? *The International Cherry Pit Spitting Championship is held annually near Eau Claire, Michigan. In 2003, Brian Krause set the North American record for spitting distance with 93 feet (28 m) and 6.5 inches (16.5 cm).*

Lansing ✪

Detroit

MINNESOTA

CAPITAL: St. Paul

LARGEST CITY: Minneapolis

POSTAL CODE: MN

LAND AREA: 79,617 square miles (206,208 sq km)

POPULATION (2010): 5,303,925

ENTERED UNION (RANK): May 11, 1858 (32)

MOTTO: *L'Étoile du nord* (Star of the north)

TREE: Red (or Norway) pine

FLOWER: Pink and white lady's slipper

BIRD: Common loon

NICKNAMES: North Star State, Gopher State, Land of 10,000 Lakes

FAMOUS MINNESOTAN: Charles Schulz, *Peanuts* cartoonist

 Lake Superior, one of the Great Lakes, forms part of Minnesota's border. Because of Lake Superior, the state has about 90,000 miles (144,841 km) of shoreline. That's more than California, Florida, and Hawaii put together!

MISSISSIPPI

CAPITAL: Jackson

LARGEST CITY: Jackson

POSTAL CODE: MS

LAND AREA: 46,914 square miles (121,507 sq km)

POPULATION (2010): 2,967,297

ENTERED UNION (RANK): December 10, 1817 (20)

MOTTO: *Virtute et armis* (By valor and arms)

TREE: Magnolia

FLOWER: Magnolia

BIRD: Mockingbird

NICKNAME: Magnolia State

FAMOUS MISSISSIPPIAN: Brett Favre, football player

 Every June, the Elvis Festival is held, in Tupelo, Mississippi, to honor hometown singing legend, Elvis Presley.

United States

MISSOURI

CAPITAL:
Jefferson City

LARGEST CITY:
Kansas City

POSTAL CODE: MO

LAND AREA: 68,898 square miles
(178,446 sq km)

POPULATION (2010): 5,998,927

ENTERED UNION (RANK):
August 10, 1821 (24)

MOTTO: *Salus populi suprema lex esto.*
(The welfare of the people shall be the
supreme law.)

TREE: Flowering dogwood

FLOWER: Hawthorn

BIRD: Bluebird

NICKNAME: Show Me State

FAMOUS MISSOURIAN: Mark Twain,
author of *Huckleberry Finn* and *The
Adventures of Tom Sawyer*

guess what? *In 2007, the three-toed box
turtle became
the official state reptile
of Missouri.*

MONTANA

CAPITAL: Helena

LARGEST CITY: Billings

POSTAL CODE: MT

LAND AREA:
145,556 square miles (376,990 sq km)

POPULATION (2010): 989,415

ENTERED UNION (RANK):
November 8, 1889 (41)

MOTTO: *Oro y plata* (Gold and silver)

TREE: Ponderosa pine

FLOWER: Bitterroot

BIRD: Western meadowlark

NICKNAME: Treasure State

FAMOUS MONTANAN: Evel Knievel,
motorcycle daredevil

guess what? *Moose live
throughout
western Montana and can
often be spotted in Glacier
National Park.*

NEVADA

CAPITAL: Carson City

LARGEST CITY: Las Vegas

POSTAL CODE: NV

LAND AREA: 109,806 square miles (284,397 sq km)

POPULATION (2010): 2,700,551

ENTERED UNION (RANK): October 31, 1864 (36)

MOTTO: All for our country

TREE: Single-leaf piñon pine

FLOWER: Sagebrush

BIRD: Mountain bluebird

NICKNAMES: Sagebrush State, Silver State, Battle Born State

FAMOUS NEVADAN: Andre Agassi, tennis player

guess what? *To build the Hoover Dam, which is 726 feet (221 m) high, circus acrobats were employed as high scalers. While hanging from ropes attached to canyon walls, they drilled with jackhammers, and packed dynamite into the rock.*

Carson City

Las Vegas

NEBRASKA

CAPITAL: Lincoln

LARGEST CITY: Omaha

POSTAL CODE: NE

LAND AREA: 76,878 square miles (199,114 sq km)

POPULATION (2010): 1,826,341

ENTERED UNION (RANK): March 1, 1867 (37)

MOTTO: Equality before the law

TREE: Eastern cottonwood

FLOWER: Goldenrod

BIRD: Western meadowlark

NICKNAMES: Cornhusker State, Beef State

FAMOUS NEBRASKAN: Standing Bear, Native American civil-rights advocate

guess what? *A section of the Nebraska National Forest is the largest hand-planted forest in the world. Known as "the Forest That Man Made," it is more than 141 square miles (365 sq km).*

Omaha
Lincoln

Montana

United States

NEW HAMPSHIRE

CAPITAL: Concord

LARGEST CITY: Manchester

POSTAL CODE: NH

LAND AREA: 8,969 square miles (23,230 sq km)

POPULATION (2010): 1,316,470

ENTERED UNION (RANK): June 21, 1788 (9)

MOTTO: Live free or die.

TREE: White birch (also known as the canoe birch or paper birch)

FLOWER: Purple lilac

BIRD: Purple finch

NICKNAME: Granite State

FAMOUS NEW HAMPSHIRITE: Bode Miller, skier and Olympic medalist

guess what? Several animals are on New Hampshire's endangered and threatened species list. They include the lynx, bald eagle, short nose sturgeon, common loon, timber rattlesnake, and Karner blue butterfly.

Concord

Manchester

NEW JERSEY

CAPITAL: Trenton

LARGEST CITY: Newark

POSTAL CODE: NJ

LAND AREA: 7,419 square miles (19,215 sq km)

POPULATION (2010): 8,791,894

ENTERED UNION (RANK): December 18, 1787 (3)

MOTTO: Liberty and prosperity

TREE: Red oak

FLOWER: Common meadow violet

BIRD: Eastern (or American) goldfinch

NICKNAME: Garden State

FAMOUS NEW JERSEYITE: Edwin "Buzz" Aldrin, astronaut

guess what? The Popcorn Park Zoo in New Jersey was founded by the Associated Humane Societies in 1977 to care for sick, injured, and abused animals.

Newark

Trenton

NEW MEXICO

CAPITAL: Santa Fe

LARGEST CITY: Albuquerque

POSTAL CODE: NM

LAND AREA: 121,365 square miles (314,335 sq km)

POPULATION (2010): 2,059,179

ENTERED UNION (RANK): January 6, 1912 (47)

MOTTO: *Crescit eundo.* (It grows as it goes.)

TREE: Piñon pine

FLOWER: Yucca

BIRD: Roadrunner

NICKNAMES: Land of Enchantment, Cactus State

FAMOUS NEW MEXICAN: William Hanna, animator

guess what? *The stunning white sand seen at the White Sands National Monument is a rare type of sand made up of white gypsum crystals.*

NEW YORK

CAPITAL: Albany

LARGEST CITY: New York

POSTAL CODE: NY

LAND AREA: 47,224 square miles (122,310 sq km)

POPULATION (2010): 19,378,102

ENTERED UNION (RANK): July 26, 1788 (11)

MOTTO: *Excelsior* (Ever upward)

TREE: Sugar maple

FLOWER: Rose

BIRD: Bluebird

NICKNAME: Empire State

FAMOUS NEW YORKER: Jonas Salk, developer of polio vaccine

guess what? *New York City was the first capital of the United States under the Constitution.*

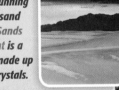

NORTH CAROLINA

CAPITAL: Raleigh

LARGEST CITY: Charlotte

POSTAL CODE: NC

LAND AREA:
48,708 square miles (126,154 sq km)

POPULATION (2010): 9,535,483

ENTERED UNION (RANK):
November 21, 1789 (12)

MOTTO: *Esse quam videri*
(To be rather than to seem)

TREE: Pine

FLOWER: Flowering dogwood

BIRD: Cardinal

NICKNAME: Tar Heel State

FAMOUS NORTH CAROLINIAN:
Dale Earnhardt Jr., NASCAR driver

guess what? North Carolina produces more sweet potatoes than any other state in the nation.

NORTH DAKOTA

CAPITAL: Bismarck

LARGEST CITY: Fargo

POSTAL CODE: ND

LAND AREA:
68,994 square miles
(178,694 sq km)

POPULATION (2010): 672,591

ENTERED UNION (RANK):
November 2, 1889 (39)

MOTTO: Liberty and union, now and forever, one and inseparable

TREE: American elm

FLOWER: Wild prairie rose

BIRD: Western meadowlark

NICKNAMES: Sioux State, Flickertail State, Peace Garden State, Rough Rider State

FAMOUS NORTH DAKOTAN:
Louis L'Amour, author

guess what? The annual Potato Bowl USA is held in Grand Forks, North Dakota, and is the biggest french fry feast in the world. A record was set in 2006 with 4,680 pounds (2,122.8 kg) of french fries served. Happy eaters also put away about 113 gallons (427.7 L) of ketchup.

OKLAHOMA

CAPITAL:
Oklahoma City

LARGEST CITY:
Oklahoma City

POSTAL CODE: OK

LAND AREA: 68,679 square miles
(177,879 sq km)

POPULATION (2010): 3,751,351

ENTERED UNION (RANK):
November 16, 1907 (46)

MOTTO: *Labor omnia vincit.*
(Labor conquers all things.)

TREE: Eastern redbud

FLOWER: Mistletoe

BIRD: Scissor-tailed flycatcher

NICKNAME: Sooner State

FAMOUS OKLAHOMAN:
Carrie Underwood, singer

guess what? *In 1988, Oklahoma chose an official state meal. It includes black-eyed peas, chicken fried steak, corn, cornbread, fried okra, strawberries, sausage and gravy, barbequed pork, squash, biscuits, grits, and pecan pie.*

OHIO

CAPITAL: Columbus

LARGEST CITY:
Columbus

POSTAL CODE: OH

LAND AREA: 40,953 square miles
(106,068 sq km)

POPULATION (2010): 11,536,504

ENTERED UNION (RANK):
March 1, 1803 (17)

MOTTO: With God, all things
are possible.

TREE: Buckeye

FLOWER: Scarlet carnation

BIRD: Cardinal

NICKNAME: Buckeye State

FAMOUS OHIOAN: Maya Lin, artist and
architect; designer of the Vietnam
Veterans Memorial

guess what? *John Glenn, the first American to orbit the Earth, was born in Cambridge, Ohio. He served as a U.S. senator for Ohio from 1975 to 1999.*

Oklahoma

OREGON

CAPITAL: Salem

LARGEST CITY: Portland

POSTAL CODE: OR

LAND AREA: 96,003 square miles (248,648 sq km)

POPULATION (2010): 3,831,074

ENTERED UNION (RANK): February 14, 1859 (33)

MOTTO: *Alis volat propriis.* (She flies with her own wings.)

TREE: Douglas fir

FLOWER: Oregon grape

BIRD: Western meadowlark

NICKNAME: Beaver State

FAMOUS OREGONIAN: Beverly Cleary, author

guess what? *The state flag of Oregon has two sides. One side features 33 stars surrounding a shield with an eagle on top, while the other side features a beaver, the state animal.*

Portland

Salem

PENNSYLVANIA

CAPITAL: Harrisburg

LARGEST CITY: Philadelphia

POSTAL CODE: PA

LAND AREA: 44,820 square miles (116,084 sq km)

POPULATION (2010): 12,702,379

ENTERED UNION (RANK): December 12, 1787 (2)

MOTTO: Virtue, liberty, and independence

TREE: Hemlock

FLOWER: Mountain laurel

BIRD: Ruffed grouse

NICKNAME: Keystone State

FAMOUS PENNSYLVANIAN: Mary Cassatt, painter

guess what? *The Declaration of Independence and the U.S. Constitution were both signed in Philadelphia, Pennsylvania, which served as the country's capital from 1790 to 1800.*

Harrisburg

Philadelphia

RHODE ISLAND

CAPITAL: Providence

LARGEST CITY: Providence

POSTAL CODE: RI

LAND AREA:
1,045 square miles (2,707 sq km)

POPULATION (2010): 1,052,567

ENTERED UNION (RANK): May 29, 1790 (13)

MOTTO: Hope

TREE: Red maple

FLOWER: Violet

BIRD: Rhode Island red hen

NICKNAME: Ocean State

FAMOUS RHODE ISLANDER:
Gilbert Stuart, artist who painted the portrait of George Washington seen on the $1 bill

 Rhode Island was the first of the original 13 colonies to declare its independence from Great Britain.

 Providence

SOUTH CAROLINA

CAPITAL: Columbia

LARGEST CITY:
Columbia

POSTAL CODE: SC

LAND AREA: 30,111 square miles (77,987 sq km)

POPULATION (2010): 4,625,364

ENTERED UNION (RANK):
May 23, 1788 (8)

MOTTOES: *Animis opibusque parati* (Prepared in mind and resources); *Dum spiro spero.* (While I breathe, I hope.)

TREE: Palmetto

FLOWER: Yellow jessamine

BIRD: Carolina wren

NICKNAME: Palmetto State

FAMOUS SOUTH CAROLINIAN:
Marian Wright Edelman, activist, founder of Children's Defense Fund

 There are high amounts of the element iodine in plants grown in South Carolina. For that reason, it is sometimes called the Iodine State.

 Columbia

SOUTH DAKOTA

CAPITAL: Pierre

LARGEST CITY: Sioux Falls

POSTAL CODE: SD

LAND AREA: 75,898 square miles (196,575 sq km)

POPULATION (2010): 814,180

ENTERED UNION (RANK): November 2, 1889 (40)

MOTTO: Under God the people rule.

TREE: Black Hills spruce

FLOWER: Pasqueflower

BIRD: Ring-necked pheasant

NICKNAMES: Mount Rushmore State, Coyote State

FAMOUS SOUTH DAKOTAN: Sitting Bull, Sioux chief

guess what? *Corn Palace, in Mitchell, South Dakota, is the only place in the world to find murals made with ears of corn. The corn is nailed to the Palace's exterior to create a scene and is replaced each year.*

TENNESSEE

CAPITAL: Nashville

LARGEST CITY: Memphis

POSTAL CODE: TN

LAND AREA: 41,220 square miles (106,760 sq km)

POPULATION (2010): 6,346,105

ENTERED UNION (RANK): June 1, 1796 (16)

MOTTO: Agriculture and commerce

TREE: Tulip poplar

FLOWER: Iris

BIRD: Mockingbird

NICKNAME: Volunteer State

FAMOUS TENNESSEAN: Dolly Parton, musician and actress

guess what? *Nashville's Parthenon, completed in 1897, is a full-scale replica of the Parthenon in Athens, Greece, which was finished in 438 B.C. The Nashville site includes an art museum and a colorful 42-foot (12.8 m) statue of Athena.*

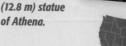

★ Nashville

TEXAS

CAPITAL: Austin

LARGEST CITY: Houston

POSTAL CODE: TX

LAND AREA: 261,914 square miles (678,357 sq km)

POPULATION (2010): 25,145,561

ENTERED UNION (RANK): December 29, 1845 (28)

MOTTO: Friendship

TREE: Pecan

FLOWER: Texas bluebonnet

BIRD: Mockingbird

NICKNAME: Lone Star State

FAMOUS TEXAN: Selena Gomez, actress and singer

guess what? *The runway of the Amarillo airport in northern Texas is so long it has been designated as an alternate landing site for the space shuttle.*

Austin ★   Houston

UTAH

CAPITAL: Salt Lake City

LARGEST CITY: Salt Lake City

POSTAL CODE: UT

LAND AREA: 82,168 square miles (212,815 sq km)

POPULATION (2010): 2,763,885

ENTERED UNION (RANK): January 4, 1896 (45)

MOTTO: Industry

TREE: Blue spruce

FLOWER: Sego lily

BIRD: California gull

NICKNAME: Beehive State

FAMOUS UTAHN: Philo T. Farnsworth, inventor of the television

guess what? *Kanab, Utah, is known as Little Hollywood because many motion pictures have been filmed in the area.*

Salt Lake City

United States

VERMONT

CAPITAL: Montpelier

LARGEST CITY: Burlington

POSTAL CODE: VT

LAND AREA: 9,249 square miles (23,956 sq km)

POPULATION (2010): 625,741

ENTERED UNION (RANK): March 4, 1791 (14)

MOTTO: Vermont: freedom and unity

TREE: Sugar maple

FLOWER: Red clover

BIRD: Hermit thrush

NICKNAME: Green Mountain State

FAMOUS VERMONTER: Joseph Smith, founder of the Mormon Church

Guess what? *Billboards are not permitted to be displayed along Vermont's highways.*

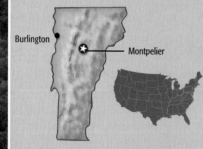

Burlington

Montpelier

VIRGINIA

CAPITAL: Richmond

LARGEST CITY: Virginia Beach

POSTAL CODE: VA

LAND AREA: 39,598 square miles (102,559 sq km)

POPULATION (2010): 8,001,024

ENTERED UNION (RANK): June 25, 1788 (10)

MOTTO: *Sic semper tyrannis* (Thus always to tyrants)

TREE: Flowering dogwood

FLOWER: American dogwood

BIRD: Cardinal

NICKNAMES: The Old Dominion, Mother of Presidents

FAMOUS VIRGINIANS: Arthur Ashe, tennis player

Guess what? *Virginia has had three capital cities: Jamestown, Williamsburg, and Richmond.*

Richmond

Virginia Beach

WEST VIRGINIA

CAPITAL:
Charleston

LARGEST CITY:
Charleston

POSTAL CODE: WV

LAND AREA: 24,087 square miles
(62,385 sq km)

POPULATION (2010): 1,852,994

ENTERED UNION (RANK):
June 20, 1863 (35)

MOTTO: *Montani semper liberi.*
(Mountaineers are always free.)

TREE: Sugar maple

FLOWER: Rhododendron

BIRD: Cardinal

NICKNAME: Mountain State

FAMOUS WEST VIRGINIAN:
Brad Paisley, musician

Guess what? *Mother's Day was first celebrated in Grafton, West Virginia, in 1908.*

Charleston

WASHINGTON

CAPITAL: Olympia

LARGEST CITY: Seattle

POSTAL CODE: WA

LAND AREA: 66,582 square miles
(172,447 sq km)

POPULATION (2010): 6,724,540

ENTERED UNION (RANK):
November 11, 1889 (42)

MOTTO: *Al-ki* (An Indian word meaning
"By and by" or "Hope for the future")

TREE: Western hemlock

FLOWER: Coast rhododendron

BIRD: Willow goldfinch

NICKNAME: Evergreen State

FAMOUS WASHINGTONIAN:
Apolo Ohno, speed skater
and Olympic medalist

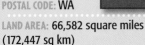

Guess what? *The first Starbucks was built in Seattle's Pike Place Market.*

Seattle

Olympia

United States

West Virginia

WISCONSIN

CAPITAL: Madison

LARGEST CITY: Milwaukee

POSTAL CODE: WI

LAND AREA: 54,314 square miles (140,673 sq km)

POPULATION (2010): 5,686,986

ENTERED UNION (RANK): May 29, 1848 (30)

MOTTO: Forward

TREE: Sugar maple

FLOWER: Wood violet

BIRD: American robin

NICKNAMES: Badger State, Dairy State

FAMOUS WISCONSINITE: Frank Lloyd Wright, architect

Guess what? *The original Barbie® doll is from the fictional town of Willows, Wisconsin. Her full name is Barbara Millicent Roberts.*

Madison • Milwaukee

WISCONSIN 1848

WYOMING

CAPITAL: Cheyenne

LARGEST CITY: Cheyenne

POSTAL CODE: WY

LAND AREA: 97,105 square miles (251,502 sq km)

POPULATION (2010): 563,626

ENTERED UNION (RANK): July 10, 1890 (44)

MOTTO: Equal rights

TREE: Plains cottonwood

FLOWER: Indian paintbrush

BIRD: Meadowlark

NICKNAMES: Big Wyoming, Equality State, Cowboy State

FAMOUS WYOMINGITE: Jackson Pollock, artist

Guess what? *Wyoming was the first U.S. state to give women the right to vote.*

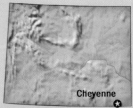
Cheyenne

Wisconsin

224

WASHINGTON, D.C.

The District of Columbia, which covers the same area as the city of Washington, is the capital of the United States. The district's history began in 1790 when Congress took charge of organizing a new site for the country's capital. George Washington chose the spot on the Potomac River, midway between the northern and southern states. The seat of government was transferred from Philadelphia, Pennsylvania, to Washington, D.C., on December 1, 1800, and President John Adams became the first resident of the White House.

LAND AREA:
68.25 square miles (177 sq km)

POPULATION (2010): 601,723

MOTTO: *Justitia omnibus* (Justice for all)

TREE: Scarlet oak

FLOWER: American beauty rose

BIRD: Wood thrush

FAMOUS WASHINGTONIAN:
John Philip Sousa, composer

CAPITAL PLACES

Many landmarks and memorials found in Washington, D.C., are monuments to people and events in U.S. history. Other impressive buildings are used by government officials. Here are a few Washington standouts.

The National Archives Building holds original copies of the Declaration of Independence, the U.S. Constitution, and the Bill of Rights.

The Lincoln Memorial pays tribute to Abraham Lincoln, President during the Civil War.

The U.S. Capitol Building is where members of the House of Representatives and the Senate meet.

The Vietnam Veterans Memorial features a wall with the names of more than 58,000 Americans who died during the Vietnam War.

The National Mall refers to the open area between the Capitol and the Lincoln Memorial, and between the White House and the Jefferson Memorial. This lawn area is surrounded by many museums, including the National Gallery of Art, the National Museum of Natural History, and the National Air and Space Museum.

United States

225

U.S. TERRITORIES

In addition to the 50 states and the District of Columbia, the United States government administers some tiny, mostly uninhabited islands around the world, including Kingman Reef, Palmyra Atoll, and Howland Island. The major U.S. territories are Puerto Rico, American Samoa, Guam, the U.S. Virgin Islands, and the Northern Mariana Islands.

AMERICAN SAMOA, a group of islands in the South Pacific, is situated about halfway between Hawaii and New Zealand. It has a land area of 77 square miles (200 sq km) and a population of approximately 67,242.

American Samoa

GUAM, in the North Pacific Ocean, was given to the United States by Spain in 1898. It has a land area of 209 square miles (541 sq km) and a population of approximately 183,286.

U.S. VIRGIN ISLANDS, which include St. Croix, St. Thomas, St. John, and many other islands, are located in the Caribbean Sea, east of Puerto Rico. Together, they have a land area of 136 square miles (351 sq km) and a population of approximately 109,666.

St. John, U.S. Virgin Islands

THE NORTHERN MARIANA ISLANDS are located in the North Pacific Ocean. They have a land area of 176 square miles (456 sq km) and a population of approximately 46,050.

PUERTO RICO is in the Caribbean Sea, about 1,000 miles (1,609 km) southeast of Miami, Florida. A U.S. possession since 1898, it consists of the island of Puerto Rico plus the adjacent islets of Vieques, Culebra, and Mona. Both Spanish and English are spoken there.

Guam

San Juan, Puerto Rico

SPOTLIGHT ON PUERTO RICO

CAPITAL: San Juan

LARGEST CITY: San Juan

LAND AREA:
3,459 square miles (8,959 sq km)

POPULATION (2011): 3,989,133

MOTTO: *Joannes est nomen eius.*
(John is his name.)

TREE: Ceiba (silk-cotton)

FLOWER: Maga (Puerto Rican hibiscus)

BIRD: Reinita (stripe-headed tanager)

FAMOUS PUERTO RICAN:
Ricky Martin, singer

U.S. MONUMENT MATCHUP

Some of these national monuments were built by humans. Others are natural wonders. But all are exciting sights to see. Match each monument to the facts about it.

 Gateway Arch **A**

 Muir Woods National Monument **B**

 Mount Rushmore **C**

 Washington Monument **D**

 Rainbow Bridge **E**

1 This South Dakota site shows the faces of four U.S. Presidents. Their faces were carved into the side of a mountain by sculptor Gutzon Borglum.

2 This Washington, D.C. attraction is 555 feet (169 m) tall. It is the tallest structure in our nation's capital.

3 At 630 feet (192 m), this monument was built to honor the historic westward expedition of the explorers Meriwether Lewis and William Clark.

4 This natural bridge is 275 feet long (84 m) and 290 feet (88 m) high. It is the largest natural bridge in the world. You can find it in Utah.

5 Sequoias are the tallest trees in the world. They touch the sky at this California spot.

Answers on page 243.

MYSTERY PERSON

I was born on September 26, 1774, in Leominster, Massachusetts. As a young man, I collected apple seeds. I cared for 1,200 acres of land. I am known for planting apple seeds as I traveled west. I also gave away seeds to pioneers. My work earned me a popular nickname.

WHO AM I? _____

Answer on page 243.

TOP 10

U.S. Baby Names
What are Americans naming their little ones? Here are the top picks for 2009.

GIRLS
1. ISABELLA
2. EMMA
3. OLIVIA
4. SOPHIA
5. AVA
6. EMILY
7. MADISON
8. ABIGAIL
9. CHLOE
10. MIA

BOYS
1. JACOB
2. ETHAN
3. MICHAEL
4. ALEXANDER
5. WILLIAM
6. JOSHUA
7. DANIEL
8. JAYDEN
9. NOAH
10. ANTHONY

United States

227

THE UNITED STATES

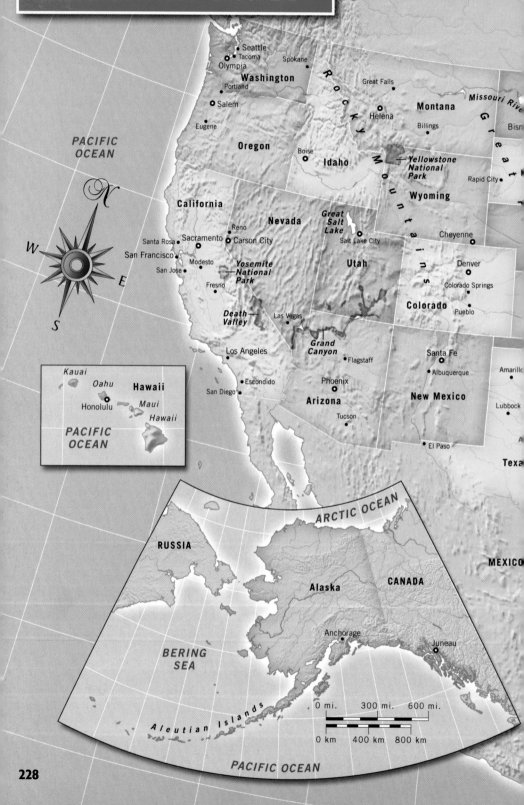

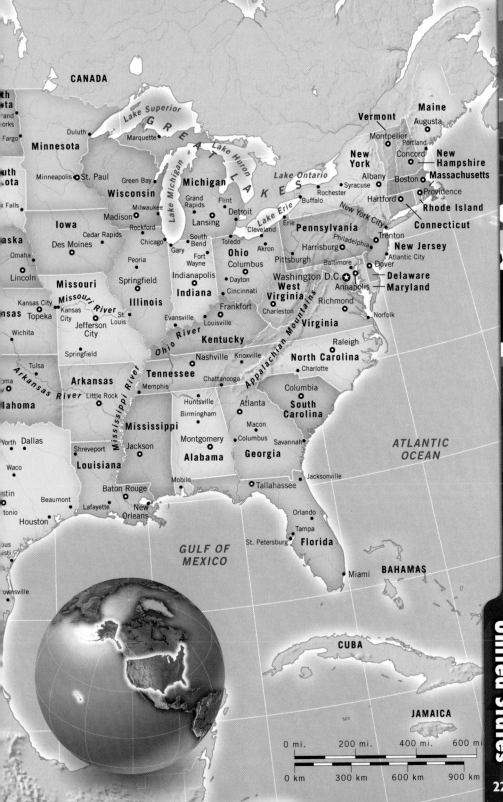

CANADA

Lake Superior

GREAT LAKES

Minnesota
Duluth
Marquette

Wisconsin
Green Bay
Milwaukee
Madison
Rockford

Iowa
Cedar Rapids
Chicago
Des Moines

Missouri
Kansas City
Topeka
Jefferson City
Wichita
Springfield

Arkansas
Little Rock

Mississippi
Jackson
Shreveport

Louisiana
Baton Rouge
New Orleans
Beaumont
Lafayette
Houston

Lake Michigan

Michigan
Grand Rapids
Flint
Lansing
Detroit
South Bend
Gary
Fort Wayne

Lake Huron

Lake Ontario

Lake Erie

Illinois
Peoria
Springfield
Indianapolis

Indiana

Ohio
Columbus
Dayton
Cincinnati
Toledo
Akron
Cleveland
Erie

Frankfort

Kentucky
Louisville
Evansville
Nashville
Knoxville
Chattanooga

Tennessee
Memphis
Huntsville
Birmingham

Alabama
Montgomery
Mobile

Columbus

Macon
Georgia
Savannah

Atlanta

South Carolina
Columbia

North Carolina
Charlotte
Raleigh

Appalachian Mountains

Virginia
Richmond
Charleston

West Virginia

Vermont
Montpelier

Maine
Augusta
Portland
Concord

New York
Albany
Syracuse
Rochester
Buffalo

New Hampshire

Massachusetts
Boston
Providence

Rhode Island

Hartford
Connecticut

New York City
Trenton

New Jersey
Atlantic City

Pennsylvania
Harrisburg
Pittsburgh
Philadelphia

Baltimore
Dover
Delaware

Washington D.C.
Annapolis
Maryland

Norfolk

Missouri River
Ohio River
Mississippi River
Arkansas River

ATLANTIC OCEAN

Tallahassee

Jacksonville

Orlando
Tampa
St. Petersburg
Florida
Miami

GULF OF MEXICO

BAHAMAS

CUBA

JAMAICA

Dallas
Waco

North

0 mi.   200 mi.   400 mi.   600 mi.

0 km   300 km   600 km   900 km

United States

229

Volunteering

FROM TIME FOR KIDS MAGAZINE

Kids Lead the Way

By Vickie An, Claudia Atticot, Brenda Iasevoli, and Kelli Plasket

Who says you need superpowers to save the world? Every year on April 22, many people worldwide celebrate Earth Day by taking part in green activities in their communities. The annual event was founded in 1970 by U.S. senator Gaylord Nelson of Wisconsin.

Volunteers help plant trees, clean up parks and beaches, collect recyclables, and more. But you don't have to wait until Earth Day to get active. You don't have to be an adult, either! Every day, young people across the globe are doing their part to keep the Earth healthy and green. These are just a few kid heroes for the planet.

MANATEE MINDER

When she was in second grade, Stephanie Cohen read about a baby manatee hit by a boat off the coast of Florida. Marine biologists at Hubbs-SeaWorld Research Institute, a nonprofit group, saved the manatee. But caring for the sea creature was costly. Stephanie took up a collection and raised $27 in one day. At 19, Stephanie still raises money to help these "gentle giants." She sells homemade manatee pins, ornaments, candles, and cards on her website. Last year, she raised $3,000. "Animals are my passion," she told TFK.

COLOR US GREEN!

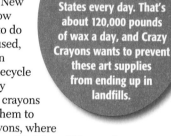

The students at Clarendon Elementary School, in Secaucus, New Jersey, know just what to do with old, used, and broken crayons: Recycle them! They collect the crayons and send them to Crazy Crayons, where they are remolded into different shapes and sizes. In the past eight years, New Jersey students have recycled nearly nine tons of crayons. "We're trying to help the Earth because too much is being wasted," 10-year-old Amanda Tabasco told TFK.

More than 12 million crayons are made in the United States every day. That's about 120,000 pounds of wax a day, and Crazy Crayons wants to prevent these art supplies from ending up in landfills.

Manatees are gentle, slow-moving herbivores, which means that they eat only plants.

TOP 5 U.S. States for Volunteering

More than 60 million Americans gave their time in 2009. In which states are volunteers most likely to give more than 100 hours a year?

1. Utah		45% of volunteers
2. Iowa		39% of volunteers
3. Minnesota		37% of volunteers
4. Alaska		37% of volunteers
5. Nebraska		36% of volunteers

SOURCE: CORPORATION FOR NATIONAL AND COMMUNITY SERVICE

GOODBYE, PAPER BAGS!

When Adrienne Boukis was in sixth grade, in Walnut Creek, California, she noticed that many of her classmates carried paper lunch bags. To help kids cut down on waste, she invented a reusable, biodegradable lunch sack. It has handles, a Velcro closure, and a front pocket. The fabric is partially made from recycled plastic bottles. "Kids like it because they can fold it up and put it in their backpacks," Adrienne told TFK. She sells the bags on her website. Some of the proceeds go to charity.

From chip bags and sandwich wrappers to disposable drink containers, the average school kid generates 67 pounds (30 kg) of lunch bag waste every year. Adrienne wants to help change that.

MAX IS ON A MISSION

Every year, Max Kesselman, of Pennsylvania, celebrates his December 3rd birthday by cleaning up the Earth. When Max was 6, he noticed trash on the side of the road. He wrote a letter to local leaders proposing a cleanup day on his birthday.

The township sponsored the first cleanup on Max's eighth birthday. More than 80 people came out to help and filled trash bags. "It's cool to see friends and people I don't know helping me and the Earth," Max told TFK.

HE'S SKIING TO SAVE THE EARTH

At 15, Parker Liautaud wanted to raise awareness about the effects of climate change on the polar regions. He set out to become one of the youngest people ever to ski to the North Pole. The teen spent nine months prepping for the difficult trek. Parker and his guide, Doug Stoup, began the Arctic expedition on April 2, 2010. They set off on foot to spread the word about the destruction of the polar regions. They did not use dogs. Instead, they pulled sleds filled with supplies. They faced freezing temperatures and whipping winds. After eight days, the harsh conditions forced them to finish the last 15 miles (24 km) of the journey by helicopter. But Parker feels he met his goal to inspire others. "All young people have the power to make a change," he told TFK.

On his birthday, Max likes to do more than receive presents. He explained, "I decided that every year around my birthday, my gift to the Earth was to help clean it up."

Volunteering

231

LEND A HAND!

Before setting out to be a volunteer, think about the cause you would like to help most. Here are a few that might be of interest.

EDUCATION

You might be able to help students from other countries speak better English. If you are good at math, tutor a younger child who is having trouble with the subject. Check with a teacher to find the best use for your time and talents.

ANIMALS

If you love animals, donate your time to an animal shelter or a pet-rescue group. You and your family might even be able to foster a pet.

HOMELESSNESS AND HUNGER

Volunteer at a shelter, soup kitchen, or for a religious group that works with people who have no place to live or who need assistance to feed their families. Gather a group and organize a canned-food or warm-clothing drive.

MUSIC

Do you enjoy singing or playing an instrument? Look for a choir or another group that performs for nursing homes, hospitals, or community centers.

KIDS AND ADULTS WITH ILLNESSES

Many hospitals and clinics have opportunities for those who want to help out. You might sit with sick children and talk with them, play with them, or read to them. You could also help serve meals, make beds, and deliver gifts to patients. Call your local health care center to find out about volunteering opportunities for students your age.

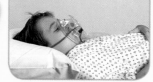

LITERACY

Share your passion for books with others. Libraries and schools welcome volunteers to read stories to younger children, and librarians always need help reshelving books!

THE ENVIRONMENT

There are countless ways you can help the environment on your own or as a group. Organize a recycling drive, have a contest to see which street in your town can recycle the most trash, or start a gardening club at school. Volunteer at a nearby state or national park, or organize a tree-planting day throughout your community.

SPORTS

If you like running, swimming, or even just walking, consider participating in a race for a cause such as cancer, AIDS, or multiple sclerosis. If you don't want to race, you can distribute water and cheer for others.

ELDERLY PEOPLE

Elderly people—whether they live alone or in group homes—can often feel lonely. A visit from a young person like you can go far toward comforting them or helping them accomplish small tasks. You might call an assisted living community to see if they need young volunteers to help out or just to hang out.

RAISING MONEY FOR DONATIONS

Often, the best way you can help people or charitable organizations is by sending much-needed money. Here are some ideas for how to raise funds for good causes.

Arrange a walk-a-thon, read-a-thon, dance-a-thon or jump-rope-a-thon. Collect pledges for each mile you walk, book you read, hour you dance, or minute you jump rope!

Host an auction. Ask people and businesses in your community to donate items or services, such as gift certificates to restaurants or baskets of products. Then invite your parents' friends and coworkers, your friends' families, and other adults to bid on the items.

Organize a car wash. Design colorful flyers and hang them up all over your town, making sure that everybody knows that the money will go to a worthy cause.

Host a bake sale. Invite lots of volunteers to help with the baking and set up your sale in a busy area. Be sure to offer lots of different types of treats.

Put on a show. Present a student talent show and charge admission to all audience members.

A LITTLE SURE CAN HELP A LOT

You may think you need to make a large contribution to a charity to accomplish something significant, but that's not the case. Here are some examples of what small donations can purchase.

ORGANIZATION	DONATION AMOUNT	WHAT IT CAN BUY
Just a Drop	about $2	a 10-year supply of safe drinking water for a child
Heifer International	$8	tree seedlings
Heifer International	$10	1/12 share of a goat, sheep, or pig
Oxfam America	$18	children's books
Oxfam America	$18	mosquito nets
Oxfam America	$20	irrigation for a farmer's land for two months
Heifer International	$20	a flock of geese, ducks, or chicks
Just a Drop	about $20	a lifetime supply of safe drinking water for one person
Oxfam America	$25	school supplies
Red Cross International	$25	five blankets for an emergency shelter
Unicef	$25	immunizations to protect a young person from the six leading childhood diseases
Heifer International	$30	a hive of honeybees
Oxfam America	$30	the planting of 50 trees
Heifer International	$60	three rabbits
Red Cross International	$75	a doctor visit for a person injured in a disaster

Volunteering

233

Weather

Tracking Tornadoes

By Brenda Iasevoli

Joshua Wurman is a meteorologist, a scientist who studies weather. He is also the head of the biggest tornado research project ever undertaken. Started in 2009, the two-year, $12 million, government-funded program is called VORTEX2. At the height of tornado season, he and about 100 other scientists equipped with high-tech weather instruments chase tornadoes across the central United States. Their mission: to learn how the fierce storms are born.

The VORTEX2 team collects data in many ways. Doppler radar systems on trucks measure the strength and size of a tornado. Scientists manning the radar stay inside the vehicles. Other team members brave the storm. Their job is to place 120-pound (54 kg) yellow discs, called pods, in the tornado's path. The pods measure the temperature, humidity, wind speed, and direction of a twister as it passes over them. A waterproof steel box protects the data.

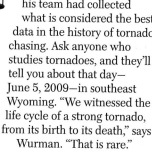

Scientists place pods like these in the path of a tornado.

CHASING THE WIND

Wurman told TFK about his experience tracking a now-famous tornado. From the mission control vehicle, the tornado looked like a big, gray triangle pointing toward the ground. The closer it came, the skinnier the tornado got, until the gray triangle looked like a twisting snake. "It was right outside the door, heading toward us," said Wurman. "At the last minute, we drove away."

But not before he and his team had collected what is considered the best data in the history of tornado chasing. Ask anyone who studies tornadoes, and they'll tell you about that day—June 5, 2009—in southeast Wyoming. "We witnessed the life cycle of a strong tornado, from its birth to its death," says Wurman. "That is rare."

TERRIBLE TWISTERS

Tornadoes are nature's most powerful storms. They can produce fierce winds of

SUPERCELL

VORTEX

COOLER AIR

WARM AIR

Guess what? While tornadoes can form at any time of the day or year, they most often occur during late afternoons in spring and summer months.

INSIDE A TORNADO

Tornadoes usually form during giant thunderstorms called supercells. Winds close to the ground are weaker than winds higher up. When the two push on the layer of air between them, the layer rotates, or spins. It forms a horizontal tube. Rising warm air lifts the tube until it is vertical. Cooler air drops down, pulling the tube to the ground. A tornado is formed. Many are black or brown from the dust and dirt they suck up through the vortex, or center.

300 miles (483 km) per hour. In late March 2010, tornadoes ripped through central North Carolina, toppling trees and tearing down houses. One witness said the tornado sounded like a freight train. Another said it "looked like a cloud of dirt coming down." No one was badly hurt, even though there was little warning of the coming twisters.

VORTEX2 scientists want to better understand how tornadoes form so they can increase warning time—and save lives. Today, meteorologists usually can give a 13-minute alert about a possible tornado strike. The goal is to push the time to 20 or even 30 minutes.

Meteorologist Greg Carbin of the Storm Prediction Center, in Norman, Oklahoma, explains that science is not yet capable of predicting how many tornadoes will happen in a given year. "Many factors

VORTEX2 scientists do not have a home base. Many of their most useful instruments are mounted on vehicles. That way, they can stay on the move. During tornado season, they can follow severe weather from state to state.

contribute to severe weather," Carbin says. "It's like putting together a jigsaw puzzle with half the pieces missing."

Karen Kosiba is a scientist working on VORTEX2. She is determined to find those missing pieces. "The most challenging and fun part of this job," Kosiba says, "is finding ways to get information despite the unpredictability of nature."

TOP 5 Tornado States

3 Kansas 55
4 Nebraska 45
5 Iowa 37
2 Oklahoma 57
1 Texas 139

About 1,000 twisters hit the U.S. each year. Many are in an area called Tornado Alley. The map shows about how many storms strike the top tornado states yearly.

1. Tornado Alley is the zone from Texas north to South Dakota. How many states is that?

2. Which state do tornadoes strike most?

3. True or false: More twisters hit Kansas than Iowa.

Answers on page 243.

KEY: ☐ Area most hit by tornadoes   ☐ Top states for tornadoes

Weather

235

WILD WIND

Tornadoes aren't the only windy weather disasters to worry about. There are also tropical storms known as hurricanes, cyclones, and typhoons. These storms have winds stronger than 75 miles (120 km) per hour. They're called hurricanes when they form in the northern Atlantic Ocean and the northeastern or southern Pacific Ocean, typhoons when they develop over the northwestern Pacific, and cyclones when they form over the Indian Ocean. No matter what they're called, they can cause serious harm.

Tropical storms are created when tropical winds gather moisture as they pass over warm water. The winds of a hurricane rotate around an eye, or center. Within the eye of the storm, the weather is calm. It can even be sunny. Outside the eye, however, the warm ocean waters give energy to the storm, causing swirling wind and pounding rain. Hurricanes are strongest when they're over water, but they can remain fierce after reaching land.

A satellite image shows a hurricane over Florida.

The eye of the storm

After Hurricane Ike in 2008, Texas residents had to clear away tons of debris.

WHERE DOES WIND COME FROM?

Winds are caused by the sun's heat falling on different parts of the Earth at different times of the day and year. The temperatures over water and land change at different rates during the day and night. In addition, warm air rises and cool air sinks. These fluctuations cause the movement of air in different patterns, creating wind.

guess what? Hurricanes are measured in categories, ranging from 1 to 5. The winds of a Category 5 storm move at more than 155 miles (250 km) per hour.

High winds batter trees along the coast of Mexico.

guess what? About 44,000 thunderstorms happen on Earth every day. A thunderstorm occurs when a huge mass of warm air collides with a huge mass of cold air.

236

DROUGHTS AND FLOODS

Not having enough water or having too much of it can both cause serious problems.

A **drought** is an unusually long period of insufficient rain or snowfall. Droughts can last for years, though most last only a few weeks or months. Warm-weather droughts affect agriculture immediately, and can lead to large

Trees and grass cannot survive without water.

crop losses. Cold-weather droughts cause trouble the following spring, when there is not enough snow and ice melting to fill rivers and streams.

During the 1930s, the states experiencing severe drought conditions became known as the Dust Bowl. The term, coined by a reporter named Robert Geiger, mostly referred to parts of Colorado, New Mexico, Texas, Oklahoma, and Kansas.

Floods are usually caused by rivers or lakes overflowing their banks, or by surges of ocean water during periods of heavy rainfall. The Galveston Flood of 1900 in Texas was caused by a hurricane surge and took the lives of more than 5,000 people. Other floods are caused by failures of engineering.

The term "flash flood" refers to a particularly dangerous type of flood that takes place very quickly and without warning. They generally occur when the water in streams or rivers in low-lying areas comes up over its banks.

In 2005, heavy rains from Hurricane Katrina raised the levels of Lake Pontchartrain. This caused the levees to break, resulting in devastating floods in New Orleans.

FIND THE FLAKES

TIME FOR KIDS **GAME**

In nature, no two snowflakes are exactly alike. But in this game, there is one identical pair. Can you find it?

Answer on page 243.

Five Fun Facts About Winter Weather

1. It is never too cold to snow.

2. Every year, about 105 storms drop snow somewhere on the continental United States.

3. Nearly every part of the U.S. has had snow—even Florida!

4. Snow changes how sound travels. A thick layer of fresh, fluffy snow absorbs sound waves. If the snowy surface is smooth and hard, it helps noise travel farther and makes sound clearer.

5. Snow appears white because visible sunlight is white.

Weather

237

What's Next?

SCIENCE AND TECHNOLOGY OUTLOOK

SEWAGE-POWERED ROCKETS

Researchers are investigating all sorts of fuel sources that will lessen the world's dependence on fossil fuels that pollute the Earth. Scientists at Stanford University have picked a particularly stinky substance to study: sewage. Bacteria thrive in sewage and give off certain gases that can be turned into rocket fuel. Perhaps in the future, you will travel aboard a plane powered by repurposed waste.

POWER FROM WITHIN

Scientists have made a breakthrough with a new kind of energy that comes from air. This renewable energy does not come from wind turbines. Instead, it's wind power from people's lungs! Flexible belts could be placed around the lungs, and the movement caused by breathing will be turned into energy to power pacemakers—devices that are implanted into some people's bodies to help their hearts keep a steady rhythm.

Experts are working to come up with a flexible material that can stretch along with the lungs as a person breathes.

LUNG POWER!

SUPERCLEAN CLOSETS

For most people, closets are simply used to store clothes. But some scientists want to make closets even more helpful. Swedish designer Michael Edenius is working to create a closet that doubles as a water-free washing machine. It would be a space-saving and water-conserving addition to houses of the future. All you would have to do is hang up your clothes at the end of the day. Sensors in the closet would scan your clothing and remove any dirt or stains using cutting-edge technology. Instead of you cleaning your closet, your closet will be doing the cleaning!

GLASSES THAT TELL YOU WHERE TO GO

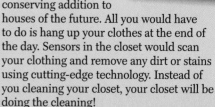

GPS systems are now pretty commonplace. They come in smartphones and cars, but soon you could be wearing one. The Wearable Personal Navigation System is shaped like a pair of glasses with a GPS and LED lights built in. Created by scientists at a university in Japan, this wearable gadget helps people keep moving in the right direction without having to constantly look down at a GPS device or smartphone. You can program a location into the glasses and put them on. Based on the direction you are facing, the lights will glow different colors to indicate which way you should go.

COLOR-CHANGING PLANTS

Plants can't get up and run away when their health is threatened, but they do respond to pollution and other factors in the environment. Scientists at Colorado State University have been working with plants to make those reactions quicker and more noticeable. A plant that changes color quickly when it comes into contact with pollution or explosives can alert people to possible threats. Bill Farland, vice president for research at Colorado State, used to be one of the top scientists at the Environmental Protection Agency. He says that the science used on the plants in the laboratory "can be applied to important problems such as environmental protection and homeland security."

Professor June Medford calls the color-changing greenery plant sentinels. *Sentinel* is another word for "guard" or "lookout." It is as if the plants are standing guard and will alert people to toxins or other dangers.

A TINY CAR THAT DRIVES ITSELF

General Motors has designed a concept for the car of the future. Called the EN-V (and pronounced like the word "envy"), it is a tiny two-seater powered by electricity and hydrogen. The car is controlled by a touch screen and does not go faster than 25 miles (40 km) per hour. Equipped with wireless technology and hooked up to a network via a GPS, the car will actually be able to drive itself! It is intended for urban environments where there is a lot of competition for parking. The car can park itself, and an owner can even use a smartphone to call the car to come pick him or her up. The EN-V is designed so that six cars could fit into the space that now fits only one.

VOICE-ACTIVATED VEHICLES

Soon, we'll all be talking to our cars. Every year, distracted drivers get into lots of accidents—accidents that could have been prevented. To keep drivers safer, carmakers are developing ways to make music, phone, and computer applications in cars respond better to voice commands. Ford Motor Company has developed Sync, General Motors has created MyLink, and other systems are also being perfected. With these new programs, drivers can control heating and air-conditioning, make phone calls, report traffic problems, use GPS devices, and change music selections without fiddling with knobs on the dashboard—and without taking their eyes from the road.

TURN UP THE MUSIC!

What's Next?

239

What's Next?

HEALTH NEWS ON THE HORIZON

NEW SOURCES OF HEALTHY FOOD

Insects are good sources of protein, vitamins, and minerals. They are also low in fat. Raising insects requires a lot less space, food, and money than raising livestock such as cows and chickens—and insects produce a lot less waste. Insects are eaten in many developing nations, and people say they've got a nice, nutty flavor, too. Some scientists are trying to spread the idea that insects are the nutritious and environmentally friendly meat of the future. If you saw crickets, worms, or beetles on the menu, would you give them a try?

MMM...FRIED COCKROACHES!

NO MORE DENTIST DRILLS!

BRUSH BRUSH BRUSH

Getting a cavity is no fun. While it is best to avoid cavities altogether by brushing your teeth and limiting the amount of sugar you eat, there could soon be a pain-free way to take care of cavities. A team of scientists in France has come up with a new gel that contains a hormone (a kind of chemical created in the body) that makes tooth cells grow. They put this gel into the mouths of mice with cavities, and the cavities disappeared. Who knows? Some day, dentists may be able to use a gel like this on humans!

RESTORING FEELING TO A MISSING LIMB

Because of injuries sustained in an accident or during a battle, some people have had an arm or leg amputated, or removed. Many amputees are fitted with a prosthetic (pross-*thet*-ik) limb, which is an artificial device designed to take the place of the missing arm, leg, hand, or foot. Some amputees complain that they still have feeling or pain in their missing limbs. The nerves that were connected to the amputated limbs are still sending messages to the person's brain. Doctors have now come up with a way to locate the nerves that are sending the incorrect messages. They can attach these nerve endings to the skin just below the surface of the amputated area. This way, the nerves can pick up on changes to that area, such as pressure put on the prosthetic or changes in temperature, giving the person the impression of having feeling in his or her prosthetic limb. This life-changing procedure may soon become commonplace for amputees.

240

FUTURE FUN!

PLAY MIND GAMES

Game makers are creating a whole new kind of video game. Instead of responding to the movements of a player's hands, these games rely on changes in brain waves. When you concentrate, your brain gives off different sorts of brain waves than it does when you are relaxing. Mattel, Inc. has a thought-controlled game called Mindflex. Players use their powers of concentration to control a floating ball and move it through hoops, into cages, and around other obstacles. One company is developing mind-controlled games for people to play during airplane flights. Don't throw away your handheld game controllers just yet, but keep your eyes out for new developments in brain wave–controlled games.

COMING SOON TO A THEATER NEAR YOU

Alvin and the Chipmunks: Chip-Wrecked
The Amazing Spider-Man 3D
The Avengers
Brave
Cinderella
The Croods
The Dark Knight Rises
Dolphin Tale
Dorothy of Oz
The Hobbit: Part 1
Ice Age: Continental Drift
John Carter of Mars
King of the Elves
The Lorax
Madagascar 3
Men in Black III
Monsters University
The Muppets Movie
Rise of the Guardians
The Seven
Snow White 3D
Star Trek 2
Stretch Armstrong
Superman: Man of Steel
Thundercats
We Bought a Zoo

Stay tuned! Alex the Lion is headed back to the big screen in *Madagascar 3*.

What's Next?

241

Answers

TIGER MATCH

PAGE 30:
MYSTERY PERSON: Francis Scott Key

PAGE 33:
MYSTERY PERSON: Washington Irving

PAGE 37:
PASS THE PIE

MYSTERY PERSON: Myles Standish

PAGE 79:
MYSTERY PERSON: Marco Polo

PAGE 95:
MYSTERY PERSON: Julia Child

PAGE 100:
MYSTERY PERSON: Matthew Henson

PAGE 129:
MYSTERY PERSON: Queen Isabella I of Spain

PAGE 133:
MYSTERY PERSON: Susan B. Anthony

PAGE 137:
MYSTERY PERSON: Benjamin Franklin

PAGE 143:
USING LANGUAGE TO WIN WARS
Send more food.

PAGE 147:
APPLE PICKING TIME!
1. 6 apples
2. 3 pies
3. 210 pounds (95 kg)
BONUS: 630 apples

PAGE 159:
MYSTERY PERSON: Wolfgang Amadeus Mozart

PAGE 169:
MYSTERY PERSON: Dwight D. Eisenhower

PAGE 175:
PIONEERS IN SCIENCE
1. Isaac Newton
2. Louis Pasteur
3. Jane Goodall
4. Rachel Carson
5. Jonas Salk
6. Marie Curie

242

PAGE 179:
ASTRO-NUTS

PAGE 195:
GIFT MIX-UP

skateboard	B
chef's hat	E
ballet shoes	G
hockey stick	A
saddle	F
dog collar	C
holiday songbook	H
football	D

MYSTERY PERSON: Dorothy Hamill

PAGE 199:
GET MOVING!

```
F U L G H Y B R I D
I R S Y N A P Q W A
E W T R A I N J U D
T L R O Z A C E L A
H P E S O K Q N G O
A K E C C J U G I R
N B T O T E D I K L
O H C P T R O N P I
L U A E X R I E M A
F O R D I G F C H R
E S U B W A Y I R F
S U P E R S O N I C
```

PAGE 227:
U.S. MONUMENT MATCHUP
1. C-Mount Rushmore
2. D-Washington Monument
3. A-Gateway Arch
4. E-Rainbow Bridge
5. B-Muir Woods National Monument

MYSTERY PERSON: Johnny Appleseed

PAGE 235:
TOP 5 TORNADO STATES
1. Five states
2. Texas
3. True

PAGE 239:
FIND THE FLAKES

Answers

Photo Credits

(ecologist); Shutterstock.com (ecologist with jar, limestone, granite, slate, magma, backgrounds). 173: Shutterstock.com (all). 174: Tim Graham/Getty Images (Tut's mask); Shutterstock.com (hieroglyphics); Library of Congress, Prints and Photographs Division (Carter); Kenneth Garrett/National Geographic/Getty Images (CT scan). 175: Kenneth Garrett/National Geographic/Getty Images (scan); Library of Congress, Prints and Photographs Division (Pasteur, Salk, Newton); AP Photo/MTI, Barnabas Honeczy (Goodall); U.S. Fish and Wildlife Service (Carson); ©Photos.com (Curie).

SPACE: 176: Shutterstock.com (border, background); NASA/National Science Foundation (background); NASA/Lynette Cook (Gliese). 177: ©iStockphoto.com/Henrik Jonsson (globe); ©iStock.com/ChristianAnthony (solar system); Shutterstock.com (Milky Way). 178: Shutterstock.com (rock); NASA (Shepard, Armstrong, Jupiter, SpaceShipOne); NASA/JPL (Mars Odyssey). 179: Shutterstock.com (Earth and sun); NASA (astronaut).

SPORTS: 180: Shutterstock.com (border); David E. Klutho/Sports Illustrated (Ohno, Ohno skating). 181: Javier Soriano/AFP/Getty Images (Pullin); Matthew Stockman/Getty Images (Czisny); Clive Rose/Getty Images (Innerhofer); Alexis Boichard/Agence Zoom/Getty Images (Goergl). 182: John Iacono/Sports Illustrated (Rodgers); Damian Strohmeyer/Sports Illustrated (Brady, Suh). 183: Robert Beck/Sports Illustrated (BCS Bowl Game); Al Tielemans/Sports Illustrated (Paterno); Bob Rosato/Sports Illstrated (Newton). 184: Rob Tringali/SportsChrome/Getty Images (Lincecum); Ronald Martinez/Getty Images (Renteria); Drew Hallowell/Getty Images (Norimatsu); Shutterstock.com (Safeco Field). 185: Darren Carroll/Sports Illustrated (Hernandez); Al Tielemans/Sports Illustrated (Halladay); John Biever/Sports Illustrated (Votto); Erick W. Rasco/Sports Illustrated (Rodriguez). 186: John W. McDonough/Sports Illustrated (Durant, Bryant, Nash). 187: Jesse D. Garrabrant/NBAE/Getty Images (Bird); D. Clarke Evans/NBAE/Getty Images (Charles); John Biever/Sports Illustrated (college basketball). 188: Lou Capozzola/Sports Illustrated (hockey, St. Louis); Lou Capozzola/Sports Illustrated (Miller); Simon Bruty/Sports Illustrated (Forlán). 189: AP Photo/Charles Krupa (auto racing); AP Photo/Terry Rena (Johnson); Nick Laham/Getty Images (Franchitti). 190: Bob Martin/Sports Illustrated (Williams); Heinz Kluetmeier/Sports Illustrated (Nadal); Mike Ehrmann/Sports Illustrated (Tseng); Al Tielemans/Sports Illustrated (McDowell). 191: Jamie McDonald/Getty Images (Sacramone); Kelly Cestari/ASP/Getty Images (Slater). 192: Bryn Lennon/Getty Images (Contador); Shaun Botterill/Getty Images (Hoff); Al Bello/Getty Images (Mitcham). 193: Bill Frakes/Sports Illustrated (Lookin at Lucky); Heinz Kluetmeier/Sports Illustrated (Super Saver); AP Photo/Anchorage Daily News, Bob Hallinen (Mackey). 194: Christian Pondella/Getty Images (Fiolek); Bo Bridges/Getty Images (Gagnon); Doug Pensinger/Getty Images (Suavé, Horgmo, Jacobellis). 195: Illustration by Steve Skelton for TIME For Kids (Holiday Gift Mix-Up); Shutterstock.com (Canada vs. Russia); Tony Triolo/Sports Illustrated/Getty Images (Hamil).

TRANSPORTATION: 196: Shutterstock.com (border); ©2010 General Motors and Wieck Media Services, Inc. (Volt); Bloomberg/Getty Images (Leaf). 197: Shutterstock.com (corn, biodiesel plant, gyroscope); ©Jank1000/Dreamstime.com (Segway). 198: Shutterstock.com (background); Library of Congress, Prints and Photographs Division (balloon, train car); NASA (airplane); Hulton Archive/Getty Images (subway). 199: Library of Congress, Prints and Photographs Division (Ford, Lindbergh); ChinaFotoPress/Getty Images (train).

UNITED STATES: 200: Shutterstock.com (all). 201: ©iStockphoto.com/LUGO (bolo tie); Shutterstock.com (mockingbird). 202–203: Shutterstock.com (all). 204: Shutterstock.com (background, Stone Mountain); NASA (Cape Canaveral). 205: Shutterstock.com (fish); David Lees/Time Life Pictures/Getty Images (Pound). 206: Ronald Reagan Presidential Foundation & Library (Reagan); Shutterstock.com (background, peony). 207: Library of Congress, Prints and Photographs Division (Buffalo Bill); Shutterstock.com (sunflower). 208: Shutterstock.com (all). 209: Official Senate Photo (Snowe); Shutterstock.com (cat). 210–211: Shutterstock.com (all). 212: Shutterstock.com (background, turtle); ©iStockphoto.com/JudiLen (moose). 213: Library of Congress, Prints and Photographs Division (Standing Bear); Shutterstock.com (Hoover Dam). 214: Shutterstock.com (background, snake); NASA (Aldrin). 215: ©Photos.com (White Sands); Shutterstock.com (New York City). 216: Shutterstock.com (all). 217: Shutterstock.com (carnations); U.S. Army photo by Sgt. 1st Class Robert C. Brogan/Department of Defense (Underwood). 218: Shutterstock.com (all). 219: Library of Congress, Prints and Photographs Division (Stuart); ©Photos.com (palms). 220: AP Photo/Doug Dreyer (Corn Palace); ©Photos.com (Parthenon). 221: Fotonoticias/WireImage/Getty Images (Gomez); Shutterstock.com (seagull). 222: Shutterstock.com (background, Williamsburg); Library of Congress, Prints and Photographs Division (Smith). 223: Shutterstock.com (all). 224: Shutterstock.com (background); Library of Congress, Prints and Photographs Division (Wright); ©Photos.com (meadowlark). 225: Shutterstock.com (all). 226: NOAA (American Samoa); ©Photos.com (Guam); Shutterstock.com (St. John, Puerto Rico). 227: Shutterstock.com (all).

VOLUNTEERING: 230: Shutterstock.com (all). 231: Courtesy Rosalind Boukis (Adrienne); Courtesy Stacey Kesselman (Max). 232: Shutterstock.com (tutor, dog, soccer, soup, piano player, books); Leigh-Anne Thompson/Cutcaster (sick child); ©Corbis/SuperStock (cleanup); ©iStockphoto.com/ShaneKato (snow shoveler). 233: Shutterstock.com (jump rope, singer, cookies); Matt Bradley/Heifer International (woman with yak).

WEATHER: 234: Shutterstock.com (border, tornado); Vortex2/Rachel Humphrey, CSWR (tornado pod). 235: TIME For Kids (Tornado States illustration); Vortex2/Herbert Stein, CSWR (storm hunters). 236: Shutterstock.com (background, hurricane); Robert Kaufmann/FEMA (Hurricane Ike); ©Pierdelune/Dreamstime.com (high wind). 237: Shutterstock.com (all).

WHAT'S NEXT?: 238: Shutterstock.com (all). 239: Courtesy Colorado State University (plant sentinels); Sam Abuesamid for General Motors/©GM Corp (EN-V); Shutterstock.com (car, boy). 240: ©Fwhb/Dreamstime.com (cockroaches); Shutterstock.com (cricket, girl with toothbrush); ©iStockphoto.com/MichaelSvoboda (runner). 241: AP Photo/Craig Ruttle (mind game); Jeffrey Mayer/WireImage/Getty Images (lion).

Index

A

AAA 400 (auto race), 189
AAA Texas 500 (auto race), 189
Aaron, Hank, 185
Abbe, Lake, 55
Abrahams, Peter, 33
Academy Awards, 152
Acela, 199
acid rain, 83
acute angles, 144
Adams, John, 115, 162, 225
Adams, John Quincy, 162
Adidas Golden Ball, 188
Adidas Golden Boot, 188
Adidas Golden Glove, 188
Adobe Photoshop, 40
Advanced Imaging Technology (AIT), 13
affect/effect, 141
Afghanistan, 47, 129, 133
Africa. See also specific countries
    history, time line, 125–29
    map, 102–3
Agassi, Andre, 213
Agnew, Spiro T., 168
Agriculture Department, U.S., 119
Airbus A380 (aircraft), 199
air-conditioning, 89
airplane flights, first, 131, 198, 199
AirPod, 137
air pollution, 83
airport security, 13
air travel, flight troubles, 8, 129
Akhenaten, 174
Alabama, 131, 200
Alaska, 200, 230
Albania, 47
Albany, New York, 215
Albuquerque, New Mexico, 215
Aldrin, Edwin "Buzz," 214
Alexander Hamilton: The Outsider (Fritz), 30
Alexander the Great, 124
algebra, 171
Algeria, 47
Ali, Zine El Abidine Ben, 9
Alice in Wonderland (movie), 152
Alito, Samuel, Jr., 120
alligators, 16
alliteration, 143
almanacs, 31
alphabet, invention of, 124
alpine skiing, 181, 194
al Qaeda, 129
Always On (Baron), 42
Amarillo airport, 221
Amazing Maurice and His Educated Rodents (Pratchett), 32
Amenhotep III, 174
America. See United States
American Civil War, 131
American Idol (TV show), 151, 152
American League, 184–85
American Music Awards, 155
American Revolution, 130
American Samoa, 226
American Sign Language, 139
Amp Energy Juice 500 (auto race), 189
amphibians, 18
Amsterdam, 68
Amtrak
    Acela, 199

Heartland Flyer, 137
Amundsen, Roald, 127
Anasazi Indians, 125
Anchorage, Alaska, 200
ancient history time line, 124
Anderson, Clay, 179
Andorra, 47
Angel, Ann, 33
Angkor, 52
angles, 144
Angola, 48
animals, 16–25
    camouflage, 21
    classification of, 18–20
    cold-blooded, 20
    communication, 24
    defenses of, 25
    endangered, 22, 23, 41
    habitats, 90–91
    insect parts, 19
    invertebrates, 19
    with jobs, 18
    pets, 17
    scientists studying, 23
    tool users, 24
    vertebrates, 18
    volunteer opportunities, 232
    warm-blooded, 20
animal shelters, 232
Annapolis, Maryland, 209
Antarctica, 96
Antarctic Desert, 90
Anthony, Carmelo, 186
Anthony, Susan B., 122
anthropology, 171
Anti-Federalists, 114
Antigua, 48
antioxidants, 95
antonyms, 143
Antro Solo, 137
aorta, 29
apartheid, 128, 129
Apple's iPad, 13, 15, 135
Appomattox Court House, 131
April (calendar), 34
April Fools' Day, 36
Arabian Desert, 100
Aral Sea, 99
Arcade Fire, 158
archaeologists, 46
archaeology, 171
archipelagoes, 100
arctic foxes, 21
Arctic Ocean, 98
area formulas, 145
Argentina, 48
Argonaut I, 198
Aristotle, 173
arithmetic, 171
Arizona, 201
    immigration bill, 11
Arizona Cardinals, 182
Arkansas, 201
Armenia, 48
    average income, 149
Armstrong, Edwin, 128
Armstrong, Neil, 178
army, largest, 62
arroyo toad, 22
arteries, 29
arthropods, 19
Arthur, Chester A., 161, 165
artificial limbs, 240

Asia. See also specific countries
    features, 96
    map, 104–5
Asia Map Match, 44
assassination of Presidents, 161
Association of Surfing Professionals (ASP), 191
astronomy, 170
Atacama Desert, 8
Atlanta, Georgia, 204
Atlanta Dream, 187
Atlantic Ocean, 98
atlases, 31
Auburn Tigers, 183
auctions, for raising money, 233
August (calendar), 35
Augusta, Maine, 209
aurora borealis, 200
Austin, Texas, 221
Australia, 48
    average income, 149
    features, 96
    map, 106–7
Australian Open, 190
Australopithecus sediba, 13
Austria, 48
autobiographies, 30
auto racing, 189
Avatar (movie), 151, 153
avocados, 93
award-winning books, 32–33
axolotls, 23
Ayers Rock (Australia), 81
Azerbaijan, 49
Aztecs, 23, 125, 126

B

"Baby" (song), 155
Babylonians, 124
baby names, 227
Bacigalupi, Paolo, 32
bacteria, 128, 175
"Bad Romance" (song), 157
Bagan, 67
Bahamas, 49
Bahrain, 49
Baikal, Lake, 99
Baikal oil fish, 99
Baikonur Cosmodrome, 61
bake sales, 233
Baku, Azerbaijan, 49, 99
bald eagles, 22, 115
Baltic states, 63
Baltimore, Maryland, 209
Baltimore & Ohio Railroad, 198
Bangkok, Thailand, 76
Bangladesh, 49
    average income, 149
    monetary value, 148
banjos, 159
bank accounts, 148
banknotes, 149
Bank of America 500, 189
Barbados, 49
Barbie®, 224
Barbuda, 48
Barkley, Alben W., 167
Baron, Naomi S., 42
baseball, 14, 184–85
basketball, 186–87
Basotho hats, 63
Bastille (Paris), 127
Baton Rouge, Louisiana, 208
Battle of Gettysburg, 131

Battle of Hastings, 125
Battle of Lexington and Concord, 130
Battle of Wounded Knee, 131
Bautista, Jose, 185
bauxite, 58
Bay of Pigs, 128
bays, 100
bedbugs, 11
Begin, Menachem, 129
Belarus, 49
Belgium, 50
Belgrade, Serbia, 72
Belichick, Bill, 182
Belize, 50
Bell, Alexander Graham, 127
Belmont Stakes, 193
Bengal tiger, 49
Benin, 50
Bering Strait, 100
Berlin Wall, 129
Berlin West Africa Conference, 127
Berners-Lee, Tim, 129
beside/besides, 141
Beyoncé, 156, 157
Bhutan, 50
bicameral structure of U.S. legislature, 117
Biden, Joe, 118, 119, 169
Bieber, Justin, 15, 154, 155, 156, 157
Biedermann, Paul, 192
Biggins, John, 132
billboards, 222
Billings, Montana, 212
Bill of Rights, 130, 225
Bingham, Hiram, 70
Bin Laden, Osama, 129
biodegradable cups, 184
biodegradable lunch sacks, 231
biodiesel, 87, 197
biofuels, 197
biographies, 30
    Internet resource guide, 44
biology, 170
biomass, 87
biomes, 90
biotechnology, 171
Bird, Sue, 187
birds, 18
    communication, 24
    tool use, 24
    top sighted, 20
Birmingham, Alabama, 200
Bishop, Nic, 32
Bismarck, North Dakota, 216
Black, Bud, 185
Black Death, 126
Black Eyed Peas, 155
black howler monkey, 50
Blind Side, The (movie), 151, 153
blood, and the heart, 29
bloodhounds, 18
Bloodless Revolution, 126
blueberries, 93
Blue Mosque (Turkey), 81
BMX, 194
body health. See health
body scanners, 13
body systems, 28–29
Boehner, John, 117
Boeing 747 (aircraft), 199
Boise, Idaho, 205
bola ties, 201

Bolívar, Simón, 127
Bolivia, 50
boll weevils, 200
Bonds, Barry, 185
bones, 27, 28, 95
Bongo, Omar, 57
books, 30–33
  award-winning, 32–33
  e-books, 15, 32
  Internet resource guide, 45
  types of literature, 30–31
Booth, John Wilkes, 131, 161
Borel, Calvin, 193
Borglum, Gutzon, 205, 227
Bosnia, 50, 129
Boston, Massachusetts, 210
Boston Celtics, 186
Boston Globe–Horn Book Award, 33
Boston Massacre, 130
Boston Tea Party, 130
botany, 170, 173
Botswana, 51
  average income, 149
Bougainville, Louis-Antoine de, 72
Bowl Championship Series (BCS), 183
Boxer Rebellion, 127
BP (British Petroleum), 10, 129, 133
Bradford, Sam, 182
Brady, Tom, 182
brain, the, 29
brass instruments, 45
Braun, Scooter, 154
Brazil, 51
  monetary value, 148
Breckinridge, John C., 164
Breyer, Stephen, 120
Bridgeport, Connecticut, 203
Britain. See United Kingdom
British Open, 190
Broadway musicals, 157
Brown v. Board of Education, 121, 124
Brunei, 51
Bryant, Kobe, 186
Bublé, Michael, 155, 158
bubonic plague, 126
Buchanan, James, 164
Buddha (Siddhartha Gautama), 124
budgeting, 148
bugs. See insects
bulbs of plant, 173
Bulgaria, 51
Bullock, Sandra, 151, 153
bull runs, 55
Bureau of Engraving and Printing, U.S., 149
Burkina Faso, 51
Burlington, Vermont, 222
Burma (Myanmar), 67
Burr, Aaron, 162
Burundi, 51
  average income, 149
Bush, George H.W., 168
Bush, George W., 133, 169
Bush v. Gore, 121, 133
Butler Bulldogs, 187
buttocks (gluteus maximus), 28
buzkashi, 47
Byzantine Empire, 126

C
Cabinet, U.S., 119
cable cars, 198
Cai Rang Floating Market (Vietnam), 79
calcium, 95
calculus, 171
Caldecott Medal, 32
Calder Memorial Trophy, 188
calendar, 34–35
Calhoun, John C., 162, 163
calico cats, 209
California, 202
"California Gurls" (song), 156
calories, 95
  burning, 27
calypso music, 76
Cambodia, 52
Camby, Marcus, 186, 203
Cameroon, 52
camouflaged animals, 21
Camp David Accords (1978), 129
Canada, 52
  monetary value, 148
canals, 100
cannibalism, 57
canyons, 100
Cape Bojador, 126
Cape Canaveral, 204
Cape of Good Hope, 126
Cape Verde, 52
Cape Wind Farm, 86
capillaries, 29
capital/Capitol, 141
Capitol Building, U.S., 225
carbohydrates, 94
carbon dioxide (CO₂), 85, 88, 89, 173
carbon footprint, 88
Carnegie, Andrew, 44
carrier pigeons, 18
cars
  alternative, 197
  electric, 13, 196
  milestones in history, 198–99
  that drive themselves, 239
  voice-activated, 239
  what's next, 239
Carson, Rachel, 175
Carson City, Nevada, 213
Carter, Helena Bonham, 152
Carter, Howard, 174
Carter, Jimmy, 121, 129, 168
Carter, Rosalynn, 123, 168
Carthage, 124
car washes, 233
Cash, Johnny, 201
cashew nuts, 59
Caspian Sea, 99
Cassatt, Mary, 218
Casspi, Omri, 186
Catching Fire (Collins), 33
cats
  biggest, 25
  popular breeds, 17
  top names, 17
Cattlewash Beach, 49
cavities, care of, 240
cedar trees, 63
cellos, 159
cell phones, 38–39, 41, 42
Census, U.S., 11
Central African Republic, 52
Central America. See also specific countries

features, 96
  map, 110–11
Central Pacific Railroad, 131, 198
cerebellum, 29
cerebrum, 29
Chad, 52
Chagall, Marc, 49
Chagas, 70
Challenger, 132
chameleons, 21
Chan, Jackie, 153
Charlemagne, 125
Charles, Tina, 187
Charles Bridge (Prague), 54
Charleston, West Virginia, 223
Charlotte, North Carolina, 216
Chase for the Sprint Cup, 189
checking accounts, 148
checks and balances, 116, 120
chemistry, 170
Cheney, Richard B. "Dick," 169
Cherokee Indians, 131
Chevy Volt, 196
Cheyenne, Wyoming, 224
chiaroscurist, 140
Chicago, Illinois, 11, 116, 206
Chicago Blackhawks, 188
Chicago World's Fair, 127
Chile, 53
  average income, 149
  mine rescue, 8
chimney rock formations, 55
chimpanzees, 24
China, 53
  average income, 149
  history, time line, 124–29
Chinese calendar, 37
Chinese language, 138, 139
Chinese New Year, 36, 37
Chisholm, Shirley, 122
chocolate, 50
Christ the Redeemer (statue), 51
Christmas, 36
Chu, Steven, 119
Chuck (TV show), 151
Chuuk Lagoon (Micronesia), 66
cichlids, 64
Cinco de Mayo, 36
circles, 145
circumference, 145
civil rights, 132
Civil War (American), 131
Clark, William, 130
Cleary, Beverly, 218
Cleveland, Grover, 165
Cleveland Cavaliers, 14, 186
Clijsters, Kim, 190
climate. See weather
climate change, 85, 173, 231
Clinton, Bill, 62, 120, 132, 168
Clinton, George, 162
Clinton, Hillary, 119, 123, 168
closets, superclean, 238
clothing drives, 232
coal, 84
cocoa, 54
code talkers, 143
Cody, William "Buffalo Bill," 207
coelacanth, 53
coelenterates, 19
coffee, 77
cold-blooded animals, 20
coleopterists, 23
Colfax, Schuyler, 164
Colfer, Chris, 153
college basketball, 187

college football, 183
college gymnastics, 191
Collins, Suzanne, 33
Cologne Cathedral, 58
Colombia, 53
Colorado, 202
color-changing plants, 239
Columbia, 133, 178, 199
Columbia, South Carolina, 219
Columbian Exposition, 127
Columbus, Christopher, 126
Columbus, Ohio, 11, 217
Columbus Day, 36
Commerce Department, U.S., 119
communication. See also Internet
  animal, 24
  Internet resource guide, 45
  wired world, 38–39
Communism, 53, 54, 62, 63, 79, 128, 132
community service. See volunteering
Comoros, 53
complex carbohydrates, 94
compost, 88
computers, 38–45. See also Internet
  electronic trends, 41
  energy use, 89
  environmental effects of electronics, 45
  high-tech activities, 39
  IMs (instant messages), 42
  Internet resource guide, 44–45
  photo-editing software, 40
  texting, 42
  Web addresses, 38
  Webby Awards, 43
  wired world, 38–39
computer science, 171
Concord, New Hampshire, 214
Confucius, 124
confused words, 141
Congo, Democratic Republic of the, 53
Congo, Republic of the, 53
Connecticut, 203
Connecticut Huskies, 187
Connick, Harry, Jr., 208
Conn Smythe Trophy, 188
Constantine the Great, 125
Constantinople, 126
Constitution, U.S., 114, 116, 118, 120, 121, 130
Constitutional Convention (1787), 114, 130
Contador, Alberto, 192
Coolidge, Calvin, 161, 166
Cooney, Joan Ganz, 201
Copernicus, 126
Copernicus, Nicolaus, 70, 126
Copper Canyon, 100
coral crisis, 82
Coretta Scott King Author Award, 32
Cornet, Henri, 192
Corn Palace (South Dakota), 220
Cortés, Hernán, 126
Costa Rica, 54
Côte d'Ivoire (Ivory Coast), 54
countries of the world, 46–81. See also specific countries
  alphabetical list of, 47–79
  cool landmarks, 80–81
CPR (cardiopulmonary resuscitation), 12

Cradle of Humankind, 13
crawfish, 208
Crawford, Chace, 151
Crazy Crayons, 230
Creamer, Paula, 190
credit cards, 132, 148
creosote, 44
cricket chirps, 170
Croatia, 54, 129
cropping photos, 40
cross-country skiing, 181
Crusades, 125
crustaceology, 140
Cuba, 54
Cuban Missile Crisis, 128, 132
Curie, Marie, 175
currencies, 148, 149
current events, 8–15
  around the country, 10–11
  around the world, 8–9
  health, science, and
    technology, 12–13
  Internet resource guide, 45
  sports and entertainment, 14–15
Curtis, Charles, 167
cycling, 192
cyclones, 236
Cyprus, 54
Cyprus mouflon, 54
Cyrus, Miley, 151, 152, 154, 156
Cy Young Award, 185
Czech Republic, 54
Czisny, Alissa, 181
Czolgosz, Leon, 161

D

Daimler, Gottlieb, 198
Dallas, George M., 163
Damascus, Syria, 75
Danakil Depression, 56
dance, 151, 157
dance-a-thons, 233
Darfur, 129
dark chocolate, 93
Dark Knight, The (movie), 153
Darwin, Charles, 127
date palm trees, 67
Davis Cup, 190
Dawes, Charles G., 166
daylight saving time, 36
Dayton, Ohio, 11
Daytona 500 (auto race), 189
DDT, 11
Dead Sea, 60, 99
death of a president, 161
December (calendar), 35
deciduous forests, 91
Declaration of Independence, 130, 218
decorator crabs, 21
Deep Green kite, 137
Deepwater Horizon, 10
Defense, Department, U.S., 119
defriend, 141
Delaware, 203
Dempsey, Jack, 202
dendrochronologists, 170
Denmark, 55
denominators, 146
Denver, Colorado, 11, 202
Denver Nuggets, 186
Department of, U.S. (Cabinet),
  Agriculture, 119
  Commerce, 119
  Defense, 119
  Education, 119

Energy, 119, 196
Justice, 119
Health and Human Services, 119
Homeland Security, 119
Housing and Urban
  Development, 119
Interior, the, 119
Labor, 119
State, 119
Transportation, 119
Treasury, 119
Veterans Affairs, 119
deposits, 148
Depp, Johnny, 152, 153
dermis, 28
Derülo, Jason, 156
deserts, 90
  largest, 100
Des Moines, Iowa, 207
DeSoto, Duane, 191
Despicable Me (movie), 152
deteriorating, 140
Detroit, Michigan, 11, 210
Detroit Lions, 182
diameter, 145
diamonds, 73, 172
Dias, Bartholomeu, 126
dictionaries, 31
  new words, 141
Diesel, Rudolf, 127
diesel fuel, 84, 85
Diggins, Jessica, 181
dinosaurs, 50
District of Columbia (Washington,
  D.C.), 225
diving, 192
Djibouti, 55
dodo birds, 66
dogs
  with jobs, 18
  popular breeds, 17
  top names, 17
dogsledding, 193
Doha Cultural Festival, 70
dolphins, 24
Dominica, 55
Dominican Republic, 55
Donovan, Shaun, 119
Dover, Delaware, 203
downloading movies and TV
  shows, 41
Dracula, 71
Drake, Francis, 130
Dreamer, The (Ryan), 32
Dred Scott v. Sandford, 121
drinking water, 95
dromedary camels, 18, 77
droughts, 237
drums, 159
Duke Blue Devils, 187
Duncan, Arne, 119
Durant, Kevin, 186
dust bowl, 237
dwarf planets, 177, 178

E

eagles. *See* bald eagles
Eannes, Gil, 126
Earhart, Amelia, 199, 207
Earnhardt, Dale, Jr., 216
Earth, 177, 178, 179. *See also*
  geography
  plate tectonics, 97
Earth Day, 36
Earth science, 170, 172–73
Easter, 36

East Timor, 55
eating habits, 92–93
e-books, 15, 32
echinoderms, 19
ecology, 172. *See also* going green
economic crisis of 2008, 129
economics, 171
ecosystems, 90–91
Ecuador, 55
Edelman, Marian Wright, 219
Edgar Allan Poe Award for Best
  Young Adult Book, 33
Edinburgh Castle (Scotland), 81
Edogawa Minami Little League,
  184
education, volunteer
  opportunities, 232
Education Department, U.S., 119
Eekoworld, 44
effect/affect, 141
Efron, Zac, 153, 202
Egypt, 55
  new discoveries, 46
  revolution, 9
Egyptians, ancient, 124
Egyptian vultures, 24
Eiffel Tower (Paris), 81
Eisenhower, Dwight D., 115, 167
elderly people, volunteering
  with, 232
electric cars, 13, 196
electronic keyboards, 159
electronics, 26, 38–39
  energy use, 89
  trends in, 41
electronic waste, 45, 88
eLEGS, 136
elephants, 24
El Salvador, 56
Elvis Festival, 211
e-mails, 41, 45
Emancipation Proclamation, 131
emeralds, 53
EMIEW2 robot, 136
EMILY (robo-guard), 135
Eminem, 155, 156, 157
"Empire State of Mind" (song), 157
encyclopedias, 31
endangered animals, 22, 23, 41
Endangered Species Act of 1973,
  22
energy, 82–89. *See also* going
  green
  Internet resource guide, 44
  nonrenewable sources, 84–85
  renewable sources, 86–87
  usage at home, 89
  usage in the United States, 87
  what's next, 238
Energy Department, U.S., 119, 196
engineering, 171
England. *See* United Kingdom
English Channel, 100
English Civil War, 126
English-teaching robots, 135
entertainment. *See also* movies;
  music; TV
  current events, 15
  Internet resource guide, 45
  what's next, 241
entomologists, 23, 170
EN-V cars, 239
environment, 82–89. *See also*
  going green
  coral crisis, 82
  effects of electronics, 45
  Internet resource guide, 44

nonrenewable energy sources,
  84–85
reducing, reusing, and recycling,
  88
renewable energy sources,
  86–87
threats to, 83
volunteer opportunities, 232
epidermis, 28
E pluribus unum, 115
Equal Rights Amendment (ERA),
  123
equator, 100
Equatorial Guinea, 56
equilateral triangles, 144
Eritrea, 56
Erskine, Kathryn, 33
Eskimo Pie, 207
essays, 30
Estonia, 56
E.T.: The Extra-Terrestrial (movie),
  153
ethanol, 87, 197
Ethiopia, 56
ethologists, 23
Europe. *See also* specific countries
  features, 96
  map, 108–9
even numbers, 146
Everglades National Park, 16
everyday math, 147
e-waste, 45, 88
Executive Branch, 116, 118–19
exercise (exercising), 27, 94
Explorer 1, 178
eye muscles, 28
Eyjafjallajökull, 8

F

Facebook, 9, 43
face transplants, 13
Fairbanks, Charles W., 166
falcons, 62
fantasy books, 31
Fargo, North Dakota, 216
Farmers' Day (Ghana), 58
Farnsworth, Philo T., 127, 221
farther/further, 141
Father's Day, 36
fats, 94
Favre, Brett, 211
February (calendar), 34
Fed Cup, 190
Federalists, 114
Federal Reserve, 149
Federer, Roger, 190
feldspar, 72
Feliz, Neftali, 185
femur, 28
few/less, 141
fiction, 30, 32–33
Fiesta Bowl, 183
FIFA Fair Play Award, 188
FIFA World Cup, 14, 188
figure skating, 181
figures of speech, 143
Fiji, 57
Fillmore, Millard, 161, 163, 164
financial crisis of 2008, 129
FINA Diving World Cup, 192
FINA World Swimming
  Championships, 192
Finland, 57
Fiolek, Ashley, 194
Firth, Colin, 152
fish, 18

Fish and Wildlife Service, U.S., 22
flag, U.S., 114
flash floods, 237
Flatbush National Bank, 132
Fleming, Alexander, 128
floods, 237
Florence + The Machine, 157
Florida, 131, 204
flowering plants, parts of, 173
flutes, 159
FM (frequency modulation), 128
fog beetles, 67
food and nutrition, 92–95
   local fare, 92
   nutrition basics, 94–95
   superfoods, 93
   what's next, 240
football, 182–83
Ford, Gerald R., 132, 161, 168
Ford, Henry, 131, 199
Ford Motor Company, 131, 199, 239
Ford 400 (auto race), 189
Forlán, Diego, 188
Fort Sumter, 131
fossil fuels, 83–85
Fountain of Wealth (Singapore), 73
fracas, 140
fractions, 146
France, 57
   average income, 149
   history, time line, 124, 126, 127, 130
Franchitti, Dario, 189
Franco, James, 152
Frankfort, Kentucky, 208
Frank J. Selke Trophy, 188
Franklin, Benjamin, 115
Franz Ferdinand, Archduke, 127
Freedom 7, 178
French fries, 216
French Open, 190
French Revolution, 127
fresh water, 99
fretted instruments, 159
frigate birds, 67
Fritz, Jean, 30
frontal lobe, 29
fruits, 92–93, 94, 95, 173
fuel cells, 87
Fukushima Daiichi nuclear plant, 8
full-body scanners, 13
funny bone, 28

G

Gabon, 57
Gaddafi, Muammar, 9
Gagarin, Yuri, 178
Gagnon, Pierre-Luc, 194
Galilei, Galileo, 126
gallo pinto, 68
gal pals, 171
Galveston Flood of 1900, 237
Gambia, The, 57
games
   Internet resource guide, 45
   mind-controlled, 241
   what's next, 241
Gamla Stan, Sweden, 75
Gandhi, Indira, 60
garbage, 83
   reducing, reusing, and recycling, 88, 231
García, Erika Villaecija, 192
Gardenhire, Ron, 185

Garden of Eden, 49
Garfield, James A., 161, 165
Garner, John, 167
garnets, 205
gasoline, 84, 85
Gates, Robert, 119
Gateway Arch (St. Louis), 227
Gator Bowl, 183
gators, 16
Gaza Strip, 128
Gecko and Sticky, The (Van Draanen), 31
Geiger, Robert, 237
Geithner, Timothy, 119
General Motors (GM), 13, 196, 239
Genghis Khan, 66, 125
geography, 96–113, 170. See also maps
   changing planet, 97
   earth vocabulary, 100
   five oceans, 98
   Internet resource guide, 44
   largest lakes, 99
   seven continents, 96
   time zones, 101
geology, 170
geometrid caterpillars, 21
geometry, 144, 171
Georgia (U.S.), 131, 204
Georgia (Asia), 57
Georgia Bulldogs, 191
geothermal energy, 87
Germanotta, Angelina. See Lady Gaga
German shepherds, 17, 18
Germany, 58
   history, time line, 127–29, 132
Gerry, Elbridge, 162
Ghana, 58
G.I. Joe: The Rise of Cobra (movie), 151
giant tortoises, 55
Gilbert Islands, 62
Gilmore, Stephanie, 191
Ginsburg, Ruth Bader, 120
Giza Pyramids, 81, 124
glaciers melt, 85
glasses with GPS, 238
Glee (TV show), 151, 153, 155
Glenn, John, 178, 217
Gliese 581g, 176
global warming, 85, 173, 231
Glorious Revolution, 126
gluteus maximus, 28
Gobi Desert, 90, 100
Goergl, Elisabeth, 181
going green
   alternative cars, 197
   baseball stadiums, 184
   basketball initiatives, 187
   electronics, 45
   exercising, 27
   healthy diet, 173
   NBA's shooting shirts, 187
   new inventions, 137
   recycling money, 149
   trash, 83
   tree plantings, 83, 188, 232
   what's next, 238–39
   World Cup tree-planting initiatives, 188
Golan Heights, 128
Golden Gate Bridge (San Francisco), 80
golden poison dart frogs, 25
Gold Rush, 131

golf, 190
Goliath frogs, 52
Gomez, Selena, 151, 152, 156, 221
Gonzalez, Carlos, 185
Goodall, Jane, 175
Gore, Albert, Jr., 121, 133, 168
gorillas, 24
Gossip Girl (TV show), 151
government, 114–21
   branches of, 116–13
   checks and balances, 116, 120
   Great Seal, 115
   Internet resource guide, 44
   separation of powers, 116, 120
   symbols of, 114–15
   U.S. Constitution, 114
   U.S. flag, 114
GPS (Global Positioning System), 41
   glasses with, 238
Grammy Awards, 158
Grand Bazaar (Turkey), 77
Grand Canyon, 100
granite, 172
Grant, Ulysses S., 131, 164
grasslands, 91
Great Backyard Bird Count, 20
Great Barrier Reef, 82
Great Bear Lake, 99
Great Britain. See United Kingdom
Great Depression, 128, 131
Great Man-Made River (Libya), 63
Great Mosque of Djenne, 65
Great Seal, 115
Greece, 58
Greeks, ancient, history time line, 124
green. See going green
green audits, 141
Green Bay Packers, 182
green-collar, 141
greenhouse effect, 85
greenhouse gases, 85, 92–93
Grenada, 58
Grenadines, The, 71
Griffey, Ken, Jr., 185
Groundhog Day, 36
Ground Zero, 10
Guam, 226
Guatemala, 58
guerdon, 140
Guinea, 58
Guinea-Bissau, 59
guitars, 159
Guiteau, Charles, 161
Gulf of Mexico, 100
   oil spill, 10, 129, 133
gulfs, 100
gusles, 67
Gutenberg, Johannes, 126
Gutenberg Bible, 126
Guyana, 59
gymnastics, 191
gyroscopes, 197

H

habitats and wildlife, 90–91
Habsburg Dynasty, 125
Hadrian's Wall, 125
haikus, 142
Haiti, 59
   earthquake, 59, 129
Halladay, Roy, 185
Hallidie, Andrew, 198
Halloween, 36
Hamilton, Josh, 185

Hamlin, Denny, 189
Hamlin, Hannibal, 164
Hammurabi, 124
handgun ban, 116
handling money, 148
hand signals, and American Sign Language, 139
handwriting, 140
Hanna, William, 215
Hanukkah, 36
hard copies, 40, 41
Harding, Warren G., 161, 166
hardware, 40
harissa, 76
harmonicas, 159
Harold II, King, 125
Harrisburg, Pennsylvania, 218
Harrison, Benjamin, 165
Harrison, William Henry, 161, 163
Harry Potter movies, 15, 150
Hartford, Connecticut, 203
Hart Memorial Trophy, 188
Harvick, Kevin, 189
Hathaway, Anne, 152
Hawaii, 205
Hawass, Zahi, 46, 174
Hayes, Rutherford B., 165
health, 26–29
   body systems, 28–29
   current events, 12–13
   exercising, 27
   Internet resource guide, 44
   sleep, 26
   what's next, 240
Health and Human Services Department, U.S., 119
health care debate, 133
heart, 27, 28, 29
heart disease, 93, 95
Heartland Flyer, 137
heart muscle, 28
Heifer International, 233
Heimlich, Henry, 203
Heisman, John, 183
Heisman Trophy, 183
Helena, Montana, 212
heliophysicists, 12
Hendricks, Thomas A., 165
Hernandez, Felix, 185
herpetologists, 23
Herzegovina, 50, 129
high-tech activities, 39
Hillary, Edmund, 68, 128
Himalaya Mountains, 50, 67
Hiroshima, 128, 132
hirz, 69
hissing cockroaches, 64
historical fiction, 31
history, 122–33
   ancient, time line, 124
   Internet resource guide, 44
   U.S., time line, 130–33
   women, time line, 122–23
   world, time line, 125–29
history books, 31
Hitler, Adolf, 128
Hobart, Garret A., 166
hockey, 188
Hoff, Kathryn, 192
Holder, Eric, 119
holidays, in 2012, 36
Homeland Security Department, U.S., 119
homelessness, volunteer opportunities, 232
home runs, 185

Homestead Act, 131
Honda, 129
Honduras, 59
honeybees, 24
Honolulu, Hawaii, 205
Hoover, Herbert C., 167
Hoover Dam, 213
Horgmo, Torstein, 194
horns, 159
horse racing, 193
hospitals, volunteer opportunities, 232
hot air balloons, 198
House of Representatives, 117, 161, 225
Housing and Urban Development Department, U.S., (HUD), 119
Houston, Texas, 221
Howard, Dwight, 186
Hu, Yadan, 192
Hubble Space Telescope, 177, 178
Hubbs-SeaWorld Research Institute, 230
Hudson, Henry, 130
Humane Society, 214
humerus, 28
Humphrey, Hubert H., 167
humuhumunukunukuapua'a, 205
Hundred Years' War, 126
Hungary, 59
hunger, volunteer opportunities, 232
Huron, Lake, 99
hurricanes, 236
Hurricane Ike, 236
Hurricane Katrina, 133, 237
Hussein, Saddam, 129, 133
Hutus, 129
hydration, 95
hydrogen, 87
hydrogen bombs, 128
hydropower, 86
hyperbole, 143
hypodermis, 28
hypotenuse, 144

I

iCarly (TV show), 152
iced tea, 78
Iceland, 59
ichthyologists, 23
Idaho, 205
Iditarod Trail Sled Dog Race, 193
Igneous rocks, 172
Iguazú Falls (Argentina/Brazil), 80
illegal immigration, 11
Illinois, 206
Illyricum, 50
immigration battles, 11
impeachment of presidents, 161
IMs (instant messages), dictionary of terms, 42
Inca Empire, 125
incomes around the world, 149
Independence Day, 36
India, 60, 128
Indiana, 206
Indianapolis, Indiana, 206
Indianapolis 500 (auto race), 189
Indian Ocean, 98
Indies Choice Award for Young Adult Book of the Year, 33
Indonesia, 60
    average income, 149
Indus River, 8
Indus River Valley, 124

Innerhofer, Christof, 181
Inouye, Daniel, 117
insects (bugs), 19
    bedbugs, 11
    camouflage, 21
    as food, 240
    habitats, 90
    parts, 19
integers, 146
interactive maps, 41
Interior Department, U.S., 119
internal combustion engines, 197, 198
International Academy of Digital Arts and Sciences, 43
International Cherry Pit Spitting Championship, 210
International Ski Federation Alpine World Ski Championship, 181
International Ski Federation Snowboard World Championship, 181
International Space Station (ISS), 178, 179
Internet
    electronic trends, 41
    IMs (instant messages), 42
    resource guide, 44–45
    texting, 42
    Web addresses, 38
    Webby Awards, 43
inventions, 134–37
    cool and new, 135–37
    White House Science Fair, 134
invertebrates, 19
iodine, 219
Iowa, 207, 230
iPad, 12, 15, 135
Iran, 60, 129
    average income, 149
    hostage crisis, 132
Iraq, 60
    Persian Gulf War, 129, 132
Iraq War, 129, 133
Ireland, 60, 127
iron, 95
Iron Man 2 (movie), 153
Islam (Muslims), 125
Isner, John, 14
isosceles triangles, 144
Israel, 60, 99, 128
ISS (International Space Station), 178, 179
Italy, 61
    history, time line, 125, 127, 128, 132
Ivan the Terrible, 126
Ivory-billed woodpeckers, 22
Ivory Coast, 54

J

Jack Adams Award, 188
Jackson, Andrew, 163
Jackson, Lauren, 187
Jackson, Mississippi, 211
Jacksonville, Florida, 204
Jacobellis, Lindsey, 194
jaguars, 22
Jamaica, 61
James, LeBron, 14, 186
James II, King, 126
James Norris Memorial Trophy, 188
Jamestown, 130
Janis Joplin: Rise Up Singing (Angel), 33

January (calendar), 34
Japan, 61
    history, time line, 127, 128, 132
    monetary value, 148
    tsunami, 8
Jasmine Revolution, 9
Jay-Z, 157, 158
Jefferson, Thomas, 115, 130, 162
Jefferson City, Missouri, 212
Jellyfish Lake, 69
Jerebko, Jonas, 186
Jerusalem, 60, 125
Jesus Christ, 125
jetpack, 136
John, King, 125
John Legend & The Roots, 158
Johnson, Andrew, 131, 161, 164
Johnson, Jimmie, 189
Johnson, Josh, 185
Johnson, Lyndon B., 128, 132, 161, 167
Johnson, Richard M., 163
Johnson Sirleaf, Ellen, 63
Jonas Brothers, 151, 154
Jones, Alphonso, II, 157
Jones, Norah, 123
Jordan, 61, 99
Jordan, Michael, 49
Joyce, James, 60
Judicial Branch, U.S., 116, 120–21
Julius Caesar, 124
July (calendar), 35
June (calendar), 34
Juneau, Alaska, 200
Jupiter (planet), 177, 178, 179
Just a Drop, 233
Justice Department, U.S., 119
Justices, Supreme Court. See Supreme Court, U.S.
Justin Bieber: Never Say Never (film), 15

K

Kadriorg Palace, 56
Kagan, Elena, 10, 120
Kaieteur Falls, 59
Kakapo Rescue (Montgomery), 32
Kalahari Desert, 100
Kanab, Utah, 221
Kane, Patrick, 188
Kang, Danielle, 190
Kansas, 207, 235
Kansas City, Missouri, 212
Karate Kid, The (movie), 152
katydids, 21
Kaymer, Martin, 190
Kazakhstan, 61
Kelo v. City of New London, 121
Kennedy, Anthony, 120
Kennedy, Jacqueline, 160, 167
Kennedy, John F., 128, 132, 160, 161, 167
Kennedy, Joseph P., 160
Kennedy Space Center, 204
Kentucky, 208
Kentucky Derby, 193
Kenya, 61
    monetary value, 148
Kerley, Jeremy, 183
Kerr, Cristie, 190
Kesselman, Max, 231
Keys, Alicia, 123, 157, 158
Khomeini, Ayatollah, 129
Khonsu, 46
Khufu, King, 124
King, Martin Luther, Jr., 36, 132

King, Stephen, 209
King, William R., 164
Kingdom of Dahomey, 50
King Fahd's Fountain (Saudi Arabia), 72
King's Speech, The (movie), 152
King Tut (Tutankhatmen), 56, 174–75
Kiribati, 62
Kitty Hawk, North Carolina, 131, 198
Knievel, Robert Craig "Evel," 212
Kobalt Tools 500, 189
Koos, Torin, 181
Korea. See North Korea; South Korea
Korean War, 128, 132
Kosovo, 62, 129
Krause, Brian, 210
Kush Kingdom, 124
Kutcher, Ashton, 151
Kuwait, 62, 129, 132
Kwanzaa, 36
Kyrgyzstan, 62

L

Labor Day, 36
Labor Department, U.S., 119
Labrador retrievers, 17, 18
Lady Antebellum, 155, 156, 158
Lady Byng Memorial Trophy, 188
Lady Gaga, 15, 155, 156, 157, 158
LaHood, Ray, 119
laid/lay, 141
lakes, largest in the world, 99
Lambert, Miranda, 158
L'Amour, Louis, 216
landfills, 45, 83, 230
landmarks. See also specific landmarks
    around the world, 80–81
    in the United States, 227
    in Washington, D.C., 225
language(s), 138–43
    American Sign, 139
    Chinese, 138
    easily confused words, 141
    figures of speech, 143
    Internet resource guide, 45
    new words, 141
    rhyming words, 142
    spelling bees, 140
    spoken in the U.S., 139
    spoken worldwide, 139
    winning wars using, 143
Lansing, Michigan, 210
Laos, 63
La Sagrada Familia (Spain), 80
Las Vegas, Nevada, 213
Latvia, 63
Lautner, Taylor, 151, 153
Laver, Rod, 190
law, as branch of science, 171
League of Women Voters, 122
Leap Day, 36
leaves of plants, 173
Lebanon, 63
Lee, Harper, 200
Lee, Robert E., 131
left atrium, 29
left ventricle, 29
Legislative Branch, 116, 117
Leo III, Pope, 125
Leptis Magna (Libya), 80
Lesotho, 63
Levi, Zachary, 151

Lewis, Meriwether, 130
Liautaud, Parker, 231
Liberia, 63
Libya, 9, 63
Liechtenstein, 64
life sciences, 170
lightening/lightning, 141
limestone, 172
Lin, Maya, 217
Lincecum, Tim, 184, 185
Lincoln, Abraham, 131, 164, 225
Lincoln, Nebraska, 213
Lincoln Memorial (Washington, D.C.), 225
Lindbergh, Charles, 199
Lion King, The (musical), 157
Lisbon, Portugal, 70
Liszt, Franz, 59
literacy volunteering, 232
literature (books), 30–33
    award-winning, 32–33
    Internet resource guide, 45
    types of, 30–31
Lithuania, 64
Little League World Series, 184
Little Rock, Arkansas, 201
local fare (locavores), 92
Locke, Gary, 119
locomotives, 198
logorrhea, 140
Lollywood, 69
Lookin At Lucky, 193
Los Angeles, California, 11, 202
Los Angeles Angels, 185
Los Angeles Lakers, 186
Los Angeles Sparks, 187
Louisiana, 131, 208
Louisiana Territory, 130
Louisville, Kentucky, 208
LPGA Championship, 190
Lucy skeleton, 56
lunch sacks, 231
lungs, power from, 238
Luther, Martin, 126
Luxembourg, 64
lyceum, 140
Lynch, Jane, 153

M

Macedonia, 64, 129
Machu Picchu, 70, 80, 125
Mackey, Lance, 193
Madagascar, 64
Madagascar 3 (movie), 241
Madison, James, 130, 162
Madison, Wisconsin, 224
magazines, online, 41
Magellan, Ferdinand, 126
Magna Carta, 125
magnesium, 95
Mahut, Nicolas, 14
Maine, 209
Major League Baseball (MLB), 184–85
malacologists, 23
Malawi, 64
Malaysia, 65
Malcolm X, 132
Maldives, 65
Mali, 65
Malta, 65
mammalogists, 23
mammals, 18
Mammoth Cave, 208
Manager of the Year, 185
manatees, 230

Manchester, New Hampshire, 214
Mandarin Chinese, 138, 139
Mandela, Nelson, 129
mantle, 97
Mao Zedong, 128
maps
    Africa, 102–3
    Asia and Middle East, 104–5
    Australia and the Pacific Islands, 106–7
    Europe, 108–9
    interactive, 41
    North America and Central America, 110–11
    South America, 112–13
    time zones, 101
    United States, 228–29
marble, 172
Marbury v. Madison, 121
March (calendar), 34
Marching for Freedom (Partridge), 33
Marco Polo, 125
Marcum, Shaun, 185
Mardi Gras, 36
Margaret A. Edwards Award, 32
mariachi music, 66
Marine Corps Memorial, U.S., 114
Marley, Bob, 61
Marovo Lagoon, 73
Mars (planet), 177, 178, 179
Mars, Bruno, 158
Marshall, Thomas R., 166
Marshall, Thurgood, 120
Marshall Islands, 65
Mars Odyssey, 178
Martin, Ricky, 226
Martin Jetpack, 136
Martin Luther King Jr. Day, 36
Maryland, 210
Massachusetts, 210
Massachusetts et al. v. Environmental Protection Agency et al., 121
mass transit, 197
Masters (golf tournament), 190
math (mathematics), 144–47. See also money
    as branch of study, 171
    common formulas, 145
    everyday, 147
    fractions, 146
    geometric terms, 144
    history of, 124
    integers, 146
    Internet resource guide, 45
Matsuo, Basho 142
Mattel, Inc. 241
Mauritania, 65
Mauritius, 66
May (calendar), 34
Mayan civilization, 125
Mayflower, 126
Mayon Volcano, 70
Mays, Willie, 185
Mbare Market (Zimbabwe), 79
McAfee Coliseum, 184
McAuliffe, Christa, 132
McCartney, Paul, 158
McCurdy, Jennette, 152
McDowell, Graeme, 190
McKinley, William, 161, 166
McNamara, Frank, 128
meat eating, 92–93
Mecca, 125
Meester, Leighton, 151
Mellouli, Oussama, 192

Memorial Day, 36
Memphis, Tennessee, 132, 220
Memphis Grizzlies, 186
Menchov, Denis, 192
Mercury (planet), 177, 179
Mesopotamia, 60
metamorphic rocks, 172
metaphors, 143
meteorology, 170. See also weather
methane, 87
Metropolis, Illinois, 206
Mexican-American War, 131
Mexico, 66
    average income, 149
    history, time line, 124–27, 130, 131
Miami Heat, 14
Michael L. Printz Award, 32
Michigan, 210
Michigan, Lake, 99
Mickelson, Phil, 190
microbiology, 170
Micronesia, 66
Middle East. See also specific countries
    map, 104–5
    revolutions, 9
Midler, Bette, 205
milk, 95, 201
Milky Way Galaxy, 176, 177
Miller, Bode, 214
Miller, Ryan, 188
Milwaukee, Wisconsin, 224
mind-controlled games, 241
Mindflex, 241
minerals, 95, 172
Ming Dynasty, 126
Minneapolis, Minnesota, 211
Minnesota, 211, 230
Minoans, 124
Minuit, Peter, 130
Miranda v. Arizona, 121
Mississippi, 131, 211
Missouri, 212
Missouri River, 130
Mitcham, Matthew, 192
Mockingbird (Erskine), 33
Model T, 131, 199
Mojave Desert, 90
Moldova, 66
mollusks, 19
Monaco, 66
Monarch caterpillars, 25
Mondale, Walter F., 168
money, 148–49
    handling, 148
    incomes around the world, 149
    paper, 149
    value of, 148
Mongol Empire, 66, 125
Mongolia, 66
monounsaturated fats, 94
Monroe, James, 130, 162
monsoons, 8
Montana, 212
Monteith, Cory, 153
Montenegro, 67, 129
Montgomery, Alabama, 132, 200
Montgomery, Sy, 32
Montpelier, Vermont, 222
Moon Over Manifest (Vanderpool), 32
moose, 212
Mormons, 222
Morocco, 67
Morton, Levi P., 165

Moscow, 71
mosquito swatting competition, 57
Most Valuable Players (MVPs), 185
Mother's Day, 36, 223
Mother Teresa, 64
MotoX, 194
mouflon, 54
Mount Everest, 68, 96, 128
Mount McKinley, 96
Mount Olympus, 58
Mount Rushmore, 227
Mount Vesuvius, 125
moustaches, 47
movies, 150–53
    Academy Awards, 152
    current events, 15
    downloading, 41
    Harry Potter, 15, 150
    highest-grossing, 153
    Nickelodeon Kids' Choice Awards, 152
    People's Choice Awards, 153
    Teen Choice Awards, 151
    Twilight, 151, 153
    what's next, 241
Mozambique, 67
MTV Video Music Awards, 157
Mubarak, Hosni, 9
Muhammad, 125
Muir Woods National Monument, 227
multitasking, 38–39
mummies, 56, 174–75
muscles (muscular system), 28
Muse, 155, 158
music, 154–58
    American Music Awards, 155
    current events, 15
    Grammy Awards, 158
    Internet resource guide, 45
    MTV Video Music Awards, 157
    Nickelodeon Kids' Choice Awards, 155
    Teen Choice Awards, 156
    volunteer opportunities, 232
musical instruments, 159
musicals, 157
Muslims. See Islam
Myanmar (Burma), 67
mystery books, 31
mythology, 58

N

Nadal, Rafael, 190
Nagasaki, 128, 132
Namibia, 67
Napolitano, Janet, 119
narcolepsy, 140
NASA, 12, 177, 178, 179, 199, 204
NASCAR, 189
Nash, Steve, 186
Nashville, Tennessee, 220
National Archives Building (Washington, D.C.), 225
National Basketball Association (NBA), 186–87
National Book Award for Young People's Literature, 33
National Football League (NFL), 182
National Hockey League (NHL), 188
National League, 184–85
National Mall (Washington, D.C.), 225
National Science Bowl, 134

National Woman Suffrage Association, 122
Natron, Lake, 76
natural gas, 84
Natural Resources Defense Council, 187
nature, Internet resource guide, 45
Nauru, 67
Navajo code talkers, 143
Navigators Islands, 72
NBA (National Basketball Association), 186–87
NCAA (National Collegiate Athletic Association), 187, 191
Nebraska, 213, 230, 235
Nebraska National Forest, 213
negative numbers, 146
Nepal, 68
Neptune (planet), 177, 179
nerpas, 99
Nestor, Daniel, 190
Netflix, 41
Netherlands, 68
neutron, 84
Nevada, 213
Nevis, 71
Nevis Peak, 71
Newark, New Jersey, 214
Newbery Medal, 32
New England Patriots, 182
New Hampshire, 214
New Jersey, 214
New Mexico, 215
New Orleans, Louisiana, 133, 208
New Orleans Hornets, 186
New Orleans Saints, 182
newspapers, online, 41
Newton, Cam, 183
Newton, Isaac, 175
New Year's Day, 36
New York (state), 215
New York City, 215
   bedbugs, 11
New York Yankees, 184, 185
New Zealand, 68, 127
NFL (National Football League), 182
NHL (National Hockey League), 188
Nicaragua, 68
Nickelodeon Kids' Choice Awards, 152, 155
Niger, 68
   average income, 149
Nigeria, 68
Nile River, 74
19th Amendment, 122, 131
9/11 terrorist attacks, 129, 133
Nissan Leaf, 196
nitrogen dioxide, 83
Nixon, Richard M., 132, 161, 167, 168
nonfiction, 30, 31
nonrenewable energy sources, 84–85
Norgay, Tenzing, 68, 128
Norimatsu, Ryota, 184
North America. See also specific countries
   features, 96
   map, 110–11
North Carolina, 216
North Dakota, 216
Northern Mariana Islands, 226
North Korea, 62, 127, 128
North Pole, 91, 127, 231
Northwest Passage, 127

Norway, 69
"Not Afraid" (song), 157
novels, 30
November (calendar), 35
Novruz, 49
nuclear energy, 84
nuclear fission, 84
nuclear war, 128, 132
numbers (numerals)
   fractions, 146
   integers, 146
   Pi, 145
numerators, 146
Nurek Dam (Tajikistan), 75
nutrition. See food and nutrition
Nyasa, Lake, 99

O
Oakland Athletics, 184
Obama, Barack, 9, 120, 133, 134, 169
Obama, Michelle, 169
oboes, 159
O'Brien, Conan, 153
obtuse angles, 144
occipital lobe, 29
Oceania, features, 96
oceanography, 170
oceans, 98
O'Connor, Sandra Day, 123
Octavian, 124
octopuses, 21
odd numbers, 146
Odyssey Award for Excellence in Audiobook Production, 32
Ohio, 217
Ohno, Apolo Anton, 180, 223
oil (petroleum), 84, 85
oil spills, 83
   Gulf of Mexico, 10, 129, 133
Oklahoma, 217, 235
Oklahoma City, Oklahoma, 217
Oklahoma City Thunder, 186
Olympia, Washington, 223
Olympic Games, 57, 195
Omaha, Nebraska, 213
Oman, 69
Omnivore's Dilemma, The (Pollan), 92–93
One Crazy Summer (Williams-Garcia), 32
online journals, 41
Oosthuizen, Louis, 190
Orange Bowl, 183
orchids, 59
Oregon, 218
Oregon Ducks, 183
Orlando Magic, 186
ornithologists, 23
ostrich eggs, 24
Oswald, Lee Harvey, 161
Ottoman Empire, 126
Oxfam America, 233
Oxford American Dictionary, 141

P
pacemakers, 238
Pacific Islands, map, 106–7
Pacific Ocean, 98
Pacific Ring of Fire, 70
Paisley, Brad, 155, 223
Pakistan, 128
Palau, 69
paleontology, 170
Palm Islands, 77
PanAm, 199

Panama, 69
Panama Canal, 100
pandanus plants, 65
Pangaea, 97
paper bags, 231
paper money, 149
Papua New Guinea, 69
Paraguay, 70
parallel lines, 144
parallelograms, 144
Paramore, 156
parietal lobe, 29
Paris Peace Accords, 129
Parks, Rosa, 132
Parthenon (Nashville), 220
Parton, Dolly, 220
Partridge, Elizabeth, 33
passed/past, 141
Passover, 36
Pasteur, Louis, 175
Paterno, Joe, 183
Pattinson, Robert, 151, 153
Paul, Chris, 186
Paulsen, Gary, 31
PCs (personal computers). See computers
peach pies, 203
Pearl Harbor, 128, 132
Peary, Robert, 127
Peloponnesian War, 124
Pemberton, John, 204
penicillin, 128
peninsulas, 100
Pennsylvania, 218
People's Choice Awards, 153
Pepsi Max 400 (auto race), 189
percussion, 159
Perkins, Frances, 119
permafrost, 91
perpendicular lines, 144
Perry, Katy, 155, 156
Perry, Ruth, 63
Persia, 60
Persian Gulf War, 129, 132
Peru, 70
   monetary value, 148
Peter I (the Great), 56, 126
Petra, Jordan, 61
Petroff, Peter, 51
petroleum. See oil
Petronas Twin Towers (Malaysia), 81
pets
   alligators as, 16
   top, 17
   volunteer activities, 232
PGA Championship, 190
Philadelphia, Pennsylvania, 11, 218
Philadelphia Eagles, 182
Philadelphia Flyers, 188
Philadelphia Phillies, 185
Philippines, 70
   monetary value, 148
Phoenix, Arizona, 201
Phoenix Suns, 186
phones. See also smartphones, 127
photo-editing software, 40
photosynthesis, 173
physical sciences, 170
physics, 170
pi, 145
pianos, 159
Pierce, Franklin, 164
Pierre, South Dakota, 220
Pike Place Market (Seattle), 223
Pilgrims, 126, 130

Pink Lake, 72
Pinnawela Elephant Orphanage, 74
Pioneer 1, 178
Pioneer 2, 178
pirates, 74
Pirates of the Caribbean (movies), 55, 153
Pittsburgh Steelers, 182
Pizarro, Francisco, 125, 126
plant sentinels., 239
plate tectonics, 97
plays, 31
Pledge of Allegiance, 115
Plessy v. Ferguson, 121
plum blossoms, 75
Pluto (dwarf planet), 177, 178
Plymouth Rock, 126, 130
Pocahontas, 130
poems, 31, 142
Polamalu, Troy, 182
Poland, 70, 128
polar bears, 22
polio vaccine, 128, 215
political science, 171
politics. See also government
   Internet resource guide, 44
Polk, James K., 163
Pollan, Michael, 92–93
Pollock, Jackson, 224
pollution, 83
polyunsaturated fats, 94
Pompeii, 125
Pony Express, 207
Popcorn Park Zoo, 214
porcupines, 25
Portland, Maine, 209
Portland, Oregon, 218
Portland Head Lighthouse, 98
Portland Trail Blazers, 186
Portugal, 70
Posey, Buster, 185
positive numbers, 146
Postage Stamp Museum (Liechtenstein), 64
potassium, 95
Potato Bowl USA, 216
potato famine, in Ireland, 127
poutine, 52
prairie dogs, 24
prairies, 91
Pratchett, Terry, 32
Preakness Stakes, 193
Predjamski Grad, 73
president pro tempore, 117
Presidents, U.S., 118, 160–69. See also specific presidents
   assassination of, 161
   death of, 161
   impeachment of, 161
   listing of, 162–69
   powers and responsibilities of, 116, 118
   State of the Union speech, 169
   succession order, 161
Presidents' Day, 36
Price Chopper 400 (auto race), 189
Príncipe, 72
Promontory Point, Utah, 131, 198
prosthetic limbs, 240
proteins, 94
Providence, Rhode Island, 219
psychology, 171
Puerto Rico, 226
Pujols, Albert, 185
Pullin, Alex, 181
pulmonary artery, 29

Pura Belpré Award, 32

Q

Qatar, 70
quadrilaterals, 144
Quayle, J. Danforth, 168
Queen Alexandra birdwing, 69
Quinnehtukqut, 203

R

Radcliffe, Daniel, 150
radius of a circle, 145
rafflesias, 65
railroads, 198
Rainbow Bridge, 227
rainbow foods, 94
rain forests, 90
raising money for donations, 233
Raleigh, North Carolina, 216
rally car racing, 194
Randall, Kikkan, 181
Randolph, Zach, 186
Ratoncito Perez, 74
Ray, James Earl, 132
Reagan, Ronald, 168, 206
Reality Check (Abrahams), 33
rectangles, 144, 145
recycling, 88, 230. *See also* going
    green
recycling drives, 231, 232
Red Box, 41
Red Cross International, 233
"red-eye" effect in photos, 40
reed dance festival, 75
reference books, 31
refrigeration, energy use, 89
renewable energy sources, 86–87
Reno, Janet, 204
Renteria, Edgar, 184
reptiles, 18
rescue dogs, 18
reusing, 88, 231
Revere, Paul, 130
Rex, Adam, 32
Rhode Island, 219
rhomboids, 144
rhombus, 144
rhyming words, 142
Richmond, Virginia, 222
Ride, Sally, 123
right angles, 144
right atrium, 29
right triangles, 144
right ventricle, 29
Rihanna, 155, 156
Ring Road (Iceland), 59
Rio de Janeiro, Brazil, 51
Robert F. Sibert Informational
    Book Medal, 32
Robert Fulton, 198
Roberts, Barbara Millicent, 224
Roberts, John, 120
robo-guards, 135
robo-teachers, 135
robot inventions, 135–36
Rockefeller, Nelson A., 168
rocks, 172
Rodgers, Aaron, 182
Rodriguez, Alex, 185
Roethlisberger, Ben, 182
roller skis, 69
romance books, 31
Romania, 71
Romans, ancient, history time
    line, 124–25
Romulus, 124

Rookie of the Year, 182, 185
Roosevelt, Franklin D., 119, 161,
    167
Roosevelt, Theodore, 161, 166
roots of plant, 173
Rose Bowl, 183
Rosh Hashanah, 36
Rush, Geoffrey, 152
Russia, 71
    history, time line, 126, 127, 131,
        178
    monetary value, 148
Russian Revolution, 127
Russo-Japanese War, 127
Ruth, Babe, 185
Rwanda, 71, 129
Ryan, Pam Muñoz, 32

S

Sacramento, California, 202
Sacramone, Alicia, 191, 210
Sadat, Anwar, 129
Safeco Field, 184
Sahara Desert, 68, 90, 100
St. Andrew, Barbados, 49
St. Basil's Cathedral (Russia), 81
Saint Bernard dogs, 18
St. Croix, 226
St. John, 226
Saint Kitts, 71
St. Louis Rams, 182
Saint Lucia, 71
St. Patrick's Day, 36
St. Paul, Minnesota, 211
St. Peter's Basilica (Vatican
    City), 78
St. Thomas, 226
Saint Vincent, 71
salamanders, 23
Salazar, Ken, 119
Saleh, Ali Abdullah, 9
Salem, Oregon, 218
Salem witch trials, 130
Salk, Jonas, 128, 175, 215
Salt Lake City, Utah, 221
salt water, 99
Salyut I, 178
Samoa, 72
San Alfonso del Mar (Chile), 53
Sanchez, Samuel, 192
Sandler, Adam, 153
sandstone, 172
San Francisco Bay, 100
San Francisco Giants, 14, 184
San Francisco 49ers, 182
San Juan, Puerto Rico, 226
San Marino, 72
Sant'Ana, 70
Santa Catrina, 70
Santa Fe, New Mexico, 215
Santo André, 70
São Jorge (Castelo), 70
São Roque, 70
São Tomé, 72
São Vicente, 70
Saqqara, Egypt, 46
saturated fats, 94
Saturn, 177, 178, 179
Saudi Arabia, 72
savannas, 91
savings accounts, 148
Sawyer, Diane, 208
scalene triangles, 144
Scalia, Antonin, 120
Schiavone, Francesca, 190
Schleck, Andy, 192

Schulz, Charles, 211
Schumacher, Cori, 191
science, 170–75
    botany and trees, 173
    branches of, 170–73
    current events, 12–13
    ecology, 172
    Internet resource guide, 45
    pioneers in, 175
    rocks and minerals, 172
    what's next, 238–39
science fiction, 31
Scott O'Dell Historical Fiction
    Award, 32
Scripps National Spelling Bee, 140
Seacrest, Ryan, 151
sea otters, 24
Seattle, Washington, 223
Seattle Mariners, 184
Seattle Seahawks, 182
Seattle Storm, 187
Sebelius, Kathleen, 119
2nd Amendment, 116
sedimentary rocks, 172
seeds, 173
segregation, 132
Segway™, 197
Senate, U.S., 117, 225
Senegal, 72
separation of powers, 116, 120
September (calendar), 35
September 11 terrorist attacks
    (2001), 129, 133
Serbia, 72, 129
Serengeti Plains, 61
sewage-powered, 238
Seychelles, 73
Shakespeare, William, 61, 142
Shakira, 155
Shang Dynasty, 124
Shendwas, 46
Shen Neng I, 82
Shepard, Alan, 178
Sherlock Holmes (movie), 151
Sherman, James S., 166
Shinseki, Eric, 119
Ship Breaker (Bacigalupi), 32
short stories, 30
Shortz, Will, 206
shyrdaks, 62
Sick Day for Amos McGee, A
    (Stead), 32
Siddhartha Gautama (Buddha),
    124
Sierra Leone, 73
sign language, 139
similes, 143
simple carbohydrates, 94
Sinai Peninsula, 128
Sinclair, Cam, 194
Singapore, 73
Singler, Kyle, 187
Sino-Japanese War, 127
Sioux Falls, South Dakota, 220
Sis, Peter, 32
Sitting Bull, 220
Six-Day War, 128
skateboarding, 194
skiing, 181, 194
skin, 28
slate, 172
Slater, Kelly, 191
slavery, 121, 131
sleep, 26
Slovakia, 73
Slovenia, 73, 129
smaragdine, 140

smartphones, 38–39, 41, 42, 238
Smith, John, 130
Smith, Joseph, 222
smog, 83
snakes, longest, 20
snow, 237
snowboarding, 181, 194
Snowe, Olympia, 209
snowmobiling, 194
soccer, 14, 188
soccer-playing robot, 134
social sciences, 171
sociology, 171
soft copies, 40, 41
software, 40
    photo-editing, 40
Solar Dynamics Observatory
    (SDO), 12
solar flares, 12
solar panels, 86
solar power, 86
solar system, 177, 179
Solis, Hilda, 119
Solomon Islands, 73
Somalia, 74
Song Dynasty, 125
sonnets, 142
Sosa, Sammy, 185
Soto, Hernando de, 130
Sotomayor, Sonia, 120
soup kitchens, volunteer
    opportunities, 232
Sousa, John Philip, 225
South Africa, 74, 129
    average income, 149
    skeleton discovery, 12
South African rhinos, tracking, 41
South America. *See also specific
    countries*
    features, 96
    map, 112–13
South Carolina, 219
South Dakota, 220
Southern Ocean, 98
South Korea, 62, 128
    history, time line, 127, 128, 132
    inventions, 135
    monetary value, 148
Soviet Union. *See also* Russia
    history, time line, 127, 128, 129,
        132
soybeans, 93
space, 176–79
    milestones in exploration, 178
    planets orbiting the sun, 179
    solar system, 177, 179
    what's next, 238
SpaceShipOne, 178
space waste, 178
Spain, 74
    history, time line, 125, 126, 127,
        131
Spalding, Esperanza, 158
Spanish-American War, 127, 131
Spanish Armada, 126
Spanish Civil War, 128
Spanish Inquisition, 126
Spanish language, 139
Speaker of the House, 117
Spears, Britney, 154
speed skating, 180
spelling bees, 140
spicy pepper soup, 68
Spider-Man (movie), 153
SpongeBob SquarePants (TV
    show), 152
sponges, 19

254

sports, 180–95. *See also specific sports*
  current events, 14
  Internet resource guide, 45
  Title IX, 123
  volunteer opportunities, 232
Springfield, Illinois, 206
Sprint Cup Series, 189
Sprouse, Dylan, 152
Sputnik, 178
squares, 144, 145
Sri Lanka, 74
Standing Bear, 213
Stanford Cardinals, 187
Stanley Cup, 188
Stanton, Elizabeth Cady, 122
Starbucks, 223
Star Maker, The (Yep), 30
stars, 176, 177
Star Wars (movie), 153
State Department, U.S., 119
State of the Union, 118, 169
stationary/stationery, 141
Statue of Liberty (New York City), 80
Stead, Erin E., 32
Stead, Philip C., 32
Stead, Rebecca, 33
stem of plant, 173
Stephens, John Paul, 120
steppes, 91
Stevenson, Adlai E., 165
Stewart, Kristen, 151, 153
stick insects, 21
Stoker, Bram, 71
Stone Mountain (Georgia), 204
straddling bus, 137
Strahovski, Yvonne, 151
straits, 100
streetcars, 198
stringed instruments, 45, 159
stromhur, 140
Stuart, Gilbert, 219
Styrofoam™, 83, 88
Suavé, Nic, 194
subway, 198, 210
Sudan, 74, 129
Suez Canal, 100
Sugar Bowl, 183
Sugru, 136
Suh, Ndamukong, 182
sulfur dioxide, 83
Sumer (Sumerians), 124
Summer Olympics (2012), 195
Summer X Games, 194
sun (sunlight), 12, 86, 173, 177, 179
Sundarbans, 49
Super Bowl XLV, 182
supercells, and tornadoes, 234
superclean closets, 238
superfoods, 93
superhero suit, 135
Superior, Lake, 99, 211
Superman, 206
super-moldable glue, 136
Super Saver, 193
Supreme Court, U.S., 120
  famous cases, 121
  newest judge, 10, 120
surfing, 56, 191
Suriname, 74
Sutter, John, 131
Swaziland, 75
Sweden, 75
  average income, 149
sweet potatoes, 216
Swift, Taylor, 155, 156

swimming, 192
Switzerland, 75
Sylvania 300, 189
synonyms, 143
Syria, 75

T

Taft, William H., 166
Tagalog, 139
taiga, 91
Taiwan, 75
Tajikistan, 75
talent shows, 233
Taliban, 129, 133
Tallahassee, Florida, 204
Tamansari Water Castle, 60
Tanganyika, Lake, 51, 99
Tanzania, 76
Tasmania, 48
Tasmanian Devil, 48
Tatum, Channing, 151
Taylor, Zachary, 161, 163
technology. *See also* computers; Internet
  as a branch of science, 171
  coolest inventions, 135–37
  current events, 12–13
  Internet resource guide, 45
  what's next, 238–39
Ted Lindsay Award, 188
Teen Choice Awards, 151, 156
telephones. *See also* smartphones, 127
television. *See* TV
Teller, Edward, 128
temperate forests, 91
Temple of Apollo (Greece), 81
temporal lobe, 29
Tennessee, 220
tennis, 14, 190
Tenochtitlán, 125
Teotihuacán, 80, 124
terrestrial planets, 177
Texas, 131, 221
Texas Christian University, 183
Texas Rangers, 14, 184, 185
texting (text messaging), 42
Thabeet, Hasheem, 186
Thailand, 76
Thanksgiving, 36, 37
Theron, Charlize, 74
thesauruses, 31
thighbone, 28
13th Amendment, 131
Thirty Years' War, 126
30 Seconds to Mars, 157
Thomas, Clarence, 120
three-toed box turtles, 212
3D movies, 15
thumb pianos, 79
thunderstorms, 234, 236
Tiananmen Square, 129
tigers, 25
timber rattlesnakes, 214
time zones, 101
Timor-Leste (East Timor), 55
Titanic (movie), 153
Title IX, 123
Tivoli Gardens (Denmark), 55
Tobago, 76
Toews, Jonathan, 188
Togo, 76
Tompkins, Daniel D., 162
Tonga, 76
tooth fairy, 74

Topeka, Kansas, 207
Tornado Alley, 235
tornadoes, 234–35
  formation of, 234
  top states, 235
Tour de France, 192
Toyota Prius, 129
Toy Story 3 (movie), 151, 152, 153
tracking animals, 41
Trail of Tears, 131
transcontinental railroad, 131, 198
transportation, 196–99
  alternative cars, 197
  coolest inventions, 137
  electric cars, 13, 196
  energy usage, 87
  milestones in history, 198–99
  what's next, 239
Transportation Department, U.S., 119
Transportation Security Administration (TSA), 13
trapezoids, 144
trash, 83
  reducing, reusing, and recycling, 88, 231
Treasury Department, U.S., 119
Treaty of Ghent, 130
Treaty of Versailles, 127
tree rings, 170
trees, 173
  global warming effects, 85
  planting, 85, 188, 232
Trenton, New Jersey, 214
Trevithick, Richard, 198
triangles, 144, 145
Trinidad, 76
Triple Crown, 193
Trojan War, 124
tropical rain forests, 90
tropical storms, 236
True Meaning of Smekday (Rex), 32
Truman, Harry S, 161, 167
Truth, Sojourner, 122
Tseng, Yani, 190
tsunami of 2004, 129
Tubman, Harriet, 209
Tums Fast Relief 500 (auto race), 189
tundras, 91
Tunisia, 76
  revolution, 9
turducken, 35
Turkey, 77
Turkmenistan, 77
Tutankhamen (King Tut), 56, 174–75
Tutsis, 129
Tuvalu, 77
TV (television), 150–53
  on the computer screen, 41
  downloading shows, 41
  invention of, 127
  Nickelodeon Kids' Choice Awards, 152
  People's Choice Awards, 153
  Teen Choice Awards, 151
Twain, Mark, 212
Twilight (movies), 151, 153
Twitter, 9
Tyler, John, 161, 163
typhoons, 236

U

Ubangi-Shari, 52
Uganda, 77
Uihlein, Peter, 190
Ukraine, 77
underwater kites, 137
Underwood, Carrie, 155, 217
Unicef, 233
Union Pacific Railroad, 131, 198
United Arab Emirates, 77
United Kingdom, 78
  average income, 149
  history, time line, 125–30
United States, 78, 200–229. *See also specific states*
  capital places, 225
  current events, 10–11
  energy usage, 87
  government, 114–21
  history, time line, 130–33
  listing of states, 200–224
  map, 228–29
  monuments, 227
  spoken languages, 139
  territories, 226
  women, time line, 122–23
United States Cross Country Ski Championships, 181
United States Figure Skating Championships, 181
universe, 170, 177
Uranus (planet), 177, 179
Urban, Keith, 156, 158
Urban II, Pope, 125
Uruguay, 78
U.S. Amateur Championship, 190
U.S. Capitol Building (Washington, D.C.), 225
U.S. Census, 11
U.S. Open, 190
U.S. Virgin Islands, 226
U.S. Women's Open, 190
U.S.A. States Map Match, 44
Usher, 154, 155, 156, 158
Utah, 221, 230
Utah Jazz, 186
Uzbekistan, 78

V

Valdés, 96
Valentine's Day, 36
Valentine's Day (movie), 151
Van Buren, Martin, 163
Vancouver, Canada, 180, 195
Van Den Broeck, Jurgen, 192
Vanderpool, Clare, 32
Van Draanen, Wendelin, 31
Vanuatu, 78
Vardzia cave city, 57
Vasco da Gama, 126
Vatican City, 78
Veasley, Willie, 187
vegetables, 92–93, 95, 173
Venezuela, 79
Venus (planet), 177, 178, 179
Vermont, 222
Verrazano, Giovanni da, 130
vertebrates, 18
Veterans Affairs, U.S., 119
Veterans Day, 36
Vezina Trophy, 188
Vice President, U.S., 117, 118, 161
Vick, Michael, 182
Victoria, Lake, 99
video games, 241

Vietnam, 79
  average income, 149
Vietnam Veterans Memorial
  (Washington, D.C.), 225
Vietnam War, 128–29, 132
Viking 1, 178
Vilsack, Tom, 119
violins, 159
Virginia, 222
Virginia Beach, Virginia, 222
vitamins, 95
Vlad Tepes, 71
voice-activated vehicles, 239
volcanoes, 8, 70, 97, 129
Volcanoes National Park, 71
Volt, 196
volunteering, 230–33
  kids making a difference,
    230–31
  raising money for donations,
    233
  sample causes, 232
  top states for, 230
vortex of tornadoes, 234
VORTEX2, 234–35
Votto, Joey, 185
Voyager, 178
vuvuzelas, 14, 141

W

Wabash, Indiana, 206
Waipio Little League, 184
walk-a-thons, 233
Wallace, Henry, 167
walnuts, 93
Walt Disney World, 49
warm-blooded animals, 20
War of 1812, 130
War on Terror, 129, 133
washing machines
  closets as, 238

energy use, 89
Washington (state), 223
Washington, D.C., 225
Washington, George, 118, 121,
  130, 162
Washington, Martha, 149, 162
Washington Monument
  (Washington, D.C.), 227
water, hydropower, 86
Watergate scandal, 132, 161
water polo, 192
Watts Race Riot, 132
WAVES (Women Accepted
  for Volunteer Emergency
  Service), 122
Wearable Personal Navigation
  System, 238
weather, 234–37
  droughts and floods, 237
  tracking tornadoes, 234–35
  wild winds, 236
Weaver, Jered, 185
Web addresses, 38
Webby Awards, 43
webisodes, 141
West Virginia, 223
whales, 24
what's next, 238–41
Wheeler, William A., 165
When You Reach Me (Stead), 33
white abalones, 22
White House Science Fair, 134
White Nile, 74
White Sands National Monument,
  215
White-throated rails, 73
Wichita, Kansas, 207
widdy widdy, 48
wildebeests, 61
wildlife. See animals
Williams, Deron, 186

Williams, Serena, 190
Williams, Venus, 190
Williamsburg, Virginia, 222
Williams-Garcia, Rita, 32
William the Conqueror, 125
Wilmington, Delaware, 203
Wilson, Henry, 164
Wilson, Woodrow, 116, 166
Wimbledon, 14
wind instruments, 159
windmills, 86
wind power, 86
winds, 236
Winter Olympics (2010), 195
winter sports, 181
winter weather, 237
Winter X Games, 194
Wisconsin, 224
withdrawals, 148
Women's British Open, 190
women's history, time line, 122–23
Women's National Basketball
  Association (WNBA), 187
Wonder, Stevie, 210
Woods Runner (Paulsen), 31
words
  easily confused, 141
  new, 141
  rhyming, 142
World Artistic Gymnastics
  Championships, 191
World Cup, 14, 188
World Figure Skating
  Championships, 181
world history, time line, 125–29
World Series, 14, 184
World Surfing Championships, 191
World Trade Center (New York
  City), 10
World War I, 127, 131
World War II, 128, 132, 143

worms, 19
Wright, Frank Lloyd, 224
Wright, Wilbur and Orville, 131,
  198
Wurman, Joshua, 234–35
Wyoming, 224

X

X Games, 194
xanthosis, 140
Xi'an, 53
Xiang Khouan, 63
XOS 2 (superhero suit), 135

Y

Yalsa Excellence in Nonfiction
  Award, 33
Yeager, Charles, 199
year in review. See current events
Year of the Dragon, 37
Yemen, 79
Yep, Laurence, 30
Yom Kippur, 36
Yom Kippur War, 129
Yoshino Mountain, 61
Young, Neil, 158
YouTube, 15, 154

Z

Zambezi River Valley, 67
Zambia, 79
zebras, 51
Zero Regrets (Ohno), 180
Zhu Yuanzhang, 126
Zimbabwe, 79
Zimonjic, Nenad, 190
zoology, 170